MAINA
GIELGUD

John Larkin is one of Australia's most distinguished journalists, having won over a dozen awards in his career, which included twenty-five years at the *Age* in Melbourne before he turned freelance. He has co-authored *The Holt Report*, an *Age* 'Insight' book on the disappearance of Prime Minister Harold Holt, *Maldon*, a pictorial history of Australia's first 'notable' town, and *Don Chipp: the Third Man*, the story of a remarkable Australian statesman. He has been writing about the performing arts for twenty years.

MAINA GIELGUD

A BIOGRAPHY

JOHN LARKIN

VIKING

Viking
Penguin Books Australia Ltd
487 Maroondah Highway, PO Box 257
Ringwood, Victoria 3134, Australia
Penguin Books Ltd
Harmondsworth, Middlesex, England
Viking Penguin, A Division of Penguin Books USA Inc
375 Hudson Street, New York, New York 10014, USA
Penguin Books Canada Limited
10 Alcorn Avenue, Toronto, Ontario, Canada M4V 3B2
Penguin Books (NZ) Ltd
182–190 Wairau Road, Auckland 10, New Zealand

First published by Penguin Books Australia 1996

1 3 5 7 9 10 8 6 4 2

Copyright © John Larkin and Maina Gielgud 1996

All rights reserved. Without limiting the rights under copyright reserved above, no part of this publication may be reproduced, stored in or introduced into a retrieval system, or transmitted, in any form or by any means (electronic, mechanical, photocopying, recording or otherwise), without the prior written permission of both the copyright owner and the above publisher of this book.

Typeset in 11/16pt Sabon by Post Typesetters, Stones Corner, Brisbane, Queensland
Printed in Australia by Australian Print Group, Maryborough, Victoria

National Library of Australia
Cataloguing-in-Publication data:

Larkin, John
Maina Gielgud : a biography.

Includes index.
ISBN 0 670 86586 9.

1. Gielgud, Maina, 1945- . 2. Australian Ballet - Biography.
3. Ballerinas - Australia - Biography. I. Title.

792.8092

CONTENTS

1 PERFORMANCE! 1
2 A DANCER PREPARES 17
3 FIRST STEPS 47
4 MUMMY 75
5 THE PROFESSIONAL 93
6 HIGHTOWER 107
7 BÉJART 129
8 NUREYEV 149
9 BEYOND BÉJART 167
10 PARTNERS 187
11 A GUEST IN OZ 199
12 FREELANCE AND FINALE 213
13 DIRECTIONS 227
14 THE TROUBLES 269
15 GOOD TIMES 319
EPILOGUE THE LAST DANCE 339
PICTURE CREDITS 352
INDEX 353

ACKNOWLEDGMENTS

My thanks to: Maina Gielgud for the time, access and attention to detail among a very busy schedule; her assistant, Dee Biggs, for so much cheerful and focused facilitation; The Australian Ballet, particularly the General Manager, Ian McRae, and the dancers, for the open door; Margaret Gee for being an ever-vigilant and helpful agent and friend; Robert Sessions, Publishing Director at Penguin Books Australia, for his enthusiasm and advice; Kerry Biram for her great skill and endurance as editor; Margot Wiburd for much help in preparing material; my partner, Dawn Davis, for her loving personal and professional support; and the dozens of people who made themselves available for interviews and so willingly gave assistance, including Gielgud's mother, Mrs Nigel Sutton, Edward Pask, and Noël Pelly, who has also given kind permission for material to be used from his book, *Zita*.

1

PERFORMANCE!

This is the holy moment that dancers hold dear and dread. With an almighty surge of breath, blood, adrenaline and anticipation, the heavy front curtain in the theatre rises slowly to reveal The Australian Ballet and the audience to each other. Overseen by the ghosts of the historic great ones stalking the wings, the performers will now create the grand illusion while at the same time exposing their inner selves. The lifting of the curtain has lifted a veil on their very souls.

No degree of suspension of the audience's disbelief can hide this process of revelation. Indeed, in the vast dark abyss beyond the stage, the observing eyes immediately become mirrors, thousands of them.

And no scrutiny will be more attentive and relentless than that by the distinguished woman with the luminous, inscrutable face sitting perfectly still near the front in her usual place. Maina Gielgud attended virtually every performance of the company for the fourteen years she was Artistic Director.

Just as consistently, Gielgud is ritually always the last to enter the theatre, reaching her seat just before the house lights go down. Her entrance is something of a theatrical event in itself. A murmur of recognition goes through the audience as they note the famous woman, with her quasi regal presence, arriving in their midst. It is an apt description, for there was no doubt who was queen during her reign with The Australian Ballet, so abruptly ended with her dethronement by the board in one of the most troubled events in the history of the performing arts in Australia.

Gielgud's invariable attendance, and her trance-like absorption, demonstrated a dedication beyond a reasonable call to duty. She never saw it thus, even though some ballet directors do not attend every show, especially once a production has settled into its season. But the habit has produced a mixture of responses. Some dancers appreciated the display of fixated dedication to their art. Others thought it excessive, and said it made them uncomfortable. This perplexed her, because she believed that was how she should be. It became one of the issues before her departure from the company, and was a measure of Gielgud's driven determination, with elements of both a blessing and a curse.

PERFORMANCE!

Without her total dedication to dance, Gielgud might not have been able to lift The Australian Ballet to become one of the leading classical companies in the world. No one could have given more. On the other hand, her single-mindedness caused problems. Having no personal life of her own made it hard for her to understand that today's generation of dancers, unlike those when she was building her own career, want to experience more of life outside of the ballet company, some believing it necessary to enrich their performance skills.

Her compulsiveness also meant she did not always trust others readily, and needed to control too much. This, together with a lack of personal communication skills, sometimes distanced her from some of the company, despite her obvious devotion to it. Dancers internalise a lot, and Gielgud is no exception. On her own admission she is shy and introverted.

Some loved her personally, some professionally, some not at all. Tension developed in the company and finally erupted. But in her final year, which ironically was possibly her best, the company has put the bad feeling behind it, and the air is clear, as though cleansed.

Right now the dancers have their minds only on themselves and the glorious ordeal of the performance ahead. This, their final night in Adelaide, after a two-month tour away from the company's home base in Melbourne, finds them both exhilarated and tired. But then, they are always tired. This is the way of a dancer, because they work twelve hours a day, six days a week, burning themselves up before their careers end, usually in their early thirties, if not before; beautiful creatures born to fade and wither early. Surprisingly, they welcome the tiredness, because they claim it gets them going, forces them to push themselves just that much further.

The other forces which shape their performances are the discipline born of a lifetime's preparation, the adrenaline coursing through their bodies at the rate of elite athletes who have Olympian training schedules, and, perhaps above all, a great addiction, for there is no drug to match the thrill of getting up on stage and performing well.

As common for the dancers as the fatigue is the pain. We in the audience would never guess, but most dancers are in constant pain for most performances. The pain varies in form and degree from a dull ache to an acute stabbing sensation. Injuries are most common in their ankles, calves, lower backs, hips, chests, necks, shoulders, knees. They can be due to tendonitis from overuse. Who would ever realise that behind the smiles, poetry, athleticism and sheer endurance of dancers in performance is not only the rigour of remembering the steps and the cues, and exposing their inner selves as they live out their characters, but also sheer agony – physically, mentally and emotionally. Dogging their every step when they are injured is the fear that on stage the affected part of their bodies will suddenly break down and fail them.

Some idea of the range of injuries among ballet people comes from the history of Gielgud herself, who, as a leading dancer of her time, suffered what is regarded as relatively few injuries. The list, nonetheless, seems excessive to the rest of us: a torn calf muscle, a sprained ankle, an elbow stress fracture, a broken toe, and in the early days, one year of severe tendonitis in one foot, and then a second and successive year of the same disorder in the other foot, both years giving her severe and constant pain. The injury meant that as a soloist she had to change some of her steps around to the other side of her body – even the difficult fouettés. This was possible because of her great technical strength.

Despite the injuries, Gielgud never stopped dancing. Indeed, her determination was such that when she was asked to be an emergency guest with The Australian Ballet in 1975, she accepted, and said nothing about her broken toe.

Tonight they are dancing a triple bill. This is one of the most popular programs in ballet, which gives the company a chance to use its classical skills in a modern idiom. The first work is *Beyond Bach*, which is choreographed by Stephen Baynes, one of the company's two resident choreographers. It is a beautifully lyrical piece, full of feeling and fluidity. The second is *Las Hermanas*, based on Garcia Lorca's play, *The House of Bernarda Alba*, choreographed by the late Sir Kenneth MacMillan. It is a darkly passionate and tragic work set to music by Frank Martin, which enables the dancers to demonstrate their dramatic flair. The last work, *In the Middle, Somewhat Elevated*, is a wild and vigorous romp of free-flowing energy by outstanding modern choreographer William Forsythe – a great climax to the evening.

The other chance for The Australian Ballet to demonstrate its quality comes in the first part of the Adelaide season with their production of the dramatic *Onegin*, one of John Cranko's most popular ballets, his 1965 adaptation of Pushkin's 1830s poem, *Eugene Onegin*, set to music by Tchaikovsky. First performed by the company in December 1976, the work is regarded by some observers as among its best full-length productions.

Now that they are in the closing stages of their time in Adelaide, there is a feeling of release, as the company prepares to return to its home base in Melbourne. Personal luggage is piled in huge heaps at one side of the stage, waiting, along with the sets and equipment, to be loaded into trucks at the end of the evening. Gielgud's is not amongst them. There never seems to be enough time for her. On the final night of *Onegin*, while others seem to be having a well-earned moment of celebration after the show, she is seen in the darkened street outside the theatre, standing alone among the swirl of the city traffic, talking on her mobile phone.

There is always an edge to each night before curtain up, especially once the half-hour call is made by the Stage Manager, who is the eye in the storm of the performance to come. Marina Milankovic has been with The Australian Ballet for a couple of years. A cool and collected young person, with a sense of humour, she started in theatre in 1980, did considerable backstage work in dramatic productions, then was assistant stage manager with the Australian Opera. She finds ballet less complicated than opera, though it seems intricate enough, as seen from her spot on a stool beside the stage in the prompt corner.

PERFORMANCE!

Much preparation has gone into having the stage ready for performance, under the technical director, Francis Croese. A month before opening, Milankovic forwards the technical schedule for each city to the theatre's production manager, and checks it when she arrives. Computers abound to handle the multiple functions, including plots for the running order, sound plots, with her following the score and watching the Conductor, Noel Smith, in the orchestra pit, on a special screen. There are plots for the stage mechanists, flying plots for the scenery, dome plots for hand-operated lights to follow the dancers from 'the gods' up in the dress circle, while the other automated lights have a plot which looks like a huge map. The crew, under Master Electrician John Berrett, work through the day to get the stage lit just as they need. It is not easy trying to set each mood well for each scene. Nothing can be taken for granted, and late-night shopping in Adelaide perversely caused a surge in the power supply in the middle of Friday's performance. The effect was of a sudden pulse racing through the place, causing a momentary power drop. The lighting system dimmed down, and then came up again, like a giant wink.

Milankovic likes working with dancers. 'There are no egos here,' she says. 'We travel so much, and we work so much as an ensemble.'

The stage crew, made up of people from both the theatre and the company, provide a down-to-earth counterpoint to the flamboyance of the dancers. Dressed in the dark uniform of their kind, they exude a gruff exterior as they prowl like meaningful phantoms among the backstage shadows, the far corners of which are littered with relics of scenery and props from such previous shows as *Hello, Dolly!*, *The Wizard of Oz*, *42nd Street* and *My Fair Lady*. The crew presents a collective persona which says that they are people of purpose, not to be messed with. They have their own clubhouse, at the far side of the stage, full of memorabilia and muffled talk, which you can sense, without being told, is off-limits. They love theatre, and are sometimes glimpsed standing in the wings, entranced by the performance.

Apart from the sixty-four dancers, the rest of the ninety-odd members of The Australian Ballet on tour are involved in management, publicity, remedial massage, and ballet staff. The whole show is a veritable juggernaut which rolls on, performance after performance, between which are dozens of activities as people prepare for the next show, and the coming repertoire in the next city, and the next season. No one is more ubiquitous than Gielgud herself.

As the crowds start to gather around the theatre, which they will fill to near-capacity, people backstage are making their final preparations for the evening's performance, the curtain keeping the two worlds apart as they approach that co-existence of intimacy and distance which creates the fantasy world of all artistic effort.

The backstage corridors are awash with movement as the orchestra arrives, their strangely shaped instrument cases, labelled 'Handle Like Eggs', stacked along walls and in corners, between which are the racks of waiting costumes hanging in their hollow finery. These have been

PERFORMANCE!

made ready by Wardrobe Mistress, Margaret Fitzsimons, and Wardrobe Master, Geoffrey Harman, two laconic individuals who lavish daily care on the clothes that transform the dancers into credible characters. After the dancers' exertions at each performance the costumes are made ready for the next, sweetened with the perfumed steam of eucalyptus oil, which so permeates the place that it smells like a convention of koalas.

The dancers who will perform tonight are doing their last-minute warm-up at the barre in the studio at the back. There is an incongruous contrast between their still being in their old practice clothes and their faces already formally made up. The air in the studio is warm from their exertion, and intense with their concentration as they study themselves one last time in the big mirrors at either end of the room, their images being repeated back and forth into infinity.

Finally, the dancers emerge in costume from their dressing rooms, hurrying past the red sign which says, 'Silence Please. Performance in Progress', with that quivering intensity of athletes and thoroughbred animals before a contest. They assemble around the stage, where the ballet staff, led by the Ballet Mistress, Wendy Walker, give final notes on performance.

One of the last preparations can be a decision about whether a dancer is able to go on or not. This depends on their injury and their determination to perform. A hurt dancer may still perform if there is no one else to do the part, and if it is estimated that despite the injury the performance will do them no further harm. Willpower and self-confidence can have a lot to do with it, too. Sometimes a dancer can dance through the pain, maybe with the affected area strapped up; pain killers and anti-inflammatory medication help too. If necessary, their sports medicine Remedial Massage Therapist, Ron Alexander, will be stationed by the side of the stage, applying acupressure to mask the pain during a performance, and keep a dancer mobile. Some dancers prefer not to block the pain with anti-inflammatory medication because they want to continue to be able to feel their bodies. Some are concerned that if they cannot sense the problem area, they might do something while on stage that will make it even worse. It is a complicated choice, and a deadly serious one, because without their bodies functioning properly, they may not be able to dance. No dancer likes to be not working. Their working life is already too short.

Gielgud is on stage, too, watching everything, making comments. She says it is traditional for the director and the ballet staff to be there every night before the curtain up. It is not usual, though, to give the Principals notes just before they dance, because they already have enough to think about. Even she is not immune from getting in the way as the place warms up with dancers appearing from all directions.

Everything is in place at last. The excitement is palpable, echoed in the buzz from the audience in front of the curtain. The Assistant Stage Manager, Guy Carrison, says loudly, 'All right, Maina.' It sounds like the formal last signal before take-off, but one of the staff confides in a stage whisper, 'What he means is, "Piss off, Maina."' It is said good-naturedly, as if they understand the Artistic

PERFORMANCE!

Director's need to be there. Gielgud leaves the stage, enters the auditorium by the small door at the side, and takes her seat just before the house lights go down. And watches.

She will come backstage to watch the final act from the wings about every fifteen performances, 'for a change'. She says she does not want the dancers to feel that she is watching them from so close because 'it can be offputting to find yourself looking at your Artistic Director's face as you turn towards a wing'. Surely, though, they are already aware of her searching presence in the audience every night. Coming backstage one night for *Onegin*, she moves around the prompt corner, and finally stands right on the edge of the stage. Even though her black clothes blend with the black side curtain, there is no missing her, with her pale face absorbed in concentration.

Being side stage enables us to see the dancers in action, to see the whites of their eyes as it were, and observe them when they come off and wait for the next cue. It is a rare and rich insight.

Beyond Bach is a superbly artistic work, with the dancers demonstrating an elegant flow of line and movement, moving to the wonderful music on a fine set designed by Andrew Carter. The exits and entrances are as enchanting as the centre stage dancing.

To the ordinary mortals watching from the audience, the dancers are creatures of great beauty, with their finely shaped bodies, the lovely lines of their legs, hips, bottoms, torsos, arms, hands, cheek bones, their straight backs and shining skin, with their freedom of movement emphasising their fresh sensuality.

But the apparent confidence of the performers belies the effort that goes into the performance. Little does the audience know that, at the start, some dancers are shaking so much that their partners can feel their hands trembling, or that others have so many butterflies in their stomachs that they feel ill.

We can see the effects of how hard they have worked as they stream off stage and line up again ready for their next entrance. Away from the eyes of the audience, they gasp and pant most inelegantly.

Ron Alexander says they are not fit in the classical sense, as are athletes, with the usual aerobic exchange of oxygen to the muscles, and back again. They function anaerobically, which means they do not predominantly use oxygen as their energy source, because they usually exert themselves in short bursts of up to three minutes at a time. Instead of oxygen, they rely on glycogen, which is stored in their muscles. They would be even fitter if they did aerobic classes, but their twelve-hour days do not allow them the time. There is also the danger that if they went to a gym in their usual tired state the extra exercise could cause their muscles to wither. But their fitness should not be underestimated. After years of doing stretching exercises, dancers are hypermobile, which means that they are very flexible, thus allowing them, for example, to lift their legs to extraordinary heights and have greater ranges of movement.

In the mundane side-stage world away from the magic, the dancers do rapid repairs to overcome the toll of their exertion, and prepare themselves for the next launch on stage. Paper tissues are taken by the handful from a box beside the stage manager, breathing passages are cleared, and sweat is mopped carefully from faces, so make-up remains undisturbed. They make little asides as they skitter off the stage. Sometimes they swear under their breath, or giggle. A beautiful female face comes into view, turns to her partner and says with a deep sigh, 'Oh, I'm buggered now!'

From the darkness further to the side we hear weird scratching sounds. The dancers are rubbing their shoes in a box of resin. Others are tying up their laces, adjusting their dress, or cutting loose bits off their shoes. Repairing their shoes during performance takes some doing as they come off stage, grab scissors from the manager's desk, cut off an offending edge, then head back on stage on cue, without missing a beat. When they get a new pair of shoes, most female dancers modify them with a knife, imposing their own personal variation on its function. Injuries can be caused by dancers not dancing properly because their shoes are not right.

Alexander says the normal weight distribution on a dancer's foot is 50 per cent on four toes, and the other 50 per cent on the big toe. If that is impossible for some reason – the character they are dancing might not allow it, or their pointe shoe is too soft or too hard – they are then likely to do surgery on the shoes. Some even remove the leather inner sole because it interferes with them bending their foot as much as they would wish, in the eternal pursuit of 'the line' as it is called – the link between leg and foot – the ideal being to make it into one continuous curve. This bending, in turn, can create other problems, because this causes the heel bone to press against the back of the tibia, so the tendons at the back of the heel can be squashed, leading to the growth of bone spurs. Physiotherapy and massage can alleviate that condition now, while in the past surgery was the only answer.

Off stage, dancers move with a waddle, their feet turned almost at right angles, their shoulders slumped forward, arms hanging down loosely. Once they begin to dance, though, any suggestion of ugly ducklings is transformed into the elegant swoops and glides of swans.

Dancers sometimes watch performances when they are particularly interested in another dancer or have a particular love for a ballet or a role. They do so either from the wings when they are waiting to go back on stage, or from the audience when they are not cast for the performance. They watch with looks of complete absorption. Tonight, people are clearly deeply moved by *Beyond Bach*. While awaiting their next cue, the dancers stand side stage perfectly still, the only movement being the heaving of their chests. The side lights from the opposite side of the stage illuminate their faces and bodies in contrast to the shadows around them. Only the front of each dancer is alight, giving them an unearthly, half-embodied appearance, beautiful nonetheless. At times they break off to flex their muscles or bend to adjust something, reminiscent of the famous paintings by Degas.

In the interval, the stage hands begin the noisy work of dismantling the set from the first act, while down in the studio they are already rolling up the floor covering and dismantling the barres ready to be transported.

PERFORMANCE!

The second work, *Las Hermanas,* is a lusty, brooding tale of five sisters thrown into disarray by the arrival of a man in their midst, resulting in tragedy at the end, with one of them hanging herself. Seen from backstage, the death scene is elaborately set up, using a substitute dancer wearing a wig, so the original one can be ready for the curtain call. The hanging looks very real, as stage hands lift the intended victim into the harness, with extra safety support from a huge rope handled by two brawny crew. In the middle of the ballet, as a cavorting couple bounce off the stage in a passionate, fornicating embrace, a stage hand waits in the wings to catch them so they do not crash into the side lights.

The final work of the triple bill, *In the Middle, Somewhat Elevated,* is a frenzy of modern movement, seen as the choreographer deconstructs the formality of classical technique and enlarges it into a new form. It provides a great release for the dancers, who hurl themselves around the empty stage with apparent abandonment to the music by Thom Willems, a deafening cacophony which booms through the blood. The effort takes a terrific toll on the dancers, who come off stage gasping. One of the lead performers is so overcome that she grabs the stage manager's stool and slumps down over it, as though dying on her feet. Her partner strokes her back in sympathy, while she fights for breath. All too soon, it is time for them to go back on stage. She thanks her partner and they join the frenzy with every bit of their being, with the audience none the wiser. Now another young dancer staggers to the corner, where she lies on the floor, also struggling to breathe. She undoes a shoe to reveal each toe covered in a little cloth cap; here is a very personal insight into how precious dancers' toes are. She adjusts each of the covers to protect her toes as much as she can, stands up, is very still for a few moments, then rejoins the melee on stage.

At last the performance is done. The audience is on its feet, the curtain calls are taken and the dancers stay to see whether they should wait for just one more. Finally, the stage manager decides and the curtain stays down. The dancers tenderly exchange hugs and kisses, then disappear, exhausted and exhilarated.

It seems to have ended so abruptly, leaving the stage suddenly empty of life, and us floundering for a few moments in that half state between illusion and reality. But they have done well tonight. The ghosts of the strict ancestors of their art have been appeased.

Any sense of sadness that it is over is dispelled within moments as the stage hands, asserting their role, pounce and start pulling up the strips holding the surface on the floor, as they would tear off a huge bandage. The big interstate trucks are standing by the stage door, their doors open and waiting to be filled with the paraphernalia of the dreams just passed. The show moves on.

The crowd outside pours itself in the direction of home, even more excited than when they arrived. The spectacle they have just seen has stirred them in a way that their usual lives cannot.

In the middle of the hustle and bustle, standing near the stage door, her face as pale as the moon, is Gielgud. Being in the crowd only makes her seem more alone than ever.

2

A DANCER PREPARES

The performance of our ballet dancers, the beauty and facility which enchant their audiences in that great act of giving which is the true spirit of theatre, has been able to happen only because of another whole world of effort which takes so much of their lives when they are not on stage. For Maina Gielgud, more than for the rest of them, there is no other life than this.

Meeting the dancers off stage and getting to know them as individuals is a deeply moving experience. They are heroic people, battling great odds, not the least the ever-present twin demons of fear of failure, and failure itself. Their existence is so controlled that many of them liken it to belonging to some kind of closeted order – a nunnery.

The analogy comes even closer to the mark when we realise that nearly all of the dancers now with The Australian Ballet have known no other artistic director than Gielgud, who has been there years longer than they have. This has given her much authority and power. The responsibility is made manifest because dancers are by nature a volatile, vulnerable mixture of artistic endeavour, physical strength, fear, courage and emotional fragility.

Dancers' lives, brief as they are, begin very early, often at four or five years of age – the earlier the better to shape their bodies and minds for the arduous journey ahead. The demands upon them develop soon enough, too, as their dedication to dance has to become more and more focused if they are to succeed. Parents, also, make many sacrifices for the sake of the art. Gielgud's own mother, Zita, who had very little money, went without many material comforts for the sake of her daughter's career.

Such are the strictures of their daily routines, which start with their arrival around 10 a.m. and finish around 11 p.m., that by the time they come down from the adrenaline rush of the performance, then eat and finally get to bed, it can be the early hours of the next morning. After a few hours' sleep, it all starts again, with them dragging themselves out of bed, often in pain, and always tired.

Tiredness being their constant condition might be surprising; we expect dancers to be as fresh as they seem when they are dancing on stage so lightly, with such enchanted expressions. The tiredness comes from the endless days and nights of practice and performance. The dancers, though, have adapted this tiredness to suit them. One says she actually needs to be tired when on stage, otherwise she is so full of energy that she finds herself literally taking off when dancing, and in danger of flying out of control.

Their lifetime of discipline has made them very hard on themselves, and none is as much a taskmaster as Gielgud, with her determination to keep on driving, day after day, night after night, both herself and her dancers. She is indeed the obsessive holy mother, whose small office in The Australian Ballet Centre in Melbourne, and small apartment in the centre of the city, are models of austerity; she has no sense of ownership about them. She calls her office, which is filled with photographs, her museum.

Gielgud's apartment is in an ordinary, anonymous building where theatre people stay when in Melbourne. Finally arriving home at all hours, she would look in the letter box, always hoping, she says, to be surprised. The corridor to her front door smells of cigars, much like the old hotels in New York. Once inside, she looks around and says, with a smile, 'Nothing's changed.' Nor had it from our last meeting there, maybe a month ago. A few flowers might be wilted in a vase, while the books on ballet that we had perused last time are still in the same place on the table where we left them.

While having a sense of home is more important to today's dancers, Gielgud uses her own home simply as somewhere to sleep. Even her bedroom, which has the feeling of being her one sanctuary, is full of her work life, with communication gadgets scattered around. She loves modern communication technology and has even had her mobile phone adapted so that she can talk while dining. She has an extraordinarily alert mind, almost mechanical in its ability to function on several levels at once, and switch like quicksilver. She has had trouble understanding why dancers these days, unlike herself, are interested in having a private life away from ballet. She has noted that even in their first year with the company, some will buy cars, while it is becoming more common for them to acquire their own house or apartment, despite being on the road for about half the year. The long absence from home makes it more complicated for those having relationships outside the company. Many of them now have mobile phones to keep in touch.

In the encounters with the dancers, they are prepared to reveal themselves readily, despite often being introverted. Having this kind of personality can be an asset for dancers because it provides the need to perform. One girl said that for her, the time of greatest stillness in her life was when she was on stage. Some dancers concentrate so hard when they perform that they say they do not hear the music from the orchestra.

A day in the life of a dancer finds them first at class from 11 a.m. to 12.15 p.m. when there is a performance that night, or earlier when there is not. Class serves as both a warm-up and a means for the dancers to develop both their bodies and their abilities. Class is usually taken by the ballet staff, including Gielgud. Each day is different, with different series of steps being devised by the teacher. Despite her limp from a troublesome hip, Gielgud demonstrates the complicated routines to the dancers. She does this with remarkable agility, and we can only wonder what she looked like when she was one of the leading ballerinas of her time.

Class is followed by rehearsal, which continues through the day. On a call sheet for the company for one day, we find Gielgud taking a dozen separate rehearsals, each running for half an hour. These can be both for ballets that are being currently danced by the company, leading up to full dress rehearsals, as well as for the future repertoires.

The morning class has Gielgud in the studio with about 30 of 'the boys' (as the males, whatever their age, are often called), while the girls are doing their class on stage with the company's Ballet Master, Paul De Masson. The stage curtain is up, revealing the empty theatre with its endless rows of red seats, resembling a huge, hungry mouth.

The atmosphere in the studio, despite the overhead fans, is soon damp and hot enough to suggest a rain forest. People are dressed stylishly, even if in old clothes. They work hard to the music played on the piano in a corner, both classical and pop, and have a glow about them, from their youth and their effort. They repeat the steps as set by Gielgud, dancing in one row, followed by the next – waves of energy washing across the room – while she watches perched up on a barre at the front.

Somehow the dancers manage to monitor themselves

in reverse, by constantly watching their every movement in the big mirrors, the images merging within themselves. Mirrors are both friend and enemy to dancers, enabling them to see when they are dancing well, but also reminding them of their faults. This constant self-observance might induce narcissism of the negative kind.

The black floor bounces to their leaps, echoing to the thudding sounds from the girls on the stage above. The boys are sweating profusely now; their shirts are wet. The air pumps with the sounds of panting.

The class comes to a close with a flourish of grandes pirouettes, the boys flying around the room like horses on a wild merry-go-round. It is a joyous exhibition, from which they come down slowly with a series of quiet stretching movements, their bodies as supple as young trees. It ends with the customary round of applause.

A dancer advises that if we want to see Gielgud as she really is, watch her in class. This is a profound and possibly most accurate observation, for she is not an easy person to get to know. Some of her colleagues describe her as a chameleon, and indeed she can change her markings as quickly as one. She can be naive and mature, warm and funny, cold and remote. Part of the elusiveness comes from her concentrating solely on what she is doing at the moment.

Virginia Woolf could have had Gielgud in mind when she once proclaimed, 'A biography is considered complete if it merely accounts for six or seven selves, whereas a person may well house as many as one thousand.' Mikhail Baryshnikov remarked at the start of his 1996 Australian tour that ballet provides endless possibilities of surprise to both the dancer and the audience. The same might be said about Gielgud. Certainly, she seems to be at her best when she is in class. 'My real life,' she says, 'is there.' She says people laugh at her love for the studio, but to her the place is sacred. It is not a common feeling, but one she shares with two of the great ballet directors for whom she danced, and from whom she learned much, Rosella Hightower and Maurice Béjart. She calls them kindred spirits.

For someone so complex, about whom the biographer as psycho-historian is trying to determine an accurate portrait, Gielgud suddenly talks about truth.

'It's the place where you can't lie; [there can be] no amount of talking, faking, or camouflaging. In some ways I feel that about performance on stage, because by dancers trying to immerse themselves in a story totally, there is a truth that comes out about them. But in the ballet studio, it's a different kind of truth. I think that those who are not really searching in the studio are the type of performers who go on stage to show off what they can do, as opposed to those who use it to express themselves, and show the present state of a never-ending search.

'So, when you think of a studio as a searching place, it makes dance and being a dancer a thousand times more meaningful. It becomes a kind of yoga. It becomes not just a physical exercise, physical polishing. It's a mental therapy, a mental discipline. I like to travel, and being in that no-man's-land between where you start and where you're going, feels a good place to be. The journey of life is interesting, and the studio is like an everlasting journey.'

'It's also a place where I feel at home. Everything drives me to the studio. When wonderful things have happened, I have to go to the studio and celebrate.' She does not drink, nor enjoy the usual social life. 'It's easier to get in there and work at the things that need to be addressed. But, on the other hand, if things are really terrible, it's the place where you can get away from them, and soak yourself in things you feel need to be done, yet which, I suppose in a funny way, are really not that important. So it's also like a drug.'

In her dancing days Gielgud, at times, like all dancers, had to force herself to work on herself in the studio, to gain enough confidence to go up on stage and do well. 'Not to work in the studio used to feel wrong. It becomes absolutely addictive, but that's my personality. When something horrible happens, I go and do a barre, and it will wash away the worst of it. To teach class is also therapy, to find new steps, new ways of getting across information, corrections, suggestions. It needs to be different for every single dancer.'

Learning from her mentor Hightower, the woman of American Indian ethnic origin living in France, how to train during a class as a dancer, and also give others the exercises, Gielgud works best when she goes into a class with no specific steps prepared in advance, but only with ideas about what is needed.

'Not just in a coaching class, but also the daily one, you have the natural format that every class has to have. But you gain your ideas about what to work on through the atmosphere of the class, and how much they are or aren't into work on that particular day, and how tired they may be. You get a feeling and also ideas from just looking at them and seeing what things they may need to work on; or remembering a performance; or there's something that has crept in – a problem you want to catch.'

The importance of a rehearsal studio to Gielgud is demonstrated in a story related by someone who saw her in action early in her time with The Australian Ballet. They were in Sydney, performing at the Opera House, after which there was a reception. Ballet receptions are regular duties which are a means by which the company meets its supporters, including the all-important sponsors, though at times after a hard night's performance it can be a bit of a grind. Dancers report that the most extraordinary conversations eventuate, when people unfamiliar with ballet unwittingly ask them very weird questions about their work. Some ask them what their real job is, or what their day job is, as though dance is something they do in their spare time. Gielgud, who is hopeless at small talk, overcomes her aversion and regularly attends these receptions.

Yet even this she will not allow to interfere with the work, for on that night in Sydney, after she finally left the reception, she was later observed in a studio in the building with three dancers, coaching them. All had changed from the formal finery worn at the reception into their work togs. It was then about 11.30 p.m. and reportedly they stayed until around 1 a.m. They were working on a ballet scheduled for later in the season. The witness says the incident was both beneficial in its sense of dedication, but ominous in its obsessiveness.

Gielgud responds: 'The episode was a sort of "dare",

as a few of the dancers were particularly dedicated. So for fun, we worked in the studio after the reception, to show that we could do both! Some of the greatest dancers of the previous generation, particularly the Russians and the Danish, were known for partying and drinking most of the night away, but were equally well known for being twice as hard working the next day, being up at dawn, having had next to no sleep, and practising before, during and after the daily class, which they never missed.'

A more typical time in the rehearsal studio finds Gielgud one morning in one of the many studios in The Australian Ballet Centre in the sprawling arts precinct on the south side of the Yarra River in Melbourne. She has a few boys and girls with her, who once again exhibit so much latent energy and beauty. They seem to fluctuate between intensity and self-deprecating good humour when they fluff a step. They work hard, with the impressive concentration so common to dancers. Nobody breaks when a mobile phone goes off among their bags by the door.

Dressed in tights and a black T-shirt which says 'Star City Hollywood', Gielgud is looking young enough herself for her fifty years, and agile despite the ever-troubling hip. People in the company desperately wish, though, that she would have it fixed.

Gielgud is common property despite her preference for privacy, and most people in the company are ready to comment about her when asked. There is great interest in whether she has any romance in her life. As one person put it, 'We would like to think that she has the joy of an intimate friendship. We feel both curiosity and concern about her.'

Music drifts in and out from the other studios, too, on this Melbourne morning, making it seem that the whole place is in concert, in contrast to the clatter of the city outside, seen in close proximity through the big windows.

Over the ninety minutes of the class, Gielgud works each person thoroughly, guiding them gently. There is incongruity between the lighthearted mood in the room and the toughness needed to get through the ordeal of the work. Dancers grimace at their mistakes while she continues to be supportive, her voice taking on a conspirator's air of encouragement: 'Yes. YES. YES !'

Colin Peasley, who has been with the company nearly thirty-five years, and still dances character roles as one of its principals, as well as teaching class, remembers when ballet was more passionate. He says it has changed now, 'because dance has become more of a business, more serious.' Historically, there has been a fight between the need for dancers to have the perfect body, and communicating emotions to the audience. 'These days, it's [like] the four-minute mile.' The top Principals back in 1962, when the company was formed, would still have the same positions today, 'but the lesser ones of us wouldn't make it. We were more like actors.'

He describes the dancers in the company being as big, open and sunny as Australia is itself. 'In those [early] days, we were a bit laid back, and now it's not [like that] – which is a good thing. We are equal to anything in the world. But I worry about dancers being cut off from life, working 11 to 11. Where's the time for the relationships, or sitting down and reading a book? In my time, there wasn't the pressure on the dancers that there is now. These days, there are larger numbers of casts. We are trying to give the dancers the appearance that they have the experience of older dancers. Standards gained have to be maintained.

'Most people think that dance is glamorous. It's not. It's hard work, and not just physical. It's the dedication you have to bring to the art form. Maina calls it "vocation".

'Dancers live a very cloistered life, because they have to think all day about the characters they will dance that night. The need is to counteract that by opening them up more often.

'Dancers are in fear of not being quite good enough. They are continually being corrected, as well as seeing themselves in the mirror. They can't achieve perfection. Dancers suffer from too much applause too soon, and too little applause too late. A lot of times when they see themselves in the mirror, they see not what they are, but what they want to be. People get into a depression about one second that has gone wrong.'

Many other, younger, dancers confirmed this constant anxiety about never being good enough. Some even went so far as to admit feeling something akin to hatred for their bodies, beautiful though they might be to the rest of us.

One senior dancer said the self-hatred was 'one reason for coming in every day, to try to refine yourself. Even in the studio, you might like to look like you're smiling, but inside you're crying out, trying to change yourself. Dancers are very good at acting, even in real life. They're also very good at picking up on other people's feelings.

When you've done a show you might feel has not gone well, if people come back afterwards and say how wonderful it was, you just know what they are really thinking.'

And it gets no better at the top. Peasley tells of talking once with Erik Bruhn, the Danish dancer who became one of the greatest in the world. It was in 1963, and they were discussing the eternal question of artists achieving such great technique that they did not have to worry any more. Bruhn told Peasley, 'It's not that at all. It's worse now for me than when I was on the way up. It's like being a gunslinger in a Wild West town, always being challenged to be the best shot.'

Wendy Walker, the Ballet Mistress, who teaches a lot of the ballets in the company repertoire, and is responsible for conducting many rehearsals, sees dancers in The Australian Ballet having the privilege of stability by being employed for fifty-two weeks of the year, unlike dancers in most other places in the world these days. Some of the Australians are unaware that this is not always commonplace in overseas companies. Walker, a vibrant, alert and friendly former Australian Ballet dancer, was recruited by Gielgud after fifteen years with the American Ballet Theatre in New York. There she found the prevailing attitude was: 'Time is money'. It had a profound effect on the production team. She is seen by some of the dancers as being sympathetic when they feel under-appreciated and under-used, by helping to influence the work being spread more evenly among them. Walker, who recognises that there are different values now among dancers, with security and material possessions being more important to them than they used to be, also personally feels the need these days, like many dancers, to be with outside people.

Frank Leo, the company Co-ordinator, and himself a former dancer, describes them as a family, understanding that they are all in the same situation. There is a lot of mutual support among them, with people being perhaps more gentle with each other than usual in such competitive circumstances. Maybe some of the dancers are rather mollycoddled by the ballet staff, whereas at times they might need to show more individual initiative. But people are proud of being in the company as they travel together, with a sense of really being something.

The interviews with the dancers themselves reveal a range of individuals who are diverse, despite the regimentation of the life. Most common among them are inordinate fears of never being good enough and the constant self-criticism, coupled with taking criticism from others very much to heart, an introverted personality, an awareness of their bodies, being very tactile, a poetic streak, a constant sense of trying to keep up with all the changes in the world of ballet, a sense of humour, friendliness, suffering regular physical fatigue and pain, and an incredible dedication to dance. Some also have a more spiritual side to them, while in worldly terms, chances are that if they have reached the high standard to be admitted to the company, they have already been toughened to some degree. First and last, they are survivors.

Lucinda Dunn has been dancing for eighteen years, since she was four. She has been with the company for nearly five years and was promoted to Senior Artist in 1995. It is a hard life, though. 'I think the person that you are is very important. It comes through on stage whether you have a warm heart.' She likes to show happiness and ease to an audience, and that she is enjoying the dance, feeling the crowd's support. Dunn speaks of her bad days at the ballet as being 'tragic', a commonly-used word, which mostly is to do with such concerns as how her body is going. She sees the whole style of classical dance moving so fast now, in movement, design, music, choreography and the demands on dancers' bodies. She drives herself, and speaks of motivation and inspiration, with the necessity of having other people around her to keep her standards up. Yet she feels free inside herself, aware of the development of both her body and her soul, through which 'you can really open up'. Outside friends are very important to her. 'It brings you back down.'

Lisa Bolte, a Principal Artist, who was a guest at Christmas 1995 of the famous Maryinsky Theatre in St Petersburg, where she danced in both *Giselle* and *Don Quixote*, speaks of feeling herself surrounded by mirrors. 'The artistic life is very volatile. It's never easy. You've always got something confronting you, learning more about yourself, how to handle different situations.' At times she feels the people around her to be warm and close, but the feelings of the company change from day to day. To her, having outside experience is appealing.

One dancer who freely admits to having always been driven is David McAllister, another Principal Artist, who joined The Australian Ballet in 1983, the year Gielgud came there. Ballet was always something he wanted to do, having at fifteen realised that it could be a way of life rather than a hobby. Immediately, though, he became aware of fear, which then became a continuous process – fear of what would happen to him.

'When I first got into the company, it was very exciting. Now I'm a bit more cynical about it. The process is harder. There's a lot more pain.'

He says sheer natural ability will keep a dancer going until they are twenty-five, but this can lead to bad technical problems being developed. McAllister says a dancer is always watching the bodies of other dancers. Once, while he was working through his doubts, he looked at his image in the studio mirror and said to himself, 'This is as good as it gets.' But then he thought, 'Well, it's not so bad . . .' What McAllister enjoys most about being a dancer, and what keeps him going, are performance, relationships with the people with whom he works closely, and being able to express himself through his body. On the negative side is the fact that the working life of a dancer is so short.

Stephen Baynes is a Leading Soloist with the company and one of its two Resident Choreographers. He finds the physical side of ballet is now being emphasised, rather than the theatricality. This leads to dancers getting to the point of doing all the movements, with technique as an end in itself. He laments that dancers today are looked upon more as athletes, and blames what he sees as a media mind set of making ballet more acceptable by comparing its prowess to such athletic pursuits as football.

Yet the people in the company are very strong, and choreographers can ask them to do more than they could a few years ago. At the same time, Baynes says, 'Dancers of this generation are so used to being shown the steps and picking it up quickly, that they have trouble with the slow process of building from nothing.' He tries to instil the idea of making some theatre. 'Dancers have to be engaged much more as actors. We have to get inside the skin of the fourth dimension, the most intangible thing that man has created, and make it three-dimensional. It's such a fine thing, to be one with the music.'

The other Resident Choreographer, Stanton Welch, who is also a Leading Soloist, definitely has dance in his blood. He is the son of famous Australian dancers Garth Welch and Marilyn Jones, and his brother, Damien, is with the company, too, as a Soloist. Welch is twenty-five, and has been with them for eight years. His new work in the 1996 repertoire is *Red Earth*, an evocative exploration of the primal impact of the Australian landscape on new settlers, set to Peter Sculthorpe's *Nourlangie* for guitar and orchestra, with the backdrop by Pro Hart. A great believer in fate, he has chosen not to have an outside life. 'I live, breathe and eat ballet.'

Justine Summers, a Principal who has been one of the girls dancing the lead role of Tatiana in *Onegin*, has at twenty-five come to a full realisation of what the way of life as a dancer involves. She says a lot of time as dancers is spent giving, including a lot more of their bodies these days. For her, one of the rewards is finding out a lot about herself while on stage, where she can throw away her inhibitions. Gielgud, when she danced, found a similar release. Summers declares that because of the need to give herself fully to her art, she has now decided she will not become involved in a serious relationship for some time.

Paula Baird, a Soloist who has been with the company for nearly ten years, was drawn to dancing because she had loved the old Fred and Ginger films and wanted to be in musical theatre, but found she could not sing. She started out with a lot of negativity about herself, but was helped through it by the great Australian dancer Lucette Aldous, who gave her self-confidence and was responsible for making her believe in herself.

Gielgud, also, has experienced what she describes as the great generosity of Aldous. It was when Gielgud, as a guest with The Australian Ballet late in 1975, was to dance for the first time the famous *La Fille mal gardée*, the Sir Frederick Ashton version. On arrival in Melbourne, she found to her dismay that there was nobody to teach it to her. It was Aldous who rescued her. Even though she was busy dancing *Black Swan* at both the matinee and evening performances, Aldous took pity on Gielgud, found a cassette player and a pianist, and recorded the whole ballet, note by note, step by step, word by mime word, through all three acts. Gielgud 'never, never forgot that. Nobody's ever done anything like that for me'.

Baird says her course through the company has been very hard emotionally. 'It's not an environment that's supportive. It never relinquishes. It requires a great deal of inner integrity. There's a lot of waiting for the next role, but there's not a lot you can do about it. What keeps me here is my love of Australia.'

She likens The Australian Ballet to an art gallery. 'When you go in and look at the paintings on the wall, the person in charge has chosen them. But, like all great galleries, there are works down below that are [also] brought out for exhibition. It's purely an artistic decision. I'm from the school where you either like a painting, or you don't, and sometimes there's no reason why.'

At the same time, she has never before known a group of dancers who have so much wanted the best thing for their company. A lot of them are prepared to make personal sacrifices because of their professionalism. More so than in other companies, the Australians do not take their personal problems on stage. She identifies three kinds of dancers who join the company: those who stay for only two or three years and leave because they do not like the lifestyle; those who find too many disappointments and are not prepared to make the sacrifices; and those who stay despite the disappointments. Most of the people Baird started with in the company have since gone, having dropped out of dance completely, usually between the ages of about twenty-five and twenty-eight.

Baird is one of the few people in the company who is married. She and her husband, who is not a dancer, organise their lives around her career. At least, she says, she can be herself in the company. She sees herself as an honest person and a survivor. She has to be, because dancers, she says, are always trying to please someone: their first teacher, the people who give them their first job, and their first choreographer. And so it goes on, the constant search for approval.

Vicki Attard, a Principal Artist, is also married. 'There's no division of my time. This comes first, and my husband knows that. While I'm here, my head is here.' While describing herself as a hard-working realist, she adds, 'What I really love about performing is [that] I love escaping. It's not to do with negativity about my life. I like to play the characters.' She has a massive struggle to get herself to performance pitch. 'Unfortunately, I set very high standards for myself, without any help.' She has a very open heart, so she cries regularly, including in the final act of *Onegin*, in which she dances the lead of Tatiana. For her this is a very good feeling.

Listening to the dancers revealing their lives, you are struck by their quality of character, eloquence, and dedication to dance. It is something of a shock, after watching them from the distance of the audience, to see up close how even more fine looking they are, and how young they appear. Some of the girls seem to have bodies not much older than children, with their small shoulders and fine limbs, though there is a sense of strength there, too, among the vulnerability, not the least of it in their willpower. Like children, they wriggle in their chairs, forever flexing their muscles, and stretching.

As if to emphasise their being not much more than children, some of the girls did not start menstruating until their early twenties. One dancer in her mid twenties had only two periods in the first five months of 1996. As happens with women in wartime, the lack of menstruation can be caused by stress or by working too hard. It is as though the body is holding onto all the nourishing material it can. Anorexia is not a popular subject around ballet companies, but this, too, can cause girls to cease menstruating.

Rebecca Yates is a Senior Artist who started dancing at the age of six, and is addicted to performing. 'A love of acting is the thing I love most about ballet.' For her, ballet begins in the mind and then enters the body. She speaks of a total interaction with the audience. 'They are sitting there and loving you, already. So, in your mind, if you are ready to take that step on stage, everything disappears, including your fears. You just become wrapped up in this huge story, then, afterwards, you might feel pain. It's like meditating. You are aware that your body's there, but your mind's off in another space. Everything melts into a Dali painting, including the music. What's unique about dancing is that you can put everything together and make one magical picture, which is fantastic, because everyone's minds are focussed, to one degree. Dancers have to make it look easy. That's the extra thing. It is hard to dance and tell a story.'

Yates has a natural technique, and the hardest part for her is the mental aspect. But she has what she calls a spark in her soul providing the will to dance. 'Shifting out of the comfort zone causes you to push yourself to dance. Some days you feel like a footballer, for example, with a very difficult role or a heavy opening night. You wake up [next morning] with a beaten feeling, as if a truck has run over you.' She agrees that she dances better when she is tired; then the adrenaline gets her through. 'The older you get, the more you have to pace yourself. It becomes as much an art as dance. Somewhere deep inside yourself you have to develop as a human being.'

All dancers are interested in eating. An army might march on its stomach, but a ballet company dances on its food. It is the one indulgence which they allow themselves, for the sheer pleasure of it as well as from knowing how good it is for their energy levels. They seem to eat constantly. Gielgud herself, who went through years of denial as a dancer, was always hungry. The best thing for her about giving up dancing has been that she can eat what she likes. A declared carnivore, she comes from the school that says meat is the best energy food. It was the same with Nureyev, with whom Gielgud often ate when they danced together, though Nijinsky, in his diary, records his abhorrence for meat.

Ron Alexander, the company's remedial massage therapist, says their diets are good, but they are still not completely following sports medicine thinking. The most important energy source comes from complex carbohydrates, such as pasta, potatoes, rice and bread – food which dancers have a few hours before performance. Protein is important, too. Today's dancers understand their bodies better than previous generations. They drink fruit juice and carry bottles of water around with them, swigging away on their treks through the long days and nights. Some are vegetarians. Some take herbs, vitamins and other supplements. A surprising number, including senior dancers, smoke tobacco, though this does not seem to affect them because their systems work anaerobically rather than aerobically.

Alexander watches the dancers carefully, monitoring their injuries. He can stop them going on, and has, but it is a 'quick and the dead' situation. Many nights people go on when they should not, because of a bad injury. Often they have to, because there is no understudy, so Alexander gives them mobilisation relief at the side of the stage so they will get through the performance. 'They are bloody heroes, some of them, what they go through. It's done with pure focus and ability.' Most of the injuries are soft tissue in nature, rather than bone problems, because they are like finely tuned machines. 'It's a fine line, whether they go on or not.'

Extra pressure comes from The Australian Ballet performance rate being reportedly among the highest in the world. The company operates for the whole year, unlike many which now run for only half that time. It is dependent on subscription because the government subsidy is not enough to sustain the company by itself.

Sometimes if a dancer who was injured the previous night then has a matinee as well as a night performance ahead of them, Alexander has to determine quickly what is wrong with them and how bad it is. If the person has an injury and cannot go on in the matinee, he will send them to the physiotherapist and still try to get them on that night. Injured dancers describe themselves to him in this way: 'Ron, we're broken dollies.'

Alexander says, 'We're finally getting through this attitude of "you're either on, or you're off – there's no grey area".' Sometimes dancers can do modified work which will help their injuries. The old idea of 'rest' is now relative, and the new thinking is that a little exercise can help.

Injury is a very important part of the life. Every night it changes. One person going off can affect up to fifteen others. Alexander sometimes has to choose his priority of the ones he feels he can help. He has to decide if he can make a change to a dancer's body in ten minutes to allow them to go on stage, and also determine if they are going to cause themselves any damage.

If someone is injured, the replacement has to learn the new part, often very quickly, as sometimes the emergency arises just before, or during the show. It changes from person to person. Some are determined to go on, regardless. Adrenaline will mask the pain, anyway. Alexander is much impressed by their sheer determination. 'They want to be better *yesterday*. I can't believe how they can do it, twelve hours a day, six days a week. They are so focused. It's awesome to be with them.'

There is considerable liaison now with the ballet staff, which previously was not always the case, and was initiated by Alexander. The medical team and the ballet staff meet once a week. Alexander, who is the only member of the medical team on tour, sees the Ballet Mistress Wendy Walker every day.

There are many stories to demonstrate the importance of the psychological side of the dancers' determination.

In 1995 in Adelaide, during the filming for a simulcast of *Manon*, a Senior Artist developed stress reactions in four bones in her foot. The girl even had trouble walking, and needed a bone scan. But she also needed to believe that she was all right, even if she was not, because nothing was going to stop her performing in *Manon*. Dancing for a couple more days, in fact, was not going to matter, so she was told she was all right, given prescription strength painkillers between acts, and as soon as the filming was finished, put on the first plane to Melbourne for a bone scan and six weeks off. It was her faith in herself which got her through.

Nicole Rhodes, a Leading Soloist, has had to fight her way back from being off for almost a year with a knee reconstruction. She actually faced the prospect of the end of her dancing career, but she is a very determined person, accepted what had happened, and set about the long road back, living one day to the next. She now has titanium staples in her knee, as a result of having had a tendon removed from the hamstring and connected to the knee to act as a cruciate ligament.

Rhodes was interviewed by Arts Editor Jason Steger, whose article on her appeared in the *Sunday Age* in June 1996 just before she opened in Melbourne as the lead in *In the Middle, Somewhat Elevated*. It is a most vigorous piece, which would test any dancer's agility. Steger wrote,

> Rhodes is darkly beautiful and remarkably composed. There is a serenity about her that disguises a strength and determination that have seen her overcome every dancer's nightmare. And she has the maturity to have gained insight from her experience.

He quotes her:

> 'It gave me a new perspective because having that time away was the first long time away from ballet that I ever had.' One moment it was rehearsal, the next a major operation. She joined the company in 1991 after spending two years at the school.

'It was a very intense time. It's hard sometimes to consider the bigger picture, to see how you're really thinking, feeling and working. When you have time out you can reassess yourself.

'I came back calmer, in a sense. I was much more focused ... In my old frame of mind if there was a ballet I didn't like, my reaction was, "Oh God", but now I ask, "What can I put into it and what can I get out of it?"'

Adrian Burnett, twenty-six, a Leading Soloist, who joined the company at seventeen, which is about as young as anyone can join, and has also danced abroad, sees the need to strike a balance in his life, the outside part of which is not given much time while dancing with this company, with its reputation of working hard. Dancing takes him out of time, and even when he has not danced well, he feels some satisfaction from being out there, and up there, doing it.

Part of the community life in the company is for dancers to be competitive. This can get them going, but it also has its dark side, when people hold themselves back from wanting to shine too much – the cutting down of tall poppies, in the Australian idiom. It is a trait Gielgud observed, to her dismay, soon after she became Artistic Director at the beginning of 1983. A senior dancer describes it in these terms: 'Don't be too good, otherwise they all attack you. You're striving, but not letting your essence come through.' Burnett does not let the tall poppy attitude bother him, and has always been obviously ambitious, and tried to be the best. 'Nobody's razzed me about it.'

James Newman, a Soloist, decided when he was six years old to be a dancer, when he saw a picture in a newspaper of The Australian Ballet. He came to the company's school at sixteen. 'I have an incredible fire in my belly to achieve a lot.' As well as his ballet career, he is doing his Master of Arts degree. 'I have a huge passion. It was as if dancing was to me a base, and enabled me to express myself artistically.' Dancing came easily to him, and at twenty-six he can still rely readily on his natural ability. 'But it's important not to. You've got to go a little bit further than God's given you [the ability to do]. As you get older, you discover there is a lot more in dance than pushing a leg to a certain height, and when you start exploring, you start realising why you're doing what you're doing.' He is reaching that point now. He says he loves working towards perfection, even though it is impossible. He has withdrawal symptoms from adrenaline. He, too, believes in having other, outside influences, 'to experience other things, and bring it into your passion of your life.'

Grant Kelley, in the Corps de ballet, is nineteen and has been with the company for nearly two years. When he does a solo, it brings out his competitive edge. 'I could just feel everybody's eyes on me. I suppose it was an ego thing. It made me feel special, but that's what you do. You're there to please the audience as well.'

The late afternoon finds Gielgud back in yet another rehearsal in the studio. It is 5.30 p.m., two and a half hours to performance, yet she still has another rehearsal after this. While the coach runs the rehearsal, it can be the decision of the dancers to stop and start again when they get it wrong. They use the time to catch their breath, resting their hands on their knees, listening to Gielgud above the sound of their breathing. They seem always to apologise before starting again, looking a bit sheepish, as though they lost the plot.

On this afternoon we see an example of how hard Gielgud is prepared to push a dancer, in this case a young boy who is only in his first year with the company. Clearly Gielgud considers him worth the effort, while to an outsider the treatment might seem harsh. She says later of him, 'If he keeps his commitment to dance and works really hard and intelligently, the potential is great, as there is a huge talent there.'

Andrew Bowman is the dancer in question – a tall, handsome young man with an excellent, willowy physique. Accompanied by the company's Principal Pianist, Stuart Macklin, he and Gielgud are rehearsing a routine from *The Sleeping Beauty* which has him hurtling at great speed around the small studio space in a series of fast jetés. But it soon becomes clear that despite his apparent agility, something is really bothering him. Finally he tells Gielgud that he is scared. She receives this news impassively, and asks him, 'Scared of what?' He replies, hesitatingly, 'Scared of falling over.'

Gielgud says, 'If you fall over, you'll know which way it is, and be able to lean the other way.' It sounds like a one-line gag until we realise she is not joking.

Bravely, Bowman keeps trying, and is breathtaking to

watch. But still Gielgud is not satisfied, and again there is an exchange between them. It becomes apparent that there is some sort of battle of wills going on. Bowman finishes his routine, looks appealingly at Gielgud, who is sitting impassive and impervious, and asks her, imploringly, 'Was that faster?' All he gets in return is a peremptory response: 'Disappointingly safe.'

She is ice cold as she makes him go further and further, and faster and faster. She talks of him feeling 'ugly' about a step, and says, 'I don't mind if you're ugly. Just push.' As he keeps trying, she suggests, very matter-of-fact, 'Just push yourself to danger point. It doesn't matter if you fall.'

By now the boy is clearly distressed, both physically and emotionally. He tries to evoke sympathy from Gielgud when he stops, blowing like a bellows, and says he needs air. By now the air in the studio is dense, and tense. Gielgud's only response is a non-committal murmur.

Bowman is now down on his knees on the floor near her, sweating and panting and grunting like a stricken racehorse. Gielgud asks him if his knee is all right. Glad of her showing some expression of concern, he says, 'Yes. It's when it's cold. I've had it for years. It's to do with growing.'

And so it goes on, only now, incredibly, both he and Gielgud are taking it in turns to suggest he does it 'one more time'. It becomes clear that they are collaborating in some sort of game to get him to break through his fear barrier.

Eventually they accomplish their goal, with Bowman finishing in a cloud of exhaustion, but triumphant. He bows.

As he composes himself afterwards, Bowman explains that he always stays back to get it right, because he has to. On the steps on the way out, he gives a little wave to the pianist. For her part, Gielgud is already working with the next dancer.

What we have seen at work here is the steel of Gielgud, a glimpse of how far she will go for the sake of the work, the end justifying the means. Some people might think it too extreme, perhaps even cruel. Watching her, though, we realise that this process of pushing beyond endurance is the same as she has always demanded of herself. She, too, had teachers just as staunch as she is today, with whom she, too, learned never to flinch, no matter how ferocious the fire of self-sacrifice, all for the sake of the art. The lineage goes on.

3
———

FIRST STEPS

Among the many exotic sights at Evian, the fashionable French resort famous for its waters, was a small girl who went there with her parents in 1948. She soon discovered there was an orchestra, and started dancing to the music. This is where Maina Gielgud gave her first public performance, at the age of three. The sight of a child so young being so animated both amused and moved the onlookers, particularly the older people, as they sat around drinking the healing water of life in the endless pursuit of slowing down the ageing process.

Gielgud herself has no recollection of the occasion, so we have to draw on the memory of her mother. 'You got the waters and the casino at the same time, and my husband and I liked to go and play a bit of roulette. It was very comfortable to leave Maina there, dancing in front of the orchestra, having asked them to keep an eye on her, which they loved doing. We used to go and gamble a bit for half an hour and come back, and there was Maina, still hopping around and absolutely adoring it.'

The event confirmed what was already assumed: that she was artistic. Even as a baby she would wobble about when she heard music, and by the time she could walk she would improvise dancing to whatever music was playing.

Gielgud, like so many of the dancers in her charge at The Australian Ballet, took her first dancing class when she was very young, five in fact, though she was already more advanced than most children her age. This happened in Brussels, where she was living with her parents, Lewis and Zita. She went to dancing classes because her best friend was going. Ballet dancers are a competitive breed, and Gielgud was no exception in her career as a ballerina. Her ambition came, though, according to her, not from the exaltation of beating others, but because she wanted to be good enough to dance all the great parts.

Her teacher in Brussels was a Russian, Madame de Zeum, and it was a proper ballet class, which had among its pupils some professionals. Being so young and small, the child stood out, but, self-possessed as always, and ballet mad, she soon fitted in. She stood at the barre next to a dancer and followed what she saw.

De Zeum said to her mother, 'I hate children. But this one can come, because she follows. She's got strong feet and legs. Buy her some pointe shoes.' This was unusual, even then. Nowadays students are generally not allowed to wear pointe shoes until they are twelve.

The teacher was one of the tribe of Russian émigrés who brought their brand of ballet to the West early this century, then stayed and taught. Many lived to a great age. Some exhibited extreme behaviour, and shouting at their students was common. Some of the best of them became Gielgud's mentors.

Born in London on 14 January 1945, the child had greasepaint in her veins from both sides of the family. She would grow tall, like all the Gielguds, with a stately bearing. She learned to speak French, as her first language, before English. She has that formal and distinctive English way of saying 'one', instead of 'I', which only adds to the sense of her reserve, and her apparent disinterest in projecting a personal self.

Her mother, with typical bluntness, says, 'As a baby, she wasn't very pretty. I must say when the nurse brought her in to show her to me I was a bit taken aback. I thought to myself, 'My God, she looks like the old Aga Khan.' I didn't know much about children, and didn't like them. I still don't, and to have given birth to Maina was not really something I wanted. Neither did her father.' Indeed, her parents had such doubts about the new family life that they considered sending the child to live with other people in the country, who could care for her better.

Her mother adds, 'I must say, she was an interesting child.' Gielgud herself says that from an early age she realised she was, in her words, odd.

Gielgud's mother, who came from a background of family wealth ravaged by war, had been an acclaimed Hungarian theatre and film actress of considerable talent through the 1930s. She uses the stage name of Zita Gordon Gielgud, and still performs occasionally. She is now in her mid eighties.

There is quite a tale to tell about Zita's name. Noël Pelly tells it, in his biography of her.

'I was born on 2 December 1911 in Gyöngyös, an important and beautiful city in the county of Heves in northern Hungary. I was the second of four children of the marriage between Ella Téven de Dévéney and Zoltán Grüszner.

'Some time before I was born, the future Habsburg king, Prince Charles, and his wife Zita paid an official visit to Gyöngyös during an important festival. My maternal grandfather, who was very influential at the time, hosted a grand ball at which, I was told, my mother was enchanting and flirted with everybody. When I came along, she decided my name should be Zita in honour of the future Queen Zita, but Father registered me as Elisabeth Clotilde Hedvidge Maria Gabriella. Much later I discovered from Aunt Böske, our elderly maiden relation who knew everything, that these were the names of his various girl friends. Mummy only found this out when I went to school and she needed a copy of my birth certificate. Until then she thought I was Zita. She was furious and appealed to the appropriate ministry to change my legal name to Zita, but by then the Habsburg reign was virtually over and, as the Hungarians hated the Habsburgs, her appeal was refused. Thus I was never officially Zita, but I have always been called by this name. In my passport, and all official papers, I am still Elisabeth Clotilde Hedvidge – the Maria and Gabriella were forgotten.'

Pelly's biography also reveals why her maiden name was so clearly non-Hungarian. Zita says she decided to get herself a professional name the night before the exams at the theatre school she was attending in Budapest after she ran away from home to become an actress. 'So I consulted the telephone directory and chose Gordon, thus keeping my Z.G. initials, and giving myself an easy international name for when Hollywood called.'

Gielgud's father, Lewis, was part of the famous Gielgud family, who had their roots in Lithuanian-Polish landowners. The family castle still stands, and Gielgud has the right to use the title of Comtesse de Gielgud but, in one of genealogy's quirks, only when she resides outside England. Lewis, who was the oldest brother, was educated at Eton and Oxford, and became Secretary-General of the International League of Red Cross Societies.

The second of the three brothers, John, became one of the leading stage and film actors of his age, much revered for his readings from Shakespeare in that wonderful rich voice, full of the peaks and valleys of human experience. When he realised that his niece was, at the age of eight, serious about becoming a dancer, he advised her to take up acting instead, because he believed it would be easier. They appeared on stage together in 1980, at a charity gala at the London Palladium, with him reading Shakespeare while she danced. They still meet occasionally when she is in England.

Val, the third brother, was an accomplished writer, and became a prominent producer at the BBC. Their sister, Eleanor, worked for a time assisting Sir John. Their mother, Kate Terry Lewis, was a niece of another famous performer, the English actress Ellen Terry, the brothers' maternal great aunt. There were many Terrys on the stage, including Ellen's sisters Mabel and Kate; Kate was Gielgud's great-grandmother and a great actress who retired in her early twenties. Ellen Terry's son, Gordon Craig, was the famous British theatre designer.

A biography by Gyles Brandreth, *John Gielgud: A Celebration*, is forthcoming about some of the Gielgud family history:

> [John's father, Frank Gielgud, was] a successful stockbroker, very much the comfortable Edwardian, despite the fact that he was of Lithuanian descent and only a second generation Londoner. Frank's father was born in England, and worked at the War Office and as a foreign correspondent, but his grandparents were Polish. One of Frank's grandmothers was an acclaimed Polish actress called Aniela Aszpergercwa. One of his grandfathers was a Polish cavalry officer called John Gielgud and it was this John Gielgud who left Poland for England in the 1830s.

FIRST STEPS

The present John Gielgud's actual first name is Arthur. He was named after his maternal grandfather, Arthur Lewis, but the Arthur was soon dropped in favour of his second name and he was known as John or Jack to his family from an early age. His mother, Kate, belonged to one of the most distinguished of all theatrical clans: the Terry's. Her immediate family included at least twenty individuals closely concerned with the theatre, of whom the best known were probably her mother, Kate Terry, her uncle, Fred Terry, her aunt, Ellen Terry, and her cousins Gordon Craig and Phyllis Neilson-Terry.

Naturally, young John was delighted with his celebrated relations: 'I was enormously englamoured by my family, particularly the ones who were still acting when I was a boy. My parents didn't encourage this very much, although they were naturally very proud of it too. My mother was the theatrical one because she was a Terry, but my father, who was partly Polish, has a curious, practical, middle-class English realism, mixed with a certain romantic *panache*.'

Zita and Lewis married in England in 1937, and because of his work did much travelling. She went into uniform at the outbreak of World War II, near the end of which their daughter was conceived, in Cairo. She was named Maina after her godmother, Maina Balfour, who worked with her mother during the war. Balfour's name was actually Mary, but she started to be called Maina by her family as a joke, after a bird of that name in India, presumably the mynah. If so, it has some resonance in Gielgud, being a bird known for making its presence felt. Her detractors might say the name is appropriate because the mynah bird is shrill and territorial, while her friends might say the bird is musical, and always ready to give of itself.

Gielgud's parents lived well in London and Paris through the 1930s, and came to know many famous people. Their daughter was taken in her early years around the diplomatic circuit, which exposed her to many writers, painters, performers and politicians. She was permitted to mingle with the guests at the various receptions, and talk with them as much as she wished. The one definite rule was that she was not to dance at the functions, where such behaviour would have been out of place.

At the same time, while meeting so many people so readily as a child in a grown-up world, she was shy and self-conscious. 'But when I was put on stage, it was really a most comfortable place.'

Gielgud's mother remembers the child being typically unimpressed when she met Winston Churchill. It would have made no difference had she known who he was. Gielgud says today she is aware of people as such, but is fortunate that she does not notice their age, sex or colour.

One person from those early years who came to influence her was Aldous Huxley, who was a great friend of Lewis, and whom the child adored. She has no direct memory of the day when she was four and he took her walking in the Luxembourg Gardens, a favourite place of his in Paris. She was still very small, while in contrast, Huxley was well over six feet tall, like a giraffe, as her mother fondly remembers him. On his request, they went to the park, and the two of them crossed the Place de la Concorde together, hand in hand, and then disappeared into the gardens, where they proceeded to play hide-and-seek.

Lewis left his daughter first editions of all of Huxley's books. A great favourite for her became *The Perennial Philosophy*, in which Huxley outlined the great spiritual teachings of the world, and showed that they each had the same essence. Although her mother was Catholic, the child was baptised Anglican, and later as a teenager used to take herself to church every Sunday. But her interest in spiritual matters, which became important to her, particularly as a part of dancing, later extended to the religions of the East.

Her parents divorced in 1950, but amicably, so much so that Zita's ex-husband was best man the following year, when she married Nigel Sutton, the Secretary-General of the Inter-Allied Reparation Agency (IARA), who in 1951 was appointed Executive Secretary of the North Atlantic Treaty Organisation (NATO). Nigel and Lewis were best friends, and the three of them got along so well that at one stage, before the divorce, they all lived together in a house in Brussels. Relating this, Gielgud shows no sense of it having been unusual. It is perhaps a sign of the sophistication of the life of which she was part.

Lewis died in 1953, and Nigel died three years later. This would bring Gielgud and her mother together in a most extraordinary and intense relationship.

Gielgud says, 'I adored both my father and stepfather, and had the benefit of the two of them.' She used to call Lewis 'Favi', and Nigel 'Fin'. They were the only names she ever used for them. How each man affected her is uncertain. Lewis Gielgud was capable of long periods of total silence, sometimes not speaking at all for weeks on end, as though he had gone deeply inside himself. Silence would become a characteristic of the daughter, too.

It took her a long time to come to terms with Lewis's death. 'For many years, there was always this feeling that I might meet my father, that he was not really dead.'

She was an earnest, serious child, who always had her head in books, even taking them to bed at night where she continued reading by torchlight under the sheets. She developed an interest in the English classics early, and read and re-read Dickens and the Brontes, along with good children's books. She adored *Little Women*, and all the works of Lewis Carroll, who would feature later in a ballet of her own creation.

'I think I looked for a father in books, in a funny kind of way, as in looking for my own species of morality. I was a real goody-goody. I can remember writing my best friend a long letter about God and the issues of life and death. It was very private. To discuss religion, or say the word "God" was enormously difficult for me.'

While she has kept an apparently strict code of personal morality, attracting no gossip for such a singular, solitary woman of much power and under public scrutiny, she is comfortable in the free and easy world of theatre. She is virtually unshockable, having seen all kinds of liaisons and heard all kinds of language. One of her most famous dance partners, Rudolf Nureyev, used to come out with 'dreadful, dreadful' things. There is a relish in her voice when she recounts them.

Gielgud as a child was alone a lot, which she actually enjoyed. She did not talk much with her contemporaries, and instead was happy in the company of older people. She had an imaginary friend, Fayelle, and there were always dogs. But no dolls.

In an interview in the *Guardian* in 1971, Gielgud was asked to respond to people with whom she worked referring to her as being 'close in'. 'Yes, it's true, I don't easily "go" toward people. Consequently, I have had so few friends. Maybe it's because as a child I was such a loner, or maybe it was due to the fact that I was dancing from an early age, and that I lived mostly with my mother.' No doubt their being constantly on the move also left little time to form friendships. Her mother says, 'Maina did everything on her own, even when she was quite, quite small. She listened to us, but there was always a distance from which she listened. Even now, when she's bored by conversation, and has had enough of it, she shamelessly looks out the window.' The characteristic is confirmed just as affectionately by Noël Pelly, who was Administrator of The Australian Ballet from 1983, the same year Gielgud started as Artistic Director, until 1991. Pelly, who knows both of them better than most, regards them as the two most powerful and remarkable women he has ever met.

He does not know how her parents' divorce affected Gielgud. She was equally fond of both her father and stepfather. 'Both were British, of a particular kind, both had been best friends all their life, and I think she leant almost exclusively to the Brit. side in her.' Despite living in Australia since the beginning of 1983, Gielgud still kept her British nationality. She says this has been for no particular reason, and that questions of nationality are irrelevant to her.

Pelly adds: 'And then, of course, you have the other influence of the fact that her education was French. So you've got those three influences in her: the Hungarian, the British and the French. An extraordinary mix.'

Suzanne Davidson, who is in charge of The Australian Ballet's operations in Sydney, and the company's film and television productions, is a close colleague and friend of Gielgud. She also has a Hungarian mother. Speaking of the troubles with the company, Gielgud once remarked to her, 'I never thought I'd say this, but I'm very glad I have Hungarian blood in me, because I think that's what's making me still stand up.'

After watching her perform as a gypsy queen in a gala event in Cannes in 1967, the great dancer, choreographer and director, Anton Dolin, of whom Gielgud was very fond, called her his 'Hungarian Goulash'. Hearing this, her mother remarked, 'She has, after all, an Hungarian bit about her somewhere.' Gielgud herself says, 'I am grateful, amongst other things, for having inherited the Hungarian strength, and the sense of humour.'

Of her emotional make-up, Gielgud says, 'I'm enormously sentimental, and not ashamed of it. It's always hard for me to say goodbye. But I start the mourning period before the parting, and it's very difficult. But then one has to get on with life.'

There is a lovely photograph of her with her mother when she was about five, showing them smiling at each other. When described as looking in it like a 'dear little girl', she responded curtly, 'I don't know about that!'

She says, 'I think, as a child, I was quite old, and later, very much younger. I think I always looked older. The tilt of the chin. As they say, "the arrogant Gielgud look". But they say it with a smile. People tend not to come to tell me their deepest secrets. Sometimes I wish they would, and sometimes I'm glad when they don't.

'In a way, I thought my parents were snobs. They spoke a lot of what was *not done*, not necessarily that I wasn't to do those things later.' She had rebellious feelings against doing the 'correct' thing, but says, 'In fact, they insisted you should know the rules, so that you can make a choice when you become an adult, as long as it does not hurt other people.'

Nigel Sutton imposed a code in the family that people must be very civilised towards each other, which meant Gielgud was taught not to make personal remarks about others, not even to compliment them on their appearance. 'These days, though, if I see somebody who's wearing what I think is a gorgeous dress, I will say so.' Yet her reserve is such that we are disinclined to be too familiar with her.

Her mother felt strongly about certain conventions, too, such as the need for women always to look very stylish. With her mother's encouragement the girl started dressing up, and was wearing make-up by the time she was fourteen, which was young for such glamour among girls in those days. Social life, though, held no attraction for her. She tried to be like other young people, but was bored at parties, seeing no point to being there. Gielgud tends to relate better to men, although there have been some significant connections with women, especially when she was younger.

Each Sunday after they moved to London from Brussels, she went to lunch with her grandmother, Kate Terry Gielgud. 'She was an awe-inspiring woman, and not someone that one would put one's arms around. She was a very elegant woman, very tall. She was always dressed in black, with some sort of lace on. I only vaguely remember my grandfather, who was also very tall, and kindly, and a beautiful man. I've always had beautiful men around me.'

Her grandparents lived in a comfortable apartment near Albert Hall. 'Minnie was the cook. There used to be roast beef, and my grandmother used to carve. But she had a terrible habit of always tasting the gravy with the serving spoon, which she licked. I used to come home and complain bitterly to Mummy.' Sutton sympathised with her daughter's predicament, but felt she had to make the effort to go there. She would drop the child at the place, and collect her afterwards. There used to be good pudding, too, because the granddaughter always loved good English food. And then there were dominoes. 'I loved playing them, like I love all games. So I always looked forward to going there, apart from the spoon business.' She and her grandmother took turns at winning. 'It would have been very important to win.' Her habit now is to play the card game of patience for hours against her computer; she becomes so immersed that she needs an alarm to tell her when to stop. She comments, 'This is something odd, that I suppose some psychologist might enjoy working out.'

An important person in Gielgud's early life was her adopted godmother, Muriel Gore. They first met when Gielgud was nine and Gore was in her sixties. She was the best friend of Nigel Sutton's first wife, who first became a friend to Gielgud's mother, but then became even closer to Gielgud herself.

'We just got on like a house on fire. She was very, very practical, and very well read. We used to talk mainly about books. She was a handsome English woman, with very large green eyes. She had a lot of Russian ballet friends, and had been involved with them a little in her earlier years. People like Lydia Lopokova [the Russian-born ballerina who was with the Diaghilev Ballet] was a friend of hers. She would have seen ballet in those days as one did in her circle, and really loved it. I can see the whole flat now, because I used to stay there. It was just off Kensington High Street, and I remember the caged lift. The apartment was on the third floor. In the bedroom there was a very, very high bed. Then there was her room, which one hardly went into. The telephone was in her room. And then the big room, with books everywhere, a dining table; the kitchen. She had her health food fads, and we would exchange health food things.' Together, they read *Prevention* magazine, which detailed 'all the gory details about things like pharmaceutical products that are being sold to you and are not really healthy. But she loved the classics, so that was our first meeting point: books. I'd always sit up at night and read, always in bed.'

It could be that Gore, who never married, was an influence on Gielgud as a single as well as a singular woman. 'I've never thought of it that way, but perhaps. She was very self-sufficient. In fact, she had some money to live on, and gave a certain amount to charity, so I had great respect for her as well. She appeared to be very proper, but she had a wonderful sense of humour, and one could tease her. She was just a little eccentric, but would never appear so unless you knew her. If I had anything to confide, she would be the one I told.

'I suppose I used her as an antidote to my mother... played one up against the other a bit, but lightly. She took my side, which was nice. I think that my mother, being pretty practical too, thought that it was healthy in a way, although a nuisance in others. My mother was very conscious that she was trying to be both mother and father to me, and Muriel was like another sensible grown-up person.'

Meanwhile, Sutton encouraged her daughter's artistic nature to develop. 'It was normal that she should go that way. I was an actress, and Lewis's family were all really artistic. In fact, I hoped, too, like John said she should, that she would become an actress, because I could see that she had that [talent] somehow... the way she talked. You could feel these sorts of things.'

But, despite her preference, Sutton did not support Sir John's advice about an actor's life being better than a dancer's. 'She was already working very seriously when he said that. My response was, I helped her in what *she* wanted to do. And she wanted to dance, from the age of five, but seriously, in the way she is now an artistic director. She hoped to do it 24 hours a day, but she knew she had to do school, so she did it, as quickly as possible, and always extremely well. For the rest, she read books, many of them on ballet, and went to see all the ballets at the time.'

Sutton jokes that she was her daughter's first choreographer. The story, from when the child was four, and already interested in a career as a dancer, gives us a glimpse of the degree of intimacy between them, with dance as the medium. Every evening, when her mother came upstairs to say good night, the child would ask her to 'make me a choreography'. The mother sat down on the bed, and did it, though she says, 'I knew absolutely nothing, except a few ballets.' But she knew enough to describe in detail how, for example, a ballerina doing a solo performance came on stage, on pointe, dancing in a circle, doing various steps, an arabesque left and right, and then finally leaving to the right, into the wings, as the curtain went slowly down.

Sutton believes the father's death enforced the very strong will in the daughter to dance. 'There was no alternative to her wanting to be a dancer. It was so clear that I didn't think any more about an easier life, or not, because Maina was so determined that this was the life that she wanted. With her having lost her father, I felt that I had to be more father than mother to her. I had to agree, and help as much as I could.'

The constant family travel between London and Paris began Gielgud's gypsy life. It gave her an early and influential experience of great ballet teachers and performances, instilling in her the strong sense of the classical dance tradition.

Edward Pask, former dancer, now dance historian, author and The Australian Ballet's archivist, has known Gielgud longer than probably anybody else in the Australian ballet world. He speaks of that lineage in the spirit of her classical ballet bloodlines, which is in fact connected ultimately with The Australian Ballet.

'It goes back to the Ballets Russes, begun by the famous impresario Sergei Pavlovich Diaghilev, which grew out of the old Imperial Russian Ballet after the Revolution, and produced many émigrés. Even prior to the Revolution, the Diaghilev company, known as the Diaghilev Ballets Russes, was performing in Paris and other parts of Western Europe from 1909.

'The first Paris performance caused a sensation. It was the eruption of an artistic volcano which was to change the entire course of the development in ballet throughout the world. It swept away all the conventions of nineteenth century ballets – the lengthy multi-act works, overdressed and bejewelled ballerinas who reigned supreme on their stages, the sometimes trite music which had been composed to coincide with every gesture and command of the choreographer, and the over-pretty chocolate-box decor. In their place were one-act ballets in which choreographer, designer, composer and scenarist worked as a team; a new wave of classical ballets and hitherto unexploited themes of folklore burst upon an unsuspecting public in a glorious riot of colour, before canvases brushed by the hands of the greatest painters of the day. And, too, the Diaghilev Ballets Russes reinstated that long-forgotten hero – the *premier danseur* – to his rightful position as a dance artist and not just as a leaning post for a prima ballerina.

'And what a galaxy of dancers appeared with the Diaghilev Ballets Russes... names that are today legends of international ballet history – Anna Pavlova, Tamara Karsavina, Olga Preobajenska, Mathilde Kschessinska, Lydia Lopokhova, Vera Nemtchinova, Olga Spessivtzeva, and Lubov Tchernicheva; the male ranks were equally impressive with Vaslav Nijinsky, Adolf Bolm, Pierre Vladimiroff, Michel Fokine, Leonide Massine, Anton Dolin, George Balanchine and Serge Lifar. The artists Bakst, Benois, Roerich, Matisse, Picasso, Gris, Laurencin and Cocteau were each associates and collaborators, as were the composers Igor Stravinsky, Maurice Ravel, Claude Debussy, Georges Auric, Darius Milhaud, Francis Poulenc and Sergei Prokofiev. His choreographers included Fokine, Nijinsky, Massine and Balanchine.

'Sergei Diaghilev was a master entrepreneur and instigator of ballet attractions, which he combined with that remarkable flair of securing the interest, patronage and financial backing of Europe's monarchs and aristocracy. Of the sixty-eight ballets staged or created by the Diaghilev company, some twenty-three remain in regular performance to this day in their original form, whilst many others have since been remade anew by latter-day choreographers. And still we have the joy of so much of the music expressly written to Diaghilev's commission.'

Diaghilev is credited with having led to the reform of dance in Europe, which in turn caused a great surge of ballet into other Western countries, including Australia. Gielgud herself says the period which fascinates her the most is the time of Diaghilev, and the coming of the Russian style to the West.

When Diaghilev died in 1929, his dancers and choreographers scattered themselves because there was nothing else they could do. This led to the formation of the various Ballets Russes companies, some of which visited Australia, the last being the Colonel de Basil's Original Ballet Russe in 1939–40.

Again, the dancers dispersed, and some stayed in Australia because of the war, and established small performing groups and schools. One of those people was the Czech-born Edouard Borovansky, who set up the Borovansky Ballet Company, which folded in 1961 after his death in 1959; Peggy van Praagh was its last Artistic Director. The Australian Ballet, with her as its first Artistic Director, was formed in September 1962. Pask was at its opening night.

Pask says that some of the former stars of the famous Maryinsky Theatre of St Petersburg (later re-named the Kirov) who were included in those Russian dancers who emigrated at the time of Diaghilev, were among the great legends of dance history with whom Gielgud studied, led there by her French education and European travels.

'To me – and Maina's feeling is exactly the same,

because we've discussed it – dance is a religion. When somebody embarks on a career in dance, they make vows, rather like a nun or a priest does, except that their vows are to themselves. I know, because I made those vows. Maina made those vows. Dance is governed by that, by that discipline. And wherever Maina was at any given time, and still to this day, the brain is active, open, on the alert to learn, not to pick and hoard, but to learn. This inner sense of tradition which has been passed to Maina, as a caretaker for the future, is the reason, the valid reason, why she thinks in the old way and works at the pace she does. It's called dedication. She is a guardian of that heritage.'

Gielgud's early life, like the rest of it, was full of ballet. While still living in London, she was taken to the best performances, and she saw an array of ballerinas. They included the Lithuanian-born British dancer Svetlana Beriosova, whom Gielgud idolised for her lyricism and line. When she was thirteen, Gielgud saw Beriosova doing a slow adagio during class one day in Monte Carlo, 'and I just cried and cried, because of the beauty of the way she was doing it. Just extraordinary.' Another favourite was the Soviet British dancer Violetta Elvin, who grew up with the Bolshoi. There was also the leading dancer Margot Fonteyn, and Elaine Fifield, an Australian who was popular both in England and in her own country.

The young girl became so engrossed in the performances that she acted them out in front of the mirror at home afterwards, pretending she had been on stage doing whatever famous role she had just seen. 'And when it actually happened, it was like a miracle.'

The performances made her ambitious, not to be a 'star', but to dance certain roles. They nurtured her definite ideas from the beginning about where she wanted to go. The signs of the ability, maturity and dedication which would chart her career also came early.

It was unusual for a child to take professional class, but Gielgud did that at the age of seven. During visits to Paris to see her father, she attended classes with Olga Preobrajenska, the famous Russian-French dancer who, at eighty-two, was still teaching, still forceful and fiery. Preobrajenska, a prima ballerina with the Maryinsky Theatre, is credited with having led ballet in Russia in the early part of this century. Later she taught several generations of the best dancers in Europe, including Youskevitch, Skibine, Golovine, Miskovitch, Baronova, Toumanova and Riabouchinska. The final three of this list were the famous 'Baby Ballerinas' who in their early teens were heading the Ballets Russes de Monte Carlo in 1933.

Also at the age of seven, Gielgud attended her first dancing school, in London, at the Hampshire School in Old Brompton Road. Run by the mother of Susan Hampshire, the film actress, it is described rather abruptly by Gielgud as a place where high society sent their children. It provided her with her first partner, who danced with her in a school show. This was Anthony Dowell, later one of Britain's finest classical dancers, and now Artistic Director of The Royal Ballet.

Another early experience for Gielgud of attending

class by a great traditionalist was with George Goncharov, the Russian dancer, choreographer and teacher, who had taught Fonteyn.

When talking of the early days, Gielgud rattles off the famous foreign-sounding names with familiarity, ease and affection, often talking too fast for them all to be noted correctly, let alone appreciated. To those of us outside the ballet world, many of them, with a few exceptions, would be unfamiliar, and Gielgud's long listing of them perhaps an overkill. Yet to her and her kind, these were the great dancers and sources of inspiration – the legends of the lineage.

Her first-hand connection with tradition was continued when she was nine and went to board at the Legat School in Tunbridge Wells, founded by Nicolai Legat and continued by his wife Nadine Nicolaeva. Both were White Russians. Legat himself was a principal at the Maryinsky Theatre around the turn of the century, and a partner preferred by the great ballerinas Pavlova, Kschessinska and Trefilova. He became Director of the Imperial Ballet School, which has had such distinguished pupils as Egorova, Preobrajenska, Sedova, Vaganova, Karsavina, Fokine, Bolm and Nijinsky. He left the USSR in 1923, became Ballet Master of Diaghilev's company, settled in London and founded his school in 1928. His students there included Fonteyn, de Valois, Nemtchinova, Danilova, Lopokova, Inglesby, Dolin and Lifar.

Gielgud remembers that Nadine Nicolaeva had the students doing very difficult things. Once, at midnight, she roused the boarders out of bed and made them do fouettés, on pointe. (A fouetté is a movement where a dancer moves the working leg to the side in a whipping motion and into the knee, while a full circle is performed.) It was useful for Gielgud's dance career that she had no fear of this difficult step.

She stayed at the school for only a few months. One day while playing leapfrog she broke her arm, but it was not discovered for three days. This did not impress her mother, who removed her immediately.

Another childhood accident happened when Gielgud was seven and was knocked on the nose by a chicken coop feeder on a farm in England, leaving her with a small bump, which remained. The Gielgud noses have always been prominent, which is usually no disadvantage on stage, but she had hers altered in mid-career, believing it was causing her to be typecast in 'bitchy' roles.

Previously there had not been much music in the family home, but through the daughter's influence it began to permeate the place. In her youthful enthusiasm Gielgud decided when she was eight that she wanted also to learn the violin, but her mother opposed it, fearing the screeching that would follow. The child had a piano in her room but this was removed because she played it all night. Instead she was given a piano accordion. Her mother wryly recalls: 'After being used for countless "Happy Birthday to You" recitals, it was eventually drowned in a cellar in Cannes in 1965, then pensioned off.'

She kept a lot to herself. Like other children, she had thoughts of life and death. She did not discuss these matters with anybody but looked for answers in books. Her sense of mortality was intensified by a constant nightmare that someone would come in her bedroom window in London and murder her.

By the time she was ten, she had definitely decided to be a dancer, and back in London went twice weekly for a mime and ballet class with the famous former Russian ballerina Tamara Karsavina, another Maryinsky Theatre legend, who was acclaimed as one of the greatest dancers in ballet history, having a profound effect on twentieth century ballet.

At the same time, Gielgud was having private classes with the noted teacher Rachel Cameron, who was Karsavina's assistant. These were in the family's apartment in Grosvenor Square, where the carpet was pulled back from the parquet floor, and a barre installed in her bedroom.

She also took class with Stanislav Idzikowsky, the Polish-born dancer who had performed with Pavlova and Diaghilev's company, and was known for his brilliant technique. One of his most famous roles was the Blue Bird in *The Sleeping Beauty*. Gielgud remembers him as a tiny, dapper man who wore patent leather shoes, in which he used to do a remarkable ten or twelve pirouettes. He taught in a church hall, and was inseparable from Madame Evina, his pianist and friend.

Part of Gielgud's becoming versed in the tradition of classical ballet was through hearing narratives about the great dancers of the past. This she did when taken to tea on Sundays hosted by a great friend of Karsavina named

Poppea Wanda, nicknamed Poppy. The illustrious company there included Karsavina herself, and Cameron, together with the esteemed English dancer, choreographer and teacher Anton Dolin. Also present were Keith Lester, another important figure in English dance who studied with Dolin, Astafieva, Legat and Fokine. Sitting there listening to them talking about the old days and dance tradition, Gielgud enjoyed the sense of being accepted at ten years of age. 'I felt grown up. It never occurred to me that they were any older than I was.'

In one of those consistent links which seem to occur regularly in the ballet world, the large house off Brompton Road which Gielgud and her mother and stepfather had before they moved to Grosvenor Square was bought by Fonteyn. Gielgud's mother recalls in her biography how the prima ballerina came to inspect the place. 'I well remember noticing the way that she walked as I led her from the Italianate hall into the garden. I had never before seen anybody walk as she did – her feet hardly touched the ground.' While she was there, Fonteyn noticed the girl's ballet tights and remarked, 'I see there's somebody in the same boat.' She talked with Gielgud and was very kind to her, understanding that she might be upset to be losing her room.

Later Fonteyn said to Gielgud's stepfather, 'It's very difficult to find a good teacher for young children. Maina now needs, as I did, good Russian teachers who not only teach you to dance, but also the love of dance.' Sutton remembered the advice when she was wondering later what to do about her daughter's training. She had considered enrolling her in The Royal Ballet School, but a letter to her from Karsavina changed her mind: 'The child is so talented, serious and advanced. Take her to Paris, take her to Lubov Egorova or Mathilde Kschessinska – any of the former Russian ballerinas who are still giving classes – because the teaching here is not quite good enough yet.'

Three months after her second husband died, Sutton packed their ten suitcases into her car and took her eleven-year-old daughter to Paris. The country where historically so much ballet had begun, and where eight years earlier the child performed so prettily in front of the patrons taking the waters at Evian, would now serve the gypsy girl well in her dancer's dreaming.

4

MUMMY

Sutton's care of her daughter intensified even more when they moved to France in 1956. They were brought together in a powerful bond by the loss of a second father and husband, so soon after the first one, the subsequent financial insecurity, the shift to the Continent, being thrown so closely together and Gielgud's needs to be given the best training in ballet, for which her mother made great sacrifices.

Our attempt to obtain an accurate portrayal of Gielgud in all her complexity must include close attention to her mother, for theirs is no ordinary relationship. Noël Pelly suggests that if we want to understand Gielgud better we must look to her mother, because the daughter's career is an extension of her own.

Both are independent, strong-willed and stoic people of the theatre. Both are basically alone, but keep in close contact, with Gielgud ringing or faxing Sutton regularly. When she falls behind in this communication, her mother laments with such remarks as, 'I'm a Friday night girl now. She rings me once a week from a railway station, or somewhere.'

It seems it may have been important for Gielgud to please her mother, though not so much in recent years. Dancers, more than most people, need approval.

There is a clear ambivalence in Gielgud towards the older woman, as there often is in offspring towards a parent with whom they are close. Indeed, when we first started our interviews, Gielgud did not always seem comfortable talking about her mother's influence, as though too much recognition of it would give it too much power; almost as if at times they were rivals. But she became easier about it as we progressed, as if she had become more reconciled and grateful towards her mother as time passed. There was even a note of what felt very like forgiveness.

Gielgud has had the habit of seeing her mother in Europe every Christmas holidays, usually meeting in Paris. While they are very pleased to be together again, within a week, according to their separate and equally rueful admission, their wills would clash in some way or another. Again, this is not uncommon among close members of a family, but in her accounts of her mother, she avoided saying anything which might possibly hurt her.

Sometimes she has confided in her; at other times she has avoided such discussions, feeling she has enough to deal with already without the added weight of her mother's strong opinions. What was most extraordinary of all was that Gielgud did not confide in her mother when she finally made the momentous decision to give up dancing. Part of it would have been because she knew her mother would be hurt, but another part of it was because she was afraid of what her mother's response would be.

Sutton can be very blunt as well as very sweet. When Gielgud had her troubles with the board of The Australian Ballet resulting in her virtual dismissal, Sutton accused her of being 'bourgeois' by staying, saying she was too attached to security. Gielgud says she has stayed for the sake of the dancers, because there was still so much to do with the company. But she has not found it easy to let go. Could it be that Gielgud's need to control so much around her is some kind of inheritance?

The intensity of their being together in those early years had for its setting a sudden and complete change of lifestyle. After having enjoyed the high life as a diplomat's wife with a staff and all the trimmings, Sutton had to face real frugality brought about by there being very little money in the estate. Yet she was prepared to do everything possible towards her daughter fulfilling her dream of becoming a dancer. She gave up smoking, and skipped meals so the child could see as many ballet performances as possible. Going to the cinema was a rare event. 'It was all hard, but just harder after having had everything,' says Sutton.

Noël Pelly says Sutton's mission was absolute. 'Zita is the very epitome of survival. Whatever she's done, she's done totally. She has not restricted herself to any one thing. She had her schooling, and her sporting life. Here was a woman who almost got to Olympic status. She conquered acting. She then had an Army career. She then had a marriage, then a family. She divorced, and married a second time. She then went on to struggle along.

'Zita was a survivor from the beginning. She ran away from home, and wanted a career as an actress, and defied parental wishes, and everything else. I think that, in a way, too, influenced her in relation to Maina's career. She had suffered lack of support in her chosen career, and with her daughter she was determined to help her in any way to achieve what she wanted.'

He speaks of the particular strength of Hungarian women, with their great capacity to deal with a problem, or with their objectives in life. 'They go straight at a thing. Hungarian women are much stronger than Hungarian men. It is a matriarchal society, in my opinion, where they are capable of devising a plan of action, and can actually see it through, and nothing will prevent them, save catastrophes. Zita could have stayed in London; she might have made a life; she might have married again.'

For her part, Gielgud says that only now does she realise what a sacrifice her mother made for her. The protectiveness was absolute. She did not, for instance, tell the child that her stepfather had cancer. Sutton says, 'I can honestly say I made every effort. You see, after my second husband died, there was nothing else for me. It wasn't a sacrifice to help Maina, who was determined, and such a hard worker. If I look back now, I have no regrets. None. I think it was my duty and it was normal.

'Also, it opened for me something quite different. I wasn't very musical. Through her, and later on through Maurice Béjart [the famous French choreographer and ballet director with whom Gielgud would work, and whose rehearsals Sutton now spends time watching in Lausanne, where his company is based], I learned about music, and I learned about dancers and dancing.'

She speaks in the voice of someone very much of the theatre. It is at once melodic, melancholy, worldly and intimate. Edward Pask describes her as 'a most wonderful lady. I adore her. I think she's an incredible person. This is not meant in a detrimental sense, but she reminds me of one of those ageless countesses who always crop up in black-and-white movies of the 1930s, 1940s and 1950s. They have an air about them. She has it, and so does Maina.'

With the stage name of Zita Gordon, she has been a considerable beauty in her day, with at times a slight resemblance to Greta Garbo. Even now, in her mid eighties, she is still reportedly an attractive woman. She lives in Lausanne, by herself except for her Yorkshire terrier. She will not travel to England or Australia now, so the dog does not have to go into quarantine.

She still works occasionally. After being interviewed for this book, she was going off to feature in a long season of a Berlin Opera Ballet production of the Béjart ballet *Le Concours*. She was playing, as she has before, the role of that dreaded, dominating breed, a ballet mother. The irony of this has not escaped her.

Her effect on Gielgud's life was not immediately apparent. Sutton says, 'It came back sometimes after years. It was very odd. Once, from Australia, Maina telephoned me, and said, "Mummy, you know, I think I'm becoming just as awful as you were."' She was referring to how, when her daughter as a dancer used to have her first nights, she sat in the first row, her knees trembling until the performance was over. Gielgud told Sutton, 'I do exactly the same thing now, with my dancers appearing on stage, some of them for the first time. You had only one. But I have sixty-five.'

Gielgud has another memory of the remark about becoming 'just as awful' as her mother. She says, 'It actually refers to my immediately wanting to go backstage after a performance, only just remembering to *first* let the dancer know of the excitement of their performance, and only *then* giving dancers notes on the things they could do to enhance their performance (because of the excitement of seeing really good performances and wanting it to be *even* better). My mother tended to criticise first of all, and I only realised when I became Artistic Director that it was not because she thought I was not good, but because she wanted it to be even better, and she *presumed* I realised how good she already thought I was!'

Gielgud now admits that her mother was probably right about some of the things she used to tell her. Sutton, in response, says, 'It does give me some pleasure because I feel I wasn't just there trying to enforce things she didn't believe in. I did, sometimes, I must say, when I thought there was danger. Not very often. I tried to advise her. I felt my duty was to stand by, to be a sort of net, like the ones under the acrobats in a circus. There weren't very many times when this net had to function.'

Pelly says, 'At one stage, I believe Zita was the mastermind. I think that role has changed now. In those early days, Maina would seek her opinion, and Zita would offer it.'

Suzanne Davidson is Hungarian-born, which means she understands more of the relationship between Gielgud and her mother. 'Both Zita and Mum came from obviously very wealthy families, whose children were never given any money. Everything was found, but [the two women] were as poor as church mice. Interestingly enough, it never occurred to either of them to go and ask for it, whereas today, most children just come and ask.'

Davidson does not entirely know what sort of mother Sutton really is. 'But I know that she's 100 per cent ready to do anything for Maina. Maina says, "My mother has a selective memory," and things like that. I don't know if she does or not, and I don't know whether it's relevant. But she knows who she is and it matters to her, and I believe she's passed that on to Maina. And to have two people who have a very strong sense of self, you have to go through a period when it doesn't work, when neither of you is good for the other close up. My mother and I have a very similar relationship. I love my mother to death.

'Not all Hungarian women are the same, but it is a particular type of person. I guess it has to do with heritage.

I think most children try to be "good", try to live up to some sort of expectation, usually of their parents. I can't speak for other people [but] I know that I had a very strong sense, from my background – and from my mother particularly, with whom I spent a lot of time – of what I should aspire to, what a good, strong person was all about. You had a strong sense of right, that you were answerable to yourself, that you should have beliefs, and not be afraid of standing up for them.'

As the early years passed, Gielgud found that in many ways Sutton had a lot of confidence in her – by letting her go off by herself when she turned professional and do things that probably a lot of other parents would not – but on the other hand, she was also very critical of her. Gielgud did not like it, but has since realised that it was useful. 'Now I know that her very definite views about my performances were because she thought I was really good, and that she wanted it to be even better. And, of course, now I know it, because I do exactly the same with my dancers – although I try to remind myself to say the good things first. I wrote to her after I came here, and said, "Now I understand."' So, there's been a little forgiveness? She laughs. 'Oh, yes.'

Gielgud has found her mother at times to be both difficult and very generous. She describes her as being very funny, and entertaining. 'She writes letters in a very witty way. She's also done travel books, short stories, and plays for radio. She's very alive, and full of stories. She's someone whom everyone finds enormously attractive physically, and as a person. People come to her with their problems. I think, actually, she both likes and dislikes it.' But the daughter has not been able to talk much about the experience of her personal self with her mother, or, for that matter, with people in general. It simply does not come naturally.

In contrast to her mother, Gielgud does not feel that people are naturally drawn to her. 'Yet I'm often surprised at the expressions of affection and support from people I haven't really done anything for. I've never put myself out for them, but they seem to like me, for some reason. It's really quite nice.'

She agrees that her mother's influence has probably helped to make her stronger. Overall, the impression is that Gielgud believes her mother's support to have been total. Sutton's first wish as a child in fact had been to be a dancer, too, but she was not allowed. 'So there was all the advantage of me being able to do what she hadn't. It wasn't imposing, because it was what I wanted to do. So it was perfect, because it all fitted into the general picture. I am truly grateful for what she put into my career. After all, she did dedicate a major part of her life entirely to it.'

She also now realises the truth behind some of her mother's forthrightness. 'You know that she's probably the only person who's actually telling you the truth. But then again, I hope I've got the relativities, the proportions, much more right now. I'm not a mother, but being a director with dancers, I think there are the same sort of possibilities and dangers. You need to be realistic to recognise a talent. Once you've done that, because you want that talent to be perfect, it's so easy for the other person only to hear negative things, without realising that they're only being told them because of the talent that is perceived. From that point of view, my mother and I are very similar. It's not because I was her daughter that she was like that. It was because of the talent she saw in me.'

When they moved to France in 1956, they first took two rooms with an English family in a large flat near the main thoroughfare beside the beach in Cannes. Its cramped conditions and their closeness to the other occupants were in painful contrast to the relative spaciousness of their former homes, but they tried to make the most of it.

Even though they did not have much money, Sutton still kept her mink coat and her jewellery, and still went to the hairdresser; all part of keeping up appearances. She had a theory that this meant getting better service. In her plain words, she did not want 'a table next to the loo.' Gielgud says, 'Now I do the same.' She dresses with exceptional style, buying either very expensive clothes, or cheap ones which look expensive; this is something that amuses her.

Gielgud's one constant piece of adornment is a finely made gold bracelet, attached to which are little gold tokens, each engraved with the name of a ballet she has danced. Here she is following the custom of her great-grandmother, Kate Terry, who similarly carried the memory of all the plays in which she had performed. Gielgud's bracelet has dozens of tokens, which shimmer like little mirrors when she moves.

After spending a wretched summer in the two rooms,

the mother and daughter then moved into the Hotel Martinez, which they discovered when out walking one day. The mother thought it would be far too expensive, but the daughter, with her usual certainty, was persistent that they should at least try. The manager was charmed by them, and gave them a room they could afford, at the back, overlooking the railway line. There the austerity continued, with them sharing the one breakfast each morning; the girl having the croissant and the milk, while the mother had the coffee. It was hard adjusting to living in small rooms, but this has become a lifelong pattern for Gielgud.

In 1957, while they were still in Cannes, Gielgud, who was twelve, worked for the first time with professional dancers. It came about one day when she and her mother returned to the hotel to find a parcel waiting for her in the lobby, containing new ballet shoes from Paris. She opened the package on the spot to see if they were the right ones. Her excitement drew the attention of a gentleman nearby in the lobby, who asked her, 'Are you a dancer?' The child looked up and, without hesitation, said, 'Yes.' Sutton, who tells the story, remarks, 'Would she be anything else?' The man explained that he was connected with a visit by the famous Marquis de Cuevas company. Gielgud had already met them when they took a class at the studio of her teacher, Julie Sedova. During their season, they were also going to do a gala in honour of Picasso. 'We need a child like you. Would you be interested?' Gielgud immediately agreed, and was led away. She was gone for so long that Sutton began to worry that maybe she had been kidnapped, and asked a hotel porter where the show was rehearsing. She finally found her daughter, as at-home as you like, happily sitting on the knee of the company's principal dancer, Vasil Tupin. He had previously been with the Ballets Russes du Colonel de Basil.

Gielgud was given the part of a child left behind when the circus packed up and moved on from a town, only to be rescued later by a clown. She danced the lost child with such feeling that Picasso himself came on stage afterwards and said to her, 'Tu m'as fait pleurer.' (You made me cry.) Sutton says, 'Well, you can imagine what happiness that was! It was a great moment.' There is a photograph of Picasso, surrounded by members of the de Cuevas company, with the girl, looking like a very pleased elf, kneeling at his feet.

At a party given by the British Council after the gala, Sutton met someone who would come to have an enormous influence on Gielgud's life. She was the dancer Rosella Hightower, who, five years later, in 1962, would open what became her famous Centre de Danse Classique in Cannes. Hightower, still today a striking figure at seventy-six, had noticed Gielgud's dancing during the show. She said to Sutton, 'Your child is very talented. Where does she learn?' Told it was with Sedova, she replied, 'Sedova is very good, but she's a bit old now and can't see very well. I think you should take her to Egorova in Paris. I can't think of anyone better.'

But Sutton could not afford for them to go to Paris, and instead took them to live in Monte Carlo, where she had been advised that there was a good teacher in Marika Besobrasova. Born in Yalta in 1891, she joined the Ballet

Russes de Monte Carlo in 1935. She formed her own company in Cannes during World War II, and taught the de Cuevas company and the Ballets des Champs-Elysées before opening her school in Monte Carlo.

In Monte Carlo, Gielgud and her mother again lived in a small hotel from June 1957 to September 1958, from which they at least had a glimpse of the beach. Being in Monte Carlo gave Gielgud access to Anton Dolin, noted for his development of British ballet as well as his princely roles, who was staying in a nearby villa in Monte Carlo. He was one of the best dancers of his generation. Gielgud had known him back in London, and he was very fond of her. Starting out as a child actor, he joined the Diaghilev production of *The Sleeping Beauty* in London in 1921, danced with Sadler's Wells, the Original Ballets Russes and Ballets Russes de Monte Carlo, before he and Alicia Markova founded the Markova-Dolin Ballet. In 1950 this became the London Festival Ballet (now English National Ballet); he was its first Artistic Director and main Principal.

He and Gielgud began a daily ritual of meeting on the beach, where she would present him with a peeled orange. 'The Orange Girl', as he called her, used to watch for Dolin every morning from her window. One day she saw the shutters of his villa were down, and her mother heard her crying, 'He's gone! He's gone!'

Their friendship would resume later, though, and he became a great supporter of Gielgud during her dancing years, uncharacteristically but enthusiastically joining the cries of 'Bravo!' at the end of some of her performances.

But Gielgud's experience in Monte Carlo with

Besobrasova, about which she had been initially most enthusiastic, was not going well any more, and after eight months it was time for her to move on. This time the destination was Paris.

Sutton still did not have enough money for the cost of travelling there, so she went to the casino. Praying all the while for help, she played roulette, choosing the date of Nigel's birthday. It came up four times consecutively, earning them what they needed.

Arriving in Paris in 1958 with their ten suitcases, they once again lived in a small hotel. It was near the Unesco headquarters, where Sutton found a job working in the gift shop. After a year in a French school, the Cours Hattemer, very near their hotel, the daughter decided to finish her education by correspondence so she could concentrate even more on her dancing, and later passed the BEPC (pre-matriculation) with distinction.

In what became a pattern, Gielgud continued her search for better teachers. 'As a dancer, I was always looking for whoever could best pass on the tradition of a role I was doing.' At last she was able to learn with Lubov Egorova, who had been recommended by both Fonteyn and Hightower. The great Russian dancer and teacher, another star of the Maryinsky Theatre, had gone to Paris in 1918, danced with Diaghilev's company, and opened a school there in 1923. Gielgud joined her in September 1958, and stayed with her for three years. Her other teachers during those years were Victor Gsovsky, Mischa Reznikov and Paul Goubé, all of whom greatly helped enhance her understanding, experience and ability. Goubé also gave pas de deux classes, where she learned all the famous adagios from the great classics such as *Swan Lake*, *The Sleeping Beauty* and *Giselle* at the age of thirteen.

But it was Egorova, teaching Gielgud in both open and private classes, who impressed her the most. The classes were held in the same studio as in the original days, through the doors of which had passed many famous dancers, including Baronova, who was one of the three famous 'Baby Ballerinas'. Gielgud distinctly remembers Madame sitting on her chair during class, dressed very formally in a blue suit and gloves, accompanied on the piano by another most impressive figure named Madame Marie.

Gielgud loved working with Egorova, who herself had been rehearsed by Marius Petipa, the choreographer of the great classics. Having her for a teacher, along with Karsavina and Preobrajenska, meant that she had learned from the very heart of the Maryinsky Theatre; she felt she could not do better than that. In her private classes with Egorova, she learnt all the major classical solos.

While she was in Paris, Gielgud had her first experience of the power of bluff to secure a role. During class one day she was offered her first pas de deux by Gerard Ohn, a respected dancer and excellent partner, who came up to her and said, 'Can you help us? Can you come to Montauban and dance the *Sylvia* pas de deux with us tomorrow?' The original partner, who had become indisposed, was Lycette Darsonval, a famous ballerina, previously from the Paris Opera, who by then was almost fifty.

Gielgud eagerly agreed to do the role. 'I didn't know

the pas de deux, the choreography, or the music. I didn't know anything. But I learned it in the train the next day on the way there, using my hands (instead of my feet) to run through the steps. He was a marvellous partner, and it was very exciting. It was an opportunity, and I had to go for it. I think it got me used to being able to dance without a whole lot of preparation, and to know that I could function on that sort of adrenaline, and rely on a certain performance instinct.'

Gielgud's experience with the Marquis de Cuevas company at the Picasso gala in Cannes had given her an important opening into the world of professional ballet. She came to know the de Cuevas dancers, and she and her mother were allowed to see the company perform whenever they wished, which they did very often. When they went to Paris to live, they saw at least forty performances of *The Sleeping Beauty*. Often Gielgud watched the company from the privileged position of the wings, where she sat in a corner and absorbed it all.

It also meant she saw Hightower, who was a principal, and the French dancer Serge Golovine, famed for his Blue Bird and Spectre de la Rose roles. Later, she was also there for the early performances of Rudolf Nureyev who joined the de Cuevas company after his defection to the West in 1961, breaking away from the Kirov Company at Paris Airport and making his dramatic and literal leap for freedom. Nureyev danced the roles of both the Blue Bird and the Prince in *The Sleeping Beauty*, the latter usually with Hightower. Gielgud watched them often.

She also did some classes with de Cuevas, where John

1 Christening. From top left: Frank Gielgud (grandfather, 'Favi's Favi'), Kate Terry Gielgud (grandmother, 'Favi's Mummy'), Zita Gielgud (mother), Maina Gielgud and Lewis Gielgud (father, 'Favi')

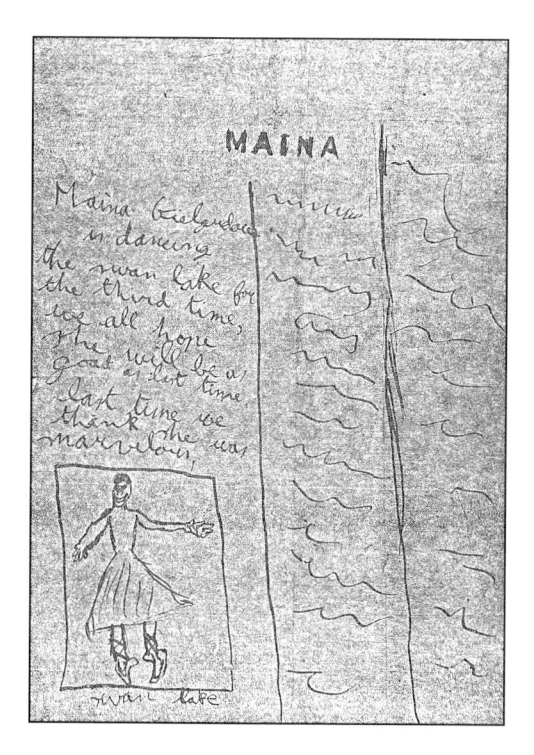

2 A review handwritten by Maina at the age of seven

3 Maina skiing before embarking on her dance career (1952)

4 Muriel Gore, Gielgud's adopted godmother

5 First practice on two fathers as a barre. Chesiere, Switzerland. From left: Nigel Sutton (stepfather, 'Fin'), Maina and Lewis Gielgud (father, 'Favi') (1946)

6 From left: Susan Hampshire, Madame Julie Sedova and Maina, holidaying in Cannes. (Pointe shoes already!) (1954)

7 From left: Gordon Craig, Zita Sutton, Maina and Nigel Sutton in Vence (1953)

8 Lewis Gielgud in Lithuania, the family homeland

9 Sir John Gielgud and his niece Maina. A gala in London, 1979: *Shakespeare Sonnets*. Choreographer Geoffrey Cauley

10 With Anthony Dowell (first partner) Hampshire School performance (1953)

11 With the De Cuevas Company, aged 17 (with original nose)

12 As Shakti in *Bhakti*. Choreographer Maurice Béjart (1969)

13 Black Swan with Peter Martins. London Festival Ballet, 1972. 'The world's best partner – dancing with him was like lying back in an armchair!'

14 With Jonathan Kelly. *Phantasmagoria* pas de deux by Domy Reiter-Soffer

15 *Les Noces*. Choreographer Maurice Béjart; with Niklas Ek (1970)

16 Serait-ce-la-Mort with Jorge Donn in *Four Last Songs*. Choreographer Maurice Béjart. One of Gielgud's most favourite roles (1970)

17 Tamara Karsavina, 1917, a very early teacher of Gielgud. She advised her mother to take her to France to be taught by the best available Russian teachers.

18 With Rosella Hightower in Cannes, mid-1970s

19 Galina Ulanova (Prima Ballerina of the Bolshoi Ballet), 'in her prime'; photograph given to Gielgud and signed by Ulanova on her visit to Australia in 1988

20 Galina Ulanova, invited by Gielgud to coach *Giselle* with The Australian Ballet; meeting Hazel Hawke, wife of the Australian prime minister, in Canberra (1988)

21 Corps de ballet of Gielgud's production of *Giselle*, with sets and costumes by great friend and outstanding designer, Peter Farmer. The Australian Ballet, in Melbourne (1986)

22 Before a 1991 performance of *The Sleeping Beauty* at the State Theatre, Melbourne

Taras, the American-born dancer and choreographer, was ballet master. She was watched in class by the Marquis himself, who then discussed her with Taras. Out of this, on the advice of Taras, came an invitation for her to join the company.

She went home on the metro thrilled with the news. But because she was still only fourteen, there was a problem. In those days ballet companies organised nothing for their dancers except travel, after which they had to find their own accommodation. The de Cuevas company was due to open soon in Lyon, but Sutton could not travel with her daughter because of her Unesco job, and there was no one else who could go with her. After discussing it with some of the members of the company, Sutton decided the offer had to be declined. It left Gielgud 'miserable and furious'.

When she was fifteen, Gielgud, drawn by the possibility of joining The Royal Ballet, went back to her British roots, back to London, and enrolled in their school. It lasted for only six weeks, after she discovered that they would not consider taking her into the company for another three years. She wanted to become professional and perform as soon as possible. 'I didn't want to spend three years in a school. I wanted to continue being taught by the people who inspired me the most.'

There was another element which put her off the school. It was something which she would also encounter later, in Australia, which would bewilder her, and distance her from some of the dancers in The Australian Ballet. 'In

England, I found that it was not done to look as though you were working hard, or to be ambitious. It was clearly frowned on, and that was a very odd experience. "Be a good sport, be a good loser, be anything but a winner."'

By now, an audition was coming up in Paris. At fifteen, she was ready to take the next critical step in her life and turn professional. But suddenly her mother, in a surge of caution, insisted that first she must do, of all things, a shorthand and typing course, just in case the career did not work out. Gielgud had no doubt about her future, but obeyed.

5

THE PROFESSIONAL

Gielgud's professional life began when she auditioned in Paris for the Roland Petit Company, in February 1961, when she was just sixteen. Out of a hundred people, ten were accepted, including her. She would start with them in the following September, in the Corps de ballet.

Petit, the French dancer, choreographer and ballet director, is one of the most flamboyant of dance creators, and toured extensively. After making his name in the 1940s, he is still a big figure. He has worked in Hollywood, and been associated with many designers and writers, bringing a certain chic style to his work.

He has not always been considered the most

traditional of choreographers, something which Gielgud, with her classical training, realised. She knew that he brought a certain theatrical sense out of his performers, and could appreciate the value of this for her, as well as learning the French theatrical style. There was the added attraction that the season would also feature André Prokovsky, who had been a Principal dancer with the de Cuevas company.

While waiting to join the company, Gielgud took another professional role by auditioning for, and then appearing in, a film being made by the stage director Raymond Rouleau, in which she performed as a ghost, painted entirely in grey.

Sutton had to sign the contract with Petit on her daughter's behalf because she was still a minor. The conditions were that Gielgud had to rehearse for three months on half pay, provide her own shoes, and pay for transport to and from rehearsals. But because the location was in one of the seediest parts of Paris, her mother came and collected her every day. There was no French dancers' union, and the conditions were common for those days. The young dancers had to agree to them if they wanted to perform.

Gielgud says the contract was signed on the understanding that it was for a season of ballet. In fact, what eventuated was more like a music hall style of performance, based on classical technique. Designed by Yves Saint Laurent, the first season, in September 1961, was at the Alhambra Theatre and featured Petit's wife, Zizi Jeanmaire, the star of many revues, ballets, and the film *Black Tights*. It included such acts as singing, juggling, some short ballets, and a longer one for Prokovsky and the Corps de ballet. Jeanmaire sang for the first time in her career, and the famous song, 'Mon Truc en Plume', was born.

'It wasn't really ballet. It was little bits and pieces of ballet, and being in the background to Zizi's singing. I realised that this wasn't going to be something that I wanted to do for any great length of time, although it was very useful.'

'The way Roland choreographed was quite peculiar to me. This was my first experience with a choreographer, and I was amazed that he just sat there on the first day of rehearsal of whatever piece he was creating, and said to the dancers, "Do something for me." And so they just improvised a few steps. And then, perhaps, he'd either take one or two of all those steps as a starting point, or he'd ask them to do something else. He always seemed to need that boost, so that they would start it off. I don't know whether it was a kick start, or to give the impression to the dancers, rightly or wrongly, that they were really creating along with him.' Petit also showed his dancers much by example.

The Alhambra was a grand old theatre, but it had no rehearsal room. With nowhere else to go, the dancers practised on a red carpet in the foyer, which was hardly ideal. Conditions were so basic that the usual class was not even provided for them, which is the centre of every dancer's daily universe. This they had to take and pay for themselves elsewhere.

Before the Paris season, they toured briefly through France and Italy, including Sicily. There were no understudies and no relief driver for the bus, so it was a rough-and-ready time on the road. Sutton took the night train from Paris to Rome and finally caught up with them on the last performance of the tour. She thought they looked like a band of gypsies. She found the dressing room crowded and Petit nonchalant about nudity, walking in with the simple announcement, 'Ladies, cover yourselves,' not caring less.

Gielgud loved the life, though she soon learned that it meant making and losing friends along the way, a common occurrence among ballet dancers. One of those was an American dancer, Laura Steele, with whom she later lost touch, to her sorrow, although they had become great friends and allies. One night when they were in their hotel room together, someone tried to break down the door. Rather than being frightened, Gielgud says she found the incident 'exciting'.

Petit told Sutton that her daughter was working very well. 'She's a good girl and she's serious about her work.' On one occasion, he cast Gielgud as an understudy of a pas de trois with Prokovsky. Then, in Paris, when one of the girls in it became ill, and Gielgud told Petit she was the only dancer in the company to know the role, he asked her to teach it to another girl, and then gave the role to the other girl. As her first experience of disappointment in the professional performing arts world, it left Gielgud shattered.

But then she got her second chance to fulfil her longing to dance with the de Cuevas company. The new director, Raymundo de Larrain, a nephew of the Marquis, who had recently died, sent a message to Sutton that he wanted to engage her. Gielgud was ecstatic, saying she had to take up the offer, and asked her mother to secure her release from the contract with Petit. But it developed into a very unpleasant situation. According to Gielgud, Petit initially said she could go, provided she came up with a replacement of the same height and proportions, and the same standard of technique. She quickly found several alternative dancers, and arranged for them to audition. On the day, though, Petit did not turn up, announcing instead that he did not want Gielgud to go. There were further ugly scenes with the manager of the Alhambra Theatre, with whom the contract had been signed. Eventually Sutton consulted a lawyer, who found that the contract was not really legal, because it had no time limit. The severance cost Gielgud a month's salary, but gained her the freedom she needed. Just the same, she learned much during those six months with Petit, and says she still has great respect for him.

But the trauma of the termination made her wary of all future contracts. This extended to more recent times, when she signed with The Australian Ballet in late 1982. Noël Pelly, who went to London for the finalisation of her contract, says she went through it in great detail, with so much niggling, that he became fed up, and asked her why she was being so pedantic. She explained what had happened with Petit, which she said could have been disastrous, and had been a very hard lesson for her.

By the time the seventeen-year-old Gielgud at last joined the de Cuevas company, in March 1962, she had a good body, and long legs, though they had a somewhat limited turnout. (This refers to the ballet position of the feet being at right angles from a forward-facing line. Taking years to develop, its purpose is to let a dancer move with ease in every direction.) She was frisky thin, which suited her unusual height. Her other attributes were a long neck, long arms, and a sense of movement. She also had the commitment and intelligence to do difficult steps, treating it all as a kind of fascinating crossword puzzle.

The Roland Petit tour had taught her to be focussed. Physically and mentally she was coming into alignment. Much of this came to her instinctively, but she had also seen many great dancers already, and was learning from them.

'Because I was taken to see as many performances as possible from an early age, I think the theatricality of it always interested me. I was very aware that the presentation – as in how you walked the stage, how you started a solo or a pas de deux, where the highlight was, and how you finished – covered a multitude of sins. You could, in fact, get away with murder. There was no intention of faking, but just using stage craft.

'You can manipulate an audience to see what you want them to see, by using your brains, though some dancers would be horrified at the thought of this. Because I was very shy at rehearsal and class, I couldn't show much emotion. Let me loose on stage, though, and there were no inhibitions. But, of course, you don't always get on stage. So I decided to develop a really strong technique, so I could get on stage in the big roles that I aspired to.'

Surprisingly, she admits to having always been a lazy

dancer, both physically and mentally, saying that it was always an effort to get up and go to class. This partly explains why she has driven herself so hard.

There was no time for any personal life, and even if there had been, it is doubtful if she would have pursued anything that was not to do with ballet. She spent a lot of time alone, and often dined by herself, sitting in cafes thinking about her work. Sometimes she ate with other theatre people, but did not go with them to night-clubs. 'I very soon found them noisy, unfriendly and basically unpleasant [places].' In the early days, the main temptation for her to go out after a performance was to be with certain people. 'But the people whom I wanted to be around usually initially didn't want to be around me, and vice versa – it's the story of my life! I've found, however, that the people I have respected and loved became true and everlasting friends. I had to work at it, and the persistence paid off.'

The discipline was intense. 'I quickly found a system for after the performance – how to get to bed as soon as possible, in terms of how many steps I did from the door to bed, also removing my make-up, and doing it all in the most compact possible way. I don't know that I slept a lot. But I looked after myself, as I've always done.'

It is probably just as well for her health that she does not drink, because the Gielguds have all had liver problems. Her inclination to be compulsive and addictive, to which she readily admits, is common among obsessive theatre people, but she keeps this aspect of herself under tight control. 'I was always serious as a girl. It's not something you learn. It's in you. I believed that I could and should only let go totally on stage, and that's what came across.

'In my generation, dancers were brought up to have a real dedication. There were a lot of teachers in the early years who tried to hand down that tradition, although there's now a push in the dance world that says that a dancer must have as "normal" a life as possible. It's not "done" any more to consider it a vocation, as much as it was in the past, when dancers had to make tremendous sacrifices. They were not very well paid, they toured a tremendous amount, and had to find their own digs. There was no free time, rehearsals were called from early in the morning, and there were also "blanket calls".' This refers to everybody in the cast being required to attend a call, regardless of whether it involved their scenes, or not. 'Unless you really loved to dance and perform, needed to dance like you needed to breathe and eat, you wouldn't contemplate it.' There was no question of feeling badly done by. 'It was just such an extraordinary situation to be able to do what I was doing, what I wanted to do, and be paid *anything* for it.'

The Marquis de Cuevas, the founder of the company that still carried his name, had been a most colourful figure who wore a long, trailing, black coat, in contrast to his very white, made-up face, altogether creating a highly theatrical effect. A gentleman of Chilean origin, he had no money of his own, but was besotted by ballet. He married a member of the Rockefeller family, from whom he received enough funds to keep his beloved company going.

Ballet companies can never pay their way completely, but his fell on harder times than most. The result was that every so often, so the story goes, his wife would tell him that he had lost so much money with his ballet that she could not give him any more. Upon hearing this news, he would immediately take to his death bed, becoming even paler than usual. Finally, his wife would become distraught and ask him what she could do. He would tell her that his last wish was to put on one more ballet. Upon hearing this, she would relent. Immediately, he would undergo a remarkable recovery, leap out of bed, and the ballet company would go on as before.

De Cuevas was an itinerant company, which had no real home base. The nearest to a home was spending a month each in Cannes and Deauville every year. Even there, they had only one studio and a very small stage. The majority of ballets were created and rehearsed there, because they toured for the rest of the time. That was how many ballet companies were in those days.

Gielgud's first ballet with de Cuevas was *Prince Igor*, when she replaced another dancer, leaving her time for only one rehearsal on stage on the day of the performance. This was with Poppa (Nicholas) Beriosoff, the ballet master, who was the father of Beriosova. 'I was supposed to lead the Corps de ballet, and I didn't know what steps I was doing, or where I was going, or anything; but there I was, flung into it. I suppose I learned from that experience, again, that it can be done, and it's wise to say, "Yes, I can," even in the Corps.' She can still remember the steps from that first performance, though she has never done it since.

She is even able to sing the music. She says that dancers carry music around in their heads. It is the music, too, which usually brings a dancer back if they forget their steps on stage.

Before joining Roland Petit, because she was burning to be in a full-length classical ballet, Gielgud had said she would do anything, even be a page. Then, when she got her wish with de Cuevas, she sent her mother a postcard from Lyon: 'When, oh when, will I cease being a page, and at least do the mazurka?'

As a page in *The Sleeping Beauty* she held Aurora's train as she came down the steps for her first entrance in the first act. 'I was very, very nervous; frightened of tripping and mucking up the ballerina's entrance. It was a huge responsibility.' The ballerina was Marilyn Jones, who was with the company with other outstanding Australians including Garth Welch and Karl Welander. They all later came back home for the first season of The Australian Ballet in 1962, where Jones eventually became the company's Artistic Director, the last one before Gielgud.

Gielgud also danced in *The Sleeping Beauty* as a nymph, and this time, it nearly did lead to disaster. The problem was that Larrain had dressed the dancers in amazing theatrical fairy-tale costumes with enormous head dresses twice the height of their heads. When Gielgud made her first jump, the whole headpiece collapsed with the elastic still clinging around her neck. She spent the rest of the performance with it all bouncing up and down. 'I spoiled almost the whole ballet. The illusion was gone. I cried all night.'

The company itself was in deep trouble. After the old Marquis had died the previous year, his nephew, who had been a designer, was struggling to keep it alive, amid legends of money being spent on such luxuries as gold leather boots. It was all to no avail; the company was literally on its last legs. It folded three months after Gielgud joined it, finishing its life in Greece at the Herod Atticus Theatre, where the final scenes were outdoors. 'It was enormously sad. It had been a great company.'

If Gielgud had been allowed to join the company when she wished, at fourteen, instead of three years later, she would have been able to work with Bronislava Nijinska, the Ballet Mistress, who was Nijinsky's sister, and whom Diaghilev had used a great deal in his company. She choreographed several major works for de Cuevas, and worked closely with Hightower.

In 1962, after the de Cuevas company folded, Gielgud went back to England and auditioned for The Royal Ballet, only to be told by the Artistic Director, Dame Ninette de Valois, that, at 5 feet 7 inches, she was too tall. There were already too many tall dancers with the company, and there was no opening for her.

Years later, when The Australian Ballet came to London in 1988, Gielgud met de Valois, The Royal Ballet's founder and retired Artistic Director, who was then nearly ninety. A British-born dancer, teacher and ballet director, who had danced for Diaghilev, de Valois is one of the most famous figures in the world of ballet. She founded the Academy of Choreographic Art in London in 1926, and its descendant, The Royal Ballet, in 1956. She was one of the people who recommended Gielgud for the job of Artistic Director of The Australian Ballet. They were together in a lift at Covent Garden, when de Valois told Gielgud that she was still sorry she had not been able to take her into the Covent Garden company when she auditioned. Gielgud was amazed that the older woman could remember the event twenty-five years later. She regards it in retrospect as an apology. She felt the need to say in response, 'It's quite okay. I had a great career, because I had such diversity, which I probably wouldn't have had if I had been at the Royal.'

Back in Paris, Gielgud had by this time been a professional for nearly a year, worked with two companies, and now had no obvious place to go. While she waited for new work, she continued her classes in Paris at the Studio Constant, with Mischa Reznikov, who was 'a wonderful, mad, Russian teacher'. Roland Petit and Zizi Jeanmaire also went there.

She was then approached by Madame Irène Lidova, the esteemed Russian-French ballet critic, and writer on dance, who told her that a small company with which she was involved was having a season in Paris. Called the Ballet de l'Étoile, it was run by Milorad Miskovitch, the noted Yugoslav dancer who had performed often with various Ballets Russes, and guested in many companies through Europe and America, partnering some of the most famous ballerinas in the world. Miskovitch, a choreographer as well as a dancer, who had also worked with Maurice Béjart, was interested in the theatre side of ballet as much as in the pure dance elements. Later, he came to follow Gielgud's career closely, and she remembers him as being 'very positive, helpful and critical in the best possible way'.

They first performed in the Theatre de l'Étoile, just off the Arc de Triomphe, in the summer of 1962, and it was here that Gielgud had her first and only experience of performing to almost empty houses. It was the holiday season, and although it was not a big theatre, with 600 seats, there were sometimes only ten or twelve people in the audience. Empty theatres are every performer's nightmare, but Gielgud used the experience to teach herself to adapt.

She was aware of the value of varied experience, as well as the status of the various companies. She certainly had more diverse work than most other dancers of her generation. This was partly because she moved around a great deal, but she insists that this was mainly circumstantial, and not necessarily on purpose. If Petit, for instance, had done a season of ballets, she might have stayed with him. Again, if de Cuevas had not folded, she might have remained there for many years. At the same time, she did not think a lot about permanency. 'The point was to do it, and then see what happened.'

Gielgud's stay with the Ballet de l'Étoile lasted only two months, but because she had become a Soloist, her name was on the posters for the first time. One of the roles turned out to be very difficult technically. Sonia Arova, famous for her brilliant technique, and another of Nureyev's first partners, gave her many helpful hints for it in a class they were both taking. It was in a ballet called *Cherche Partenaire* (Look for a Partner). Gielgud says, with a wry edge in her voice, 'I later decided that this was the story of my life!' The remark is tantalisingly ambiguous, until we realise she is speaking solely about her life as a dancer.

6

HIGHTOWER

Among the hundreds of photographs which Gielgud has recording the span of her dance career, there is one of her together with Rosella Hightower which reflects the great feeling that has existed between them. It shows the younger woman and her mentor walking by water, striding out with the vigour and supple ease so common to dancers. These two, though, seem to have more of a spring to their step than most. There are the similarities of their respective lean builds, long limbs and classical features. They have an intensity about them within the carefree mood of the day. Most of all, they seem happy.

Whenever Gielgud speaks of Hightower, her voice

takes a special tone, an intimacy to which few others are privileged. Within the voice we can hear love, respect, admiration and gratitude. No one else in Gielgud's memoirs is given quite as much. She was the guide at the critical time of Gielgud's reaching adulthood, extending over four years.

Hightower, who was born in Oklahoma in 1920, with Red Indian ancestry, which, Gielgud says, accounts for some of her stoic personality, has been much admired for her technical brilliance and artistry, her creation of many roles, and her teaching ability. She had danced with the Ballets Russes de Monte Carlo, then with Massine's Ballets Russes Highlights and the Original Ballets Russes. She also featured with the Nouveau Ballet de Monte Carlo, and, after the death of the Marquis de Cuevas, in 1962 founded her Centre, the Centre de Danse Classique, in Cannes.

At the beginning of 1963, Gielgud decided to leave Paris and go to Cannes, after Hightower had invited her to dance in some gala performances there, and study with her for a few weeks.

On the way to Cannes she stopped off in Marseille, in what turned out to be a mere momentary career *divertissement*. On a suggestion by Irène Lidova, she called in to do an audition with a company there led by a contemporary choreographer whose work was based in the classical style. She found it to be a madhouse, with nobody seeming to know what was happening, and the place seething with intrigue. She quickly got back on the train.

One of the immediate attractions for Gielgud of going to Cannes was that she had been told that she would be one of the Leading Sylphs in a gala production of *La Sylphide*. It was being staged by Erik Bruhn, who would also be dancing the leading role of James, with Hightower dancing the title role.

In Gielgud's office at The Australian Ballet headquarters in Melbourne, there are two particular photographs which are outstanding. One is of Nureyev on his last visit to Australia. He is sprawled beneath a barre, with his arms stretched up holding it, looking exhausted, but smiling. The other is a serious portrait of Bruhn, a young man of very fine features, and most intense. These men, two of the world's greatest dancers, became companions. Bruhn died in 1986, seven years before Nureyev.

The other draw for Gielgud going to Cannes was that it would give her the chance to study with Hightower. 'It was a wonderful time, and a discovery, to work with Rosella, and the teachers she had there, at the centre. It was a bit of a revelation, the way she taught, with the focus on the individual dancer, and their particular possibilities.

'Most teachers work from the premise that you have the perfect physique for dance, as in perfect proportions and perfect turnout. They don't take into account that there are things that you are supposed to do in a certain way, and some physiques can't!

'Rosella has been an enormously hard worker all her life. She wasn't what one would normally call naturally gifted, but has a huge determination and willpower, working with her own physique and just knowing how to make the most of it. She was a very strong technician as well as a great artist, and a very exciting dancer. She knew how to sell her technique, her virtuosity. She made her career, a very prominent one, mainly in France.

'I have huge admiration and awe for the two strands – instinct and intelligence; for people who have extraordinary natural talent that is God-given (and inexplicable by anything except reincarnation if there's any justice in the universe); and also for people who have worked for *everything* that they have, who don't have natural attributes, and who've really strived to achieve; but, best of all, of course, are people who have the natural attributes *and* strive to develop them to the ultimate.

'It's often unfair. Some will have to strive and work harder to become a Corps de ballet dancer than someone else to become a Principal. That's something you come across and feel awful about when you're directing a company, because you see people who are worthy in terms of talent, of being given roles and promotions, but who do very much less work in terms of time, energy and thought, than others who work twice as hard and who simply are not going to make it out of the Corps de ballet. It's the injustice of the world, isn't it?

'Rosella was very interested in teaching, and still is. I felt that I had a great deal to learn from her. Having been a professional for a little while, I also had more of an idea of what was lacking; what I should work on in a class situation.'

Although she has lived virtually all of her life in France, Hightower still has a strong American accent, which comes through even when she speaks French. Gielgud says she is not obviously physically beautiful, but describes her this way: 'She has very large and extraordinary turquoise eyes. She takes no care of herself outside of performing. I mean, she hardly ever wears make-up. She has quite nice casual clothes. But she's a woman who, when you speak with her, is immensely attractive. She's one of those people who really lights up with the interest of what they're talking about. On stage she has tremendous glamour. With just two lines, those eyes take over her entire face.'

Hightower inspired the people working at her Centre. After the gala performances of *La Sylphide*, which went very well, Gielgud decided to stay there and continue working with her. It was idyllic, being able to concentrate on studio work, as well as performing, and she did not look anywhere else for work.

Gielgud and three other girls, the 'Rosella groupies', as she calls the four of them, all worked very hard at the Centre together. There Gielgud made friends with some of those dancers who, like herself, were fascinated by the work. Among them was the American, Lee Wilson, and the Australian, Louise Naughton, with whom Gielgud still has occasional contact. Other great friends and influences on her life and career at that time were Alfonso Cata and Wilhelm Burman.

'Apart from the morning and evening classes, there was another, which was exclusive, and wonderful. It was entirely dedicated to doing pointe work and was extraordinarily good and strengthening. Rosella devised exercises which were not necessarily beautiful aesthetically, but which really got you onto your legs, and helped you with your technique and style. She had a huge repertoire herself, having worked with extraordinary people like Nijinska, and sometimes used extracts from ballets that she'd danced.' The lessons had such an impact on Gielgud that she still gives her dancers some exercises today that she remembers from those times. It was tough work, but she loved it.

While at the Centre, Gielgud, for only the second time in her life, had her portrait painted, by Jean Robier, who is Hightower's husband, and a stage designer and painter. The portrait, which hangs in her mother's apartment in Lausanne, shows Gielgud naked from the waist up. Sutton loves to shock people with it. On other occasions, when more delicate visitors have arrived, she has covered it with a scarf. That portrait is a far cry from the other, much more formal, one of Gielgud which used to hang in the board room at The Australian Ballet Centre in Melbourne, now a meeting room. Indeed, in an idle moment of mischief, we might wonder what possible influence the Robier picture might have had with the board if it had been looking down on them when they discussed Gielgud.

Hightower would also have a profound effect on Gielgud's attitude to ballet itself. Even though she had seen it as a career, Gielgud had few stars in her eyes. 'As a young student of classical ballet, it did seem to me somewhat frivolous as an occupation.'

Even now, she warns against 'taking it all too desperately seriously. It doesn't work, because you become too tight and too worked up about the technique. You have to be a little bit objective about it, and keep a sense that, in a way, it's all pretty silly, really. I mean, you put on these pink tights and pointe shoes and flowers and crowns, and whatnot. Basically, we're all playacting, even in contemporary ballets, though some people would *kill* me for saying it! I think one has to keep that in mind.'

Gielgud has no problem with these remarks being in such apparent contrast to some of her other statements which express such reverence for her art.

'Yes, I do contradict myself, often. Both are true. Ballet – and anything one chooses to do with one's life – is both extremely serious and extremely frivolous, depending on how one is looking at it. I believe it is very important to keep that at the back of one's mind; to keep the perspective continually.' In fact, in those early years, Gielgud imagined that she would stop dancing when she turned thirty, and had dreams of 'doing something useful', such as working with Albert Schweitzer. But Hightower believed in the power and importance of dance, and through that influence Gielgud came to realise that it could be a worthwhile career for her over a much longer time than she had previously imagined.

Resonating with her as a kindred spirit, Hightower seemed to reach right inside her with the personal combination of her dedication to dance, her resilience, and her refusal to dwell on negative things. It became something of a mantra for Gielgud, who also seeks to embody those qualities.

For her part, Hightower has described Gielgud as her best dance disciple. This is saying a lot, considering her ballet centre in Cannes attracts dancers from all over the world.

Sutton says her daughter was mightily impressed when she once overheard Hightower say to a dancer who was complaining that she could not perform, 'A dancer only doesn't dance when she's dead.'

Sutton observes, 'In my opinion, Rosella has been the most important person in Maina's professional and private life. I don't think she's done a ballet – or anything – without first talking about it with Rosella, who really in some ways has been more of a mother to her than I.' She likes to quote Hightower's assistant, José Ferran, who was once a star dancer with Roland Petit. He once gave Sutton what in her view is the most appropriate description of Hightower: 'She is something out of the Bible.' By this he meant that she has saintly qualities.

Gielgud vividly remembers when she was fifteen and travelling with Hightower in the back of a car, when suddenly she started talking about reincarnation, as though it was the most natural thing in the world. It made a big impact on her, not the least because the other woman was a practical and realistic person. As a result, she started reading many theosophical books on Eastern teachings. She dreamed of going to India, and later did, to dance. She wants to return there.

Previously, Gielgud had found it almost impossible to talk about religion and God. What Hightower said that day 'struck a big chord. This was like something that I'd been waiting for, to bring together the two aspects, my interior life and what I was intent on doing with my dancing. Rosella made a yoga of dance. It's not only the physical dance. It's the striving for unattainable perfection of yourself physically, mentally and spiritually. Rosella's way was giving me a way within my already chosen path, without going outside and looking for a spiritual path; it was all very simple. It was right there, in my work.'

The gala performances in France where Gielgud worked with Hightower were billed: 'Hommage au Marquis de Cuevas'. The new shows used the defunct company's repertoire, costumes, sets and some of their principal dancers. Out of this came a series of overseas tours over the next four years, giving Gielgud much valuable experience.

The focus, as always, would be on her professional life. The personal one, as always, is minimal. But now she is seventeen. It might be reasonable to wonder if there is anybody waiting in the wings. She responds to any talk of romance lightheartedly.

'Oh, I fell in love from when I was twelve. It was very obsessive, of course, and it wasn't said to the various people, always kept secret.' Each time it lasted two or three years. 'Oh, I'd carry on so much if I fell in love. I'd get very annoyed with my mother, because she'd say, "Forget about him. Just get out of the house and get on with your work." But there were not very many available men in the dance world, or I was too young and they were too old.

'I still have never really fallen seriously in love. I've thought I was. I still have a dream of one day . . . maybe a man. I still think I might marry.' She pauses. 'I've a sort of fatalistic attitude. If he's meant to turn up, then it will happen. But it doesn't matter if I don't marry, and never has. To me, it seems so extraordinary that people, more often than not, make do with someone who isn't their soul mate, rather than not have anyone. Just because most people are looking for him or her, it seems to be often presumed that they must appear on the horizon, but if they don't by a certain age, then it is better to have *someone* than *no one* to share one's life with: Why?'

As for passion for its own sake: 'Well, these things can last a short time. It doesn't have to be lifelong.' She says she has had that attitude since she was seventeen. But presumably she had not lived entirely like a nun, even though her little apartment in central Melbourne has some of that feeling? 'No.' That was as good as this pale attempt at prying was going to get. Back, as always, to ballet . . .

Being with Hightower was what Gielgud calls an amazing time for her in Cannes, with the studying, watching the classes and the other dancers, and making the most of learning from Hightower and the other teachers. It was so interesting to be able to observe Hightower put her ideas into practice. 'I was always fascinated to watch her and the different students or professionals, how they worked, what their physical and technical problems were, and how they dealt with them, and trying to put those into practice myself.

'I used to work alone, already from that time. I used to go to a studio on Sunday – I must say, with the hope that I might be seen, and gain points for being hard-working. It was seeking approval in one way, but only to do something that I really wanted. I knew that working by myself was very valuable. I found out things then that I couldn't in normal class, where things went too fast. And it really helped me to think that I would be considered a hard worker. It seemed to me a good thing to work hard, and it was difficult. So, in a curious way, I used that need to seek approval to help myself improve. It's something that I've tried to do as a director, to let people know that I could *see* when they work hard. But most people don't seem to want that, or need it. I believe it's good to work hard; it's also interesting.'

She admits to being competitive, but not on a personal level. 'It was great if I had somebody who was competition. I suppose I was what they now call an achiever. I would use that person to drive me harder. So, if they're doing five pirouettes, why on earth shouldn't I do five, or even six. If that person can lift their legs up to here, okay, I can't get up that far, but I'm going to get it just that much higher than I can now, and perhaps I can find something else that they can't do. So it was a very unashamed *using* of that person, in a positive way, for the achievements that I wanted, but not doing them any harm. If they weren't there, it was that much harder, and I had to find it within myself.'

It was the same with whatever obstacles came her way, including not being cast in a ballet that she wanted to do. She determined, 'Okay, so I'll go at the back; I'll go to every bloody rehearsal; I'll show them that I would have been better, or at least that I could do it, too. And perhaps I'll get it that way, and perhaps I won't. But at least I will have improved, anyway, and not hurt anyone in the process.'

She says sadly that she could not share that with most of the dancers at The Australian Ballet. 'It's just not a conception. It's like, "Competition? Oh, no, no, no! That's a bad thing! That's treading on other people. The killer instinct." And that's not what I mean, but I can't get that across.

'People say, "Are you really a workaholic, and do you mind being thought of as such?" I think, "No, that's what I want to be." A workaholic is somebody who loves to work, and can't get enough of it. Nowadays it's apparently "correct" to separate your life between work and leisure. But when your work *is* your leisure – your hobby and your profession – then where do you draw the dividing line, and why should you?'

In Gielgud's view, most people in the world do not have the good fortune to enjoy their work. 'They want to make as much money as they can, so that they can have as much to play with as possible. Hence the greed for money. It takes over. Because I love my work, that's something I don't understand. I don't preach about it, but I've never asked for a raise in my life. I couldn't.'

Before the company left France, the Hommage au Marquis de Cuevas company gave a series of galas all over the country, often doing various *divertissements*. Gielgud danced a Balanchine pas de trois with Floris Alexander, who later partnered her many times in Maurice Béjart's company.

Then, one day, Hightower asked Gielgud to do the pas de deux *Soirée Musicale*, choreographed by John Taras. It was a landmark for her. She was amazed that

Hightower had such confidence in her, because it was her pas de deux, and she was the only one who danced it. Gielgud was so overwhelmed that she cried, 'and then rushed to the studio to try and make it look what I thought was halfway decent'. She went into a week's rehearsal, 'and worked out how to do it technically, but also how to sell it.' The expression 'sell' seems incongruous for one so artistic.

'There are certain dances and movements that are known to be particularly difficult technically. But somebody who's not a great technician may actually not have much difficulty with some of them, but have great difficulty with something else. The Black Swan pas de deux and solo is known to be a technical virtuoso pinnacle, whereas I found the White Swan solo to be one of the hardest in the entire repertoire; it depends on an equal balance both to the right and to the left, as well as the lyricism, to carry it through. It's almost impossible to do without a blemish, even just on a technical basis. You hope the public won't notice as such, but, of course, dancers know. One of the things that can make it exquisite is how a dancer refines it. In fact how you deal with whatever happens on the moment, is what really matters.'

Their first tour, in 1964, was a great adventure for the small band of dancers who went to many places, including North Africa, the Middle East, South-East Asia, Canada, Italy, and India. In South-East Asia, they were also able to watch the dancers of other cultures. In Canada, it was supposed to be an 'all French' company, so Gielgud changed her name to 'something French'. 'I took an unlikely name: Maryse Thevenon!'

Dancers back then, everywhere, had to put up with conditions which people nowadays might consider bad enough to cause them to refuse to perform. On tour, performance venues were often picture theatres. Poor flooring was common, with many of the stages being old. They had one advantage, they were springy. But with the dancers already having enough to think about with all the demands of performance, bad flooring was not only hard to navigate, but also dangerous. There were splinters as well as nails. The stages were often slippery, too, especially in South-East Asia, where they were not necessarily used to classical ballet, and the floors were sometimes polished. In the old days, it was a tradition for the most junior member of the company to have the task of sprinkling the floor with water. The famous paintings of ballet dancers by Degas show the watering can as it was used. Gielgud and her colleagues learned a trick of preparing the dance surface with a mixture of cola and resin. It made a very sticky mess, but saved them many a fall.

'The first thing you did when you arrived, even before you got any accommodation, was to go to the theatre, put your bags down at the stage door, and go and look at the stage. You needed to see where the holes were, and the ridges, and if there were any nails sticking up. You would then work out a plan of how you were going to avoid them when you were dancing. The stages didn't have any floor covering. Traditionally, you danced on wood.'

Thankfully, this has now changed with the coming –

mainly through contemporary dance, and dancing barefoot – of tarkett, a linoleum type of floor which most ballet companies now use.

Gielgud credits much of her ability to deal with her injuries to her training with Hightower. 'Rosella was an amazing example. It was something I followed on through my dance career. She would never say that she was tired or ill, or not feeling well. And, like the other things, I copied that. I came to the conclusion that her reason was if you start to say that you're tired, you start feeling even more tired, and sorry for yourself. If I got aches and pains that really started looking serious, I would go on my own into a studio in front of a mirror, and work very slowly and try to see what I was doing wrong, and try to correct it.'

When they were in North Africa, on the Hommage au Marquis de Cuevas tour, Hightower gave Gielgud a piece of advice that has stayed with her. Gielgud, in her first time in the role, had the second lead as the Queen of the Wilis in *Giselle*, and the Principal role in *Bal de Nuit*, thus positioning her between Soloist and Senior Artist rank.

'I was terribly worried about where I should exit in *Giselle* because of where the wings were, and I'd only rehearsed it in the studio. So I went to ask Rosella, who was dancing Giselle, where I should go out, because there was this line of Wilis, the Corps de ballet dancers, and I thought the Queen should probably not go out between them. Instead, she gave me about the shortest reply I ever received from her. She said, "Oh, don't exaggerate," as in: "Work this out for yourself."'

The North African trip took them to Algiers, then still occupied by the French. 'It was extraordinary. We were in an open-air theatre once, doing *Suite en Blanc*, and it was absolutely chockablock. There were people everywhere, walking on the canvas of the tent, and even going on the stage, because there was no room anywhere else. One of the dancers, Principal Lyane Dayde, ran to her partner, Michel Renault, for a lift, and a policeman who was trying to keep order came between them. It was wild!'

In 1965, they went again to South-East Asia, including Vietnam, as well as to China, before going on to Australia. Later, they toured the United States. The company was now calling itself the Grand Ballet Classique de France. In fact, they were still using the sets, costumes and repertoire from the de Cuevas company, only now the number of dancers had expanded from seven to twenty-eight. Dancers often included Hightower and Prokovsky.

South-East Asia was still in the middle of the war, and the dancers heard bomb explosions while they were performing in Saigon. Gielgud's mother became very anxious about her daughter being in a war zone, and contacted the impresario and said, 'How are they doing?' He replied, 'Oh, it's great. The box office is fantastic.'

The China tour was the first cultural exchange with France, and was considered important by both countries. The company met the then-Premier, Chou En-lai, and visited many parts of the country. They were taken to collective farms, and dancing and performing arts schools, which Gielgud found to be fantastic. 'When the Russians were there, they brought in all their tremendous, terrific teachers, and trained them in the Russian system. Then, when they left, they took all their teachers away. But the Chinese, being as clever as they are, had taken most of it in, and by now they've transformed it, to a certain degree, to suit them. The tragedy was that during the Cultural Revolution, a lot of the dancers were sent off to work on the farms, and missed one, two, three years of training, which, of course, can never be picked up again. It was disastrous.'

These days, they have two very good companies: the Central Ballet of China, in Beijing, and the Shanghai Company. In 1995 a competition was held in Shanghai, to which The Australian Ballet sent two of its dancers, Lucinda Dunn and Andrew Murphy. The company has already visited China twice, and went there again in 1996.

Gielgud says dancers in the communist countries have generally been very well treated, even though this has been far from Western standards, with people living collectively in small rooms.

She was impressed by the tradition of the Peking Opera and by the Central Ballet of China, with its mixture of traditional repertoire and revolutionary ballets, as an item of history, 'where you had these women in baggy shorts and pointe shoes, and guns, and going... arabesque, arabesque, arabesque, shoot, shoot. Amazing. There was no real difference in the style or the steps. It was just the way they were dressed and the story they were trying to tell.'

The tour went off, in Gielgud's words, wonderfully,

even if the Chinese audiences sometimes had trouble understanding what was happening. They performed the full-length *Giselle* on this tour, and the Chinese audiences clearly did not understand the conventional mime, since when Albrecht swore his love for Giselle, they laughed loudly, as they also did when Gielgud crossed the stage on pointe as the Queen of the Wilis, making her first entrance, covered in her white veil.

While in China they were blissfully unaware of world events, because there were no foreign newspapers. One night they got a rude awakening when they attended a performance in Shanghai of *divertissements*, with jugglers and acrobats. A Chinese woman came out in front of the curtain, as usual, to announce the show, but she got a more than typically enthusiastic response. 'Everybody around us got up and started shouting, gesticulating and screaming, and looking terribly happy. When we asked our interpreter, she said, "We've got the atomic bomb!"'

Reviews of the Australian tour singled out Gielgud. Frank Harris, in the *Daily Mirror*, was boisterous, Sydney style. He said the company was short on shine. However, in his last paragraph came this: 'For my money, the star of the future in this company is Maina Gielgud, niece of Sir John, and if I'm wrong, I'll pirouette down Martin Place.'

In Adelaide, the *News* was more restrained in its language, though no less enthusiastic, under the heading: 'Refined And Moving *Giselle*. In the middle of the review, the critic described Gielgud as an imperious Queen of the Wilis, 'her polished movements being a shining example for the stately white maidens of the Corps de ballet. The precision and control of hands and arms was of a particularly high standard.'

Gielgud vividly remembers her first impression of Melbourne, where she would come to live and work many years later. 'Everything seemed to close up at six o'clock. There wasn't a restaurant open. And the food was so bad – worse than the English provinces. My goodness, how it's improved now – to some of the best in the world.'

She would feel drawn back to Australia because of the audiences. 'They really had tremendous warmth, and were fabulous. They were probably the best audiences I have ever danced for.' She laughs. 'Now it's a complete turn-around. The audiences are not as demonstrative, and the food is fantastic.' There was a lot of knowledge of the ballet, and it was very popular. She later realised this was due first to Pavlova's visits, then to the Ballets Russes de Monte Carlo having come during World War II, and stayed for some years, and then the influence of Borovansky. It was also gratifying that the great interest in ballet there at that time encouraged many of that generation's children to dance, 'although that still doesn't explain the innate artistry and qualities that Australian dancers have'. Australians are a great mixture of athleticism and poetry.

While visiting Perth at the end of the Australian part of the tour, Gielgud came down with a bad attack of bronchitis and had to be hospitalised. 'It was horrible, because I'd never been ill before. I literally could not get up. I could not perform. And I had the unpleasant experience of the management not believing me.'

All the tours, but especially the North American one in 1965, provided invaluable professional experience to Gielgud. The only thing missing was feedback about the performances. 'You'd dance night after night, and no one would say whether you were going the right way or the wrong way.'

What about the critics, the reviews? 'You don't count that, not as feedback for your performance . . . well, I suppose to a degree, because I have always paid attention, but you're just getting from a reviewer what they see, as your one-off performance, not knowing you as a dancer.' Not having the feedback made her 'hanker for it, feeling that I would go in a direction and probably pull back when perhaps I didn't need to, and try another direction without developing further the ideas about a role, so I found that very frustrating. But it *was* wonderful to do a role so many times; to dance six or seven times a week, for nine weeks.'

She loved the organisation of the American tour, and enjoyed the one-night stands in various towns and cities, which were usually thought of as horrific. There were proper meal breaks, and wake-up calls, and air-conditioned buses with toilets at the back. There were union regulations, too, which were unfamiliar, because in France there were no such organisations for dancers. Gielgud felt her rights were impinged, and went ahead and worked when she felt like it. 'I never abided by any union rules,' she says, rather primly. 'I have only felt strongly about one right, that of those who want to work. Although she added, 'They need protection nowadays,' her attitude was hardly likely to endear her later to the more union-minded members of The Australian Ballet, which in 1981, prior to Gielgud's arrival, went through a traumatic strike by the dancers.

The company made an extensive sweep of America, including down through the South, and were very well received, with much curiosity about who they were. The reviews went well. 'Maina Gielgud, whose graceful movements looked like a porcelain statue come alive, carried much of the weight of the show.' (*Evansville Press*). 'The most interesting dancer is Maina Gielgud (niece of Sir John Gielgud and Ellen Terry). She is a willowy girl with a good technique and a definite stage presence.' (*Chicago American*).

Dance Magazine, the world's largest dance publication, from New York, said the company was 'displaying the charm and chic of French ballet as well as its exaggerated carelessness about the details of ballet technique.' It went on to say that the company had some excellent dancers, notably Marianna Hilarides and Maina Gielgud.

The esteemed *Los Angeles Free Press* said, 'Mlle. Gielgud was superb stylistically and in subtlety of humour.' After the review described the ballet *Noir et Blanc* as hanging 'between the grandeur and the cobwebs of the Paris Opera and the cerebralism and dryness of Balanchine', and being only lukewarm about the overall performance, it resumed its rapture about Gielgud: 'At this point this reviewer found himself waiting on Mlle. Gielgud's entrances, and her special quality that one looks for and so rarely finds in the ballet.' The reviewer wrote of her 'Danilova-like profile,' and said of her in *Giselle*:

'Dancing an accurate, authoritative Queen of the Wilis, she was the essence of that most difficult role.' The comments on *Les Sylphides* would make any dancer glow: 'Mlle. Gielgud was outstanding in the valse, displaying elevation, balance and a love for what she was doing to such a degree that one began to love it, too.'

7

BÉJART

In what seemed a natural course of events for Gielgud after her awakening with Hightower to seeing ballet as something of a spiritual pursuit, she next joined the Ballet of the Twentieth Century (Ballet du XXème Siècle) company in 1967. It was run by the famed Maurice Béjart, who brought together the spiritual and physical side of dance, and this gave her a much deeper experience of it, heightening her appreciation and her striving for expression.

She would stay there four years, which also gave her the stability of being with a permanent company.

Gielgud had seen her first Béjart ballet in Paris when she was fourteen. It was the *Rite of Spring*, a highly exotic and erotic ballet, which caused great controversy when it was first staged there in 1913 by the Ballets Russes de Sergei Diaghilev. The Béjart version had a profound effect on Gielgud, though it never occurred to her that she might join that company, since the ballet seemed to her at that time so removed from classical.

She and her mother were guests in the box of the British ambassadress, who at the end turned to the girl and asked her, somewhat rhetorically, if she had enjoyed it. To the older woman's amazement, Gielgud answered resoundingly in the affirmative.

Béjart, who was French-born, and established an international reputation as a dancer and choreographer, in 1960 became Director of a company based at the Theatre de Monnaie, in Brussels. He was much acclaimed for the spectacle of his productions, which were held in such public places as circuses, stadiums and bullrings, and attracted audiences which normally would never have attended ballet.

His ballets resonated deeply with the young Gielgud. They helped give her direction. 'They appealed to me tremendously as a way of communicating things that you can't express verbally, to such a *wide* variety of people. That made sense of being a dancer, because you were performing for people of all kinds.'

She had encountered Béjart in Cannes when he was a guest teacher at Hightower's Centre. He told her that he wanted her in the company, but there was no immediate possibility of a place. As she waited, she continued dancing with the Grand Ballet Classique de France, and continued to study with Hightower and live in Cannes. But she was determined to join Béjart. 'I didn't know when I was going to have a place with him. It would be at least a year. But, my God, was I there! I was not going to let this man forget me. No way!

'I went everywhere that Béjart's company went, often with my tutu in my hand, which was really very funny, because Béjart supposedly despised tutus and the decoration of classical ballet. I remember getting off the train, going straight to the theatre, going to find Maurice, and his saying, "Well, leave your things here, and I'll take you in (to the theatre)." So I left my tutu in Maurice's dressing room, which was really outrageous. It was in a kind of plastic bag, but the shape was absolutely unmistakable.' Years later Gielgud was wielding another plastic bag when she met with Béjart for lunch in London. It was an incongruous accessory to the fur coat she was wearing at the time, causing him to call her a 'snob gypsy'.

Gielgud watched every Béjart performance that she could, especially in Paris. She paid particular attention to *Romeo and Juliet*, which had just been created, and the *Ninth Symphony*, which she found extraordinary. She particularly admired his male dancers. They included Paolo Bortoluzzi, who was already established, and had remarkable control of his technique and sense of movement, which Béjart used to the ultimate. There was also Jorge Donn, who was just emerging as a huge personality. Younger than Gielgud, about eighteen, he was not as strong or as clean a technician as Bortoluzzi, yet she found his personality and charisma amazing.

Watching the Béjart company perform served to fuel Gielgud's ambition to join the company. She wanted Béjart to choreograph for her, to have works created for her, as opposed to taking on repertoire that was done before. 'Almost every dancer is desperate to have ballets created on them. It's one of the most exciting things for them, and often their career is made by a choreographer who believes in them and brings out their special qualities.'

Béjart wanted to improve the standard and to have more material from which to work at that time, so a few other classical dancers were brought into the company as well as Gielgud. They included Floris Alexander, Daniel Lommel and Lorca Massine – the son of the famous Leonide Massine – with whom Gielgud studied in Paris with Gsovsky. 'It was known as a very original company, very contemporary, and Béjart's name was getting very hot, as they say, especially in France, Germany and Italy. He was getting huge audiences, even though he had not yet been to America with the company, or England. It was made up of dancers from all over the world.'

When Gielgud first joined, in 1967, Béjart created a ballet called *Mass For The Present Time*, in which she had a tiny solo, using her technical virtuosity. Almost immediately she was given the great role of Queen Mab in *Romeo and Juliet*, which was rehearsed in Brussels and opened in Avignon. It was one of the most notoriously difficult female solos in Béjart's repertoire, and there was much rehearsal with the ballet master. The old guard in the company felt that she was 'too classical' and did not know or understand the Béjart style, but Béjart himself was very enthusiastic.

She did feel type cast, though, as Queen Mab. 'I was an evil thing, which tended to happen to me.' For this she partly blamed her nose with the bump on it. Indeed, photographs of her as Queen Mab show an exotic, treacherous-looking character.

Her solo ran to twenty minutes, as opposed to the usual classical one, which lasts three minutes. 'It was exhausting. I used to be sick afterwards, and nearly fainted at the end of each performance.

'Queen Mab was dressed in all-over silver tights, stiff and very uncomfortable, with little spangles all over it, silver shoes and a skull cap, and a little plastic globe with a light inside it. Because I was in a later cast, I had never rehearsed with all the characters. When it came to performance, I had to run past Mercutio, but I didn't know which side. So I ran into him with my globe and fell on my backside, and the globe exploded. But I was used to falling. I often fell, and usually on a first night. Nobody minded. Anyway, everyone loathed the costume, and later Béjart changed it to red and gold.'

Gielgud's arrival at Béjart's company came when he was particularly interested in bringing mysticism into ballet, using many influences from places like India. The first ballet he created for Gielgud was *Bhakti*, in 1968, for which he went to India to prepare. Gielgud remembers it was a time of the hippy culture and there was much interest in things Indian. She was given the role of Shakti, the goddess counterpart to Shiva, the god of destruction. The ballet depicts gods and contemporary figures as mirror images. The music is folkloric Indian. It is basically three pas de deux, of which the one involving Shakti and Shiva has since been best known. The role further developed Gielgud's interest in Eastern teachings. 'I was the goddess of destruction, and it was a solo focused on that, and needed to be very strong.

'In the solo, every pose was made quite distinctly, and that was hard, because you have to rev up the machine for every step, rather than letting one flow into the other, as you would in a classical piece. The work did not try to replicate Indian dancing, only the essence of it. This was the way Béjart worked when he used themes from other countries. People are always astounded at the way he seems to capture the feeling without using any actual part of the traditional dancing.'

Gielgud's costume was a mixture of a temple statue design and all-over body tights, made into a bikini style, with a considerable amount of her flesh bare. She had very black hair in a bun with two long loose strands, and very dramatic make-up.

On the first night, she and her partner – in this instance, Lommel, although the piece was created for her and Germinal Casado – started off in the pose of idols, with her sitting on top of Shiva. Suddenly, the elastic on her costume broke, 'and I could feel it going down my bottom, showing the crack between the two cheeks. So I had to do the whole thing with the elastic coming off!' She made her movements even more vigorous to compensate, and hoped the audience would not notice. Presumably the *Dancing Times* did not, because they called her 'the very embodiment of destruction as Shakti'.

Bhakti was later made into a film. 'It was Béjart at his most revolutionary. He had shots of butcher's shops and meat hanging up and all sorts of things, and we went up and down supermarket escalators as part of the preamble, showing the difference in cultures: the "dreadful" West and the "wondrous" East.' In its review of the film, the *Montreal Star* said, 'Maina Gielgud as Shakti . . . is a burning, splendid . . . dancer, who dominates the screen every moment she is on it.'

Also in 1968, they did *Ni Fleurs, Ni Couronnes* (Neither Flowers nor Crowns), taking the themes from well-known parts of *The Sleeping Beauty*, which Gielgud already knew. 'Béjart used a bit of the Lilac Fairy solo, the theme, to piano, and for me the beginning of the Rose Adagio, also to piano. It was well known to be the hardest. He used also the beginnings of the Blue Bird, and of the famous Act III wedding pas de deux. He changed it musically, adding to it, making it more contemporary, making the choreography evolve in short little segments. So, at first it would be *"ta dum, ta dum, ta dee, ta dum, ta dum, ta dee da, da dee da, da dee da, stop."* And then it would be piano, with a bit of percussion, and the steps with some added contemporary feel to it, and getting harder and harder as it became more and more quirky. And then adding the boys for the famous promenades and balances of the Rose Adagio. That was enormously hard. He did it to challenge all of us so that our techniques would get stronger; and to make use of those of us who came from a classical background.

'Béjart, himself, of course, was trained classically. He

was adamant that his dancers should have the best possible teachers, and brought, amongst others, Asaf Messerer from the Bolshoi to guest teach in the early days of his company. All too often the fringe population of the ballet world are not aware of how firmly entrenched the roots of most contemporary choreographers are in the tradition and vocabulary of classical ballet.'

The following year they did a Béjart ballet on Baudelaire. Described as a spectacle in nine scenes, it uses poems by Baudelaire, songs by Debussy, and excerpts from Wagner's *Tannhauser* as its mainstream. Part of it is choreographed as a normal ballet, and the rest is improvised to guidelines; what Gielgud calls the 'hippy' part. It opened in an amazing new theatre outside Grenoble that used a huge turntable on which the audience was seated, so they could be turned around to see dancers on different parts of the stage – even at the back. An outer circle, on which the dancers would also perform, could be turned in the opposite direction. 'It was a huge success. Béjart is just the most extraordinary theatrical wizard. People would sit mesmerised, crying, and still be in their seats half an hour after the performance was over.'

Because it was a long way from Grenoble, this was also the only time when she had the pleasure of sleeping in a theatre where she was performing. There were three dressing rooms with beds in them where a few of them stayed. 'It was great fun. It's always been my dream to live, eat and sleep in the theatre where I perform.'

Gielgud's role was as one of the five women in Baudelaire's life. To her chagrin, her solo was set to percussion. They were in all-over tights of different colours. Gielgud was in mauve, with a matching wig. 'It was certainly very sexy. I was always doing sexy women.' Indeed, there was a certain slinky sensuality about her as she has appeared in photographs and films from her dancing years. Part of it was in the long willowy limbs and the fluidity of movement, as well as the exotic beauty of that pale face, flowing hair, and the dark-rimmed doe-eyes.

But there is no Bambi about Gielgud, nor for that matter bimbo, for she abhors coquettishness. Indeed, she still recalls with distaste the example of a French ballerina who joined them on the previous American tour. She was young and talented, with a strong technique, but not of the kind Gielgud liked. The young lady hammed it up to the audience to catch their attention; anything for success, even playing the coquette. This demonstrated to Gielgud 'the difference between seeing some of the top ballerinas and *premiers danseurs* with great elegance, as opposed to a nightclub artist type.' Yet, while Gielgud is so down on vulgar display, there is a suspicion that she enjoyed some mischievous exhibitionism of her own.

At twenty-four, she was still not expecting romantic roles with Béjart, wanting instead merely to work with him, though she would have eagerly taken the chance of dancing to more of the great melodies.

'But I certainly had the feeling of getting a lot of experience and diversity. It was a golden era of his company, and it was a golden time for my career. It was very creative. I was getting some of the most interesting roles for women that Béjart was creating.' In 1970, she was at last given a romantic role, in *Four Last Songs*, with music by Richard Strauss, creating a pas de deux with Jorge Donn.

She was soon admitted to the 'inner circle' of the company. This was composed of a select few dancers, and one or two outside people who were close to Béjart. They spent a lot of time together, sharing to an even greater degree than the rest of the company a great love of dance and the feel of being a part of something very important that was being created by Béjart. Later, while retaining her friendship with Béjart, she was not so involved with that group, but found other friends in Catherine Verneuil, who was in and out of that group, and Itomi Asakawa, who was often Donn's partner.

That year, Peter Williams wrote in *Dance and Dancers* of having had the first chance to see Gielgud, about whom he had heard so much. 'She really looks like a Balanchine girl, physically, with her long neck and sleek lithe body. But, doubtless due to her French training with Hightower, she is able to take the old Russian classics in her stride. I loved her – she has a really grand manner, great speed and a brilliant technique.

'I think that with greater attention to her arms, which had a tendency to spikiness, she could become one of the great ballerinas of Europe. Possibly a few months with Madame Dudinskaya in Leningrad would put these faults right. She is tall, and tall girls need to extend their line with more fluid arm movements, and greater attention to épaulement. Nevertheless, I get a thrill from her work that is rare with dancers of the West.'

In late 1970, prior to their proposed trip the next year

to New York, Béjart told Gielgud before a performance that if she danced really well that night he had a surprise for her. It turned out that he was going to create a solo for her for the advance publicity tour, the role of Lady Macbeth, to a recording of Maria Callas. It was an exciting prospect.

Gielgud, her mother, Béjart and Donn then went away for a memorable holiday in Capri, where Gielgud went on fascinating long walks with the Director. He was a highly creative person, charismatic and full of knowledge. 'I love being around knowledgeable people. I don't pick it up, unfortunately, but I enjoy hearing it. Then I don't remember it, which is annoying!'

When they returned to Brussels, her name went up on the notice board for rehearsal and she got to the studio early, as was her habit, to warm up and be ready for Lady Macbeth. She read the play, despite not being fond of Shakespeare, about which, because of her uncle, she is slightly embarrassed. To her bemusement, the sound man put on a very strange tape, which to Gielgud came across as being full of squeaks and grunts. After listening to this tape for the third time, Gielgud asked if she could hear the Lady Macbeth music, only to be told that this was the right tape for the rehearsal.

Then Béjart arrived, and informed Gielgud that he was going to do a ballet based on the piece, which was written by the French pioneer composer of concrete music, Pierre Henry, with whom Béjart had often collaborated. The work was called *Variations pour une Porte et un Soupir* (Variations for a Door and a Sigh). Béjart, who had previously worked an improvisation ballet to it, wanted to use sections for a solo.

'I wouldn't have even called it music,' Gielgud says. 'I was absolutely devastated, but of course couldn't show anything. I think he did virtually the whole thing in that one session. I went home and cried. This was after *Four Last Songs*. I was going to have some real music again, and meaty, emotional stuff. And yet, no, there it was: *Forme et Ligne*, or *Squeaky Door*, as it came to be called, was born.' When she calmed down, she at least acknowledged that the piece was amusing. 'But I had no idea what it would end up doing for my career.'

Indeed, *Squeaky Door* was a great success. It revealed Gielgud's versatility, and did much for her reputation. Both funny and stark, it allowed her to show a droll sense of humour as her body was contorted convulsively to the concrete music, while she maintained very cool facial expressions, as though wearing a mask.

That experience came to the fore almost twenty-five years later, when Gielgud gave the same part to a dancer in The Australian Ballet. As they rehearsed together in a studio in Sydney, Gielgud could see the dancer, Nicole Rhodes, was struggling with the eccentricity of the role, even though it suited her perfectly. She took her into the office and said, 'Look, I can see how you're feeling about this. But I'm wanting you to do it on purpose, because we don't know what's going to happen later on in terms of the company [this was in 1995, after the board's decision not to reappoint her as Artistic Director after 1996] – who they will like or dislike. I, too, was very disappointed when this role first came my way, but, in fact, if you make it your own, in your own way, it can be very useful. As happened with me, it can lead to your being asked to dance in galas here, there and everywhere. It's something that is yours, that no one else does, and is very different from all the virtuoso pas de deux that everybody does all over the world.'

Squeaky Door was performed, and filmed, for the advance promotional tour in the United States. Gielgud later guested everywhere with it, after dancing classical pas de deux on the same evening. The film today still stands up very well, with Gielgud as a slightly manic figure immersed in a solo which made her look like a puppet which had lost its way under the spell of a hidden force.

When the casting for the American tour was announced, Gielgud felt she was not being given enough work. She raised her concerns with Béjart, who agreed that she dance the pas de deux *Webern Opus 5* by the Austrian composer Anton Webern. This puzzled Gielgud, because when she had danced the role previously, in Brussels, Béjart had not seemed to like it. 'He said something about my being like a dancer from The Royal Ballet. That was not a compliment!' Nonetheless, the work became one of her absolute favourites. 'I found the music, in a curious way, very melodious, although it was very plinky and plonky, and quite dry at times.' Béjart had broken down some of her resistance to contemporary scores through his unique use of this kind of music.

The Béjart season in America was a huge public success, though, according to Gielgud, 'as usual for Béjart in both New York and London, the critics demolished it.'

Well, not all of it. *Variety* said, 'Maina Gielgud comes on and steals the show. She is a very great dancer, both technically and expressively.'

The *Village Voice* said:

> The dancers are splendid, but... Béjart allows some of his best men... to throw far too many come-hither glances at the audience. This, in part, is what gives the Las Vegas effect. Maina Gielgud does it too, although she too is a splendid dancer.

A year before, during *Squeaky Door*, the magazine called her 'a real star'. In the *New York Times*, the critic Clive Barnes said, 'I was most taken with the steely forcefulness of Maina Gielgud.'

Winthrop Sargeant, in the *New Yorker*, listed 'a tremendous array of fine females, led by Maina Gielgud'. He continued:

> The ballet began with the thirty-two fouettés from *Swan Lake*, performed by Miss Gielgud – or perhaps 'tossed off' is a better description, since this series of steps, usually regarded as difficult, was done in an offhand manner, as if to say: 'We can do all that if necessary, but let's get on with something more up to date.'

Gielgud, meanwhile, received a telephone call from Lincoln Kirstein, the illustrious grandfather of the New York City Ballet, who in 1933 had brought to America

George Balanchine, the famous Russian dancer and Diaghilev's chief choreographer. Balanchine became the Artistic Director when the company was formed in 1948. Gielgud had met Kirstein some years before through her uncle, John Gielgud. Now he told her that Balanchine would be very happy if she came and did class with the company. Delighted with the invitation, Gielgud went ahead.

She might well have been advised to have first consulted Béjart, though, for when she came back to rehearsal later that day, he ignored her. 'I realised later that he knew I'd gone to do class with Balanchine, and he probably thought I was being disloyal, and trying to get into the New York City Ballet. But I had told Lincoln Kirstein that I was very happy at Béjart, and wasn't really interested, but I'd love to go and do class with them. Some lovelies must have said to Béjart, "She's gone off to New York City Ballet; she's trying to go there." They might even have said I was playing tit for tat because he had taken Suzanne Farrell into the company, who had been a favourite of Balanchine.'

On the return to Belgium, Gielgud decided to talk to Béjart, because she felt she was not getting very much to do, and was not happy about it. She went to see him in his flat. It was to be a most unpleasant experience.

'The suggestion came about in the conversation – I think by me – that I should take a year's leave, because nothing was really happening. He presumed I meant in a year's time. But I meant right then and there, which was heartrending for me. But there wasn't really any hesitation. That's what I had to do. I had to go. I felt he wasn't as interested in me. I wasn't developing any further, and not getting the roles. I just seemed to have struck a ceiling there, or hiatus, and I wasn't prepared to walk on the spot, treading water.

'I had things to go further with, to develop, which were the reason I had gone there. And, of course, there was also a disappointment at the apparent change of policy, because this was a company which traditionally had no stars, no principals as such.' She is referring to him having brought in Farrell, who in London was given the leading role in *Rite of Spring*, instead of it being given to Tania Bari, for whom it had been created. When the casting appeared on the notice board, 'a few of us – the believers – felt that something had gone terribly wrong. This wasn't the company that we'd joined.'

Many times during their meeting Béjart used the expression, 'Vous n'avez rien compris' (You haven't understood anything). Gielgud says, 'I *think* I now know what he meant . . .

'When I decided to take the leave, he said, "Yes, go. Go as far as you possibly can go." It didn't mean as far from his company, or him. It was something else. He gave me a book afterwards, when I left, which was *Swan*, poems by Gandhi, and he inscribed in it: "Envolez vous loin, très loin" (Fly away far, very far). It was funny; I flew away to Australia. But that was a long time later.

'I remember leaving his flat absolutely devastated, because I hadn't gone there thinking I was actually going to leave. But it happened, and it was clear, and it was what had to be.

'I got into the lift and howled like a dog. Then I got to the restaurant where my mother, who was visiting at the time, was waiting, and I howled all through the meal. I was so full of the horror of having to leave a company that had meant so much to me, of leaving Maurice, who still and always does mean so much to me. My mother was fully understanding, as she always has been when I've made decisions that had to be made.' This last remark seems at odds with evidence that at times Sutton clearly questioned her career moves. What seems to be the case, though, is that her mother accepted her daughter's decisions and supported her once Gielgud had made up her mind.

'And that was that. We left for London, which was my last season with them.' It was also her debut in the city of her birth, and clearly made an impact.

Vogue described her as 'a long pale ivory Madonna with Titian hair', who was 'bewitched by Béjart's fierce modernism'. Of the Béjart dancers in that last season, at the London Coliseum, she was the one identified as having a sense of 'terrific drama.' Richard Buckle said in the *Sunday Times* that she was 'marvellous'.

The *Guardian*, writing about her in a feature piece, described her as the impressive young ballerina of the Béjart company. It noted her resemblance to a younger version of her famous Uncle John, and, indeed, in the accompanying photograph, it was there very noticeably. The article said she 'has the same melancholy eyes, the same characteristic profile, the same almost pedantic way of shaping words'. It went on: 'She is 26 and, at 5ft. 7in., fairly tall for a dancer. She wears hot pants, black open neck sweater over sparse bosom, high heels, and black mesh tights covering legs which seem to terminate somewhere beneath her armpits.'

Photographs of her at the time revealed her luscious physicality. On stage, her long limbs seemed to be perfectly controlled, while she danced with apparent abandon. In a London park, she was pictured striding out on strong, long legs, edged by hot pants, with a wide belt, looking most self-possessed. As always, the eyes were rimmed with dark make-up making them glow, in contrast to the translucent skin.

In a voice as fashionably French existential as those eyes, she told the *Guardian* interviewer that it was futile to think about the past or the future. 'We Capricorns have no need for any philosophies. We are quite simply hard working and solitary. We know exactly what we want to do. I want to dance forever and forever, and a bit more. And then perhaps, try some acting. Maybe one day I'll cross over into my uncle's territory. He always said I should.'

On an even more personal note, an earlier extended profile as a 'career story' of Gielgud by Estelle Herf in the London dance magazine, *Ballet Today* in 1968 said, in retrospect somewhat prophetically,

> She shrinks from any public parade of her feelings, from words like 'dedication', from petty intrigues, and self-advancement. The seed of her forebears is there, if only Maina can overcome her own wall of reserve and allow her personality to shine through and become articulate.

For this, to Maina, will be the last enemy to overcome in her career. If and when she does, she will combine the great gifts of her heredity, with all the sweat and tears that have gone into training as a classical ballet dancer, and become a great artist.

The article went on to say that the most important step towards this goal was her engagement by Maurice Béjart for his Twentieth Century Ballet Company.

In an interview in London in June 1971 for the *Guardian*, Gielgud commented on Béjart as she left his company:

> Certainly, Béjart has been accused of placing spectacle before dance. But then, this is what he is aiming for. He wants a new public, a young public, a wider, bigger public. He's doing a private crusade on behalf of Terpsichore.

This referred to one of the nine Muses of Greek mythology, the custodian of choral dance and song, who has featured in several ballets. 'Béjart's work does what Wagner does: it takes you there,' – prodding the pit of her stomach – 'this peculiarly schizophrenic emotion of angst and elation.'

Gielgud later danced more Béjart ballets, with Donn and Lommel as her partners. 'He allowed me to dance his ballets, and he lent me his dancers, and that was wonderful. Then, about two years later, he asked me if I would be interested in coming back. I was in Monte Carlo, and wrote him a very long letter, explaining why I just couldn't, however much I loved him, and continued to love his work. I tried to put into words that I felt this chapter was over, and it wouldn't be right to get back into it. It would have been wrong for both him and me.' Gielgud later guested with the Béjart company, twice, which was unusual. She did her old roles of Queen Mab and the pas de deux *Webern Opus 5*.

She says they are still great friends, and very much in contact. She has produced his work at different times, the latest being *Le Concours*, which toured in The Australian Ballet's 1995 repertoire. Béjart is strictly protective of his ballets and allows only three directors from other companies to stage them. As one of those, Gielgud says she had hoped to bring his *Ninth Symphony* to Australia for the Olympic Games year 2000. It is a melancholy story, now that she is leaving the company in 1996; all the more so for giving us some measure of how far ahead she had been planning.

8

NUREYEV

They were both dancers, and both in Paris, but little did Gielgud dream, when Nureyev defected, that she would one day dance with him, and indeed, still be working with him thirty years later, again in Paris, close to his death in 1993. Not only that, but she had no idea that the wild Kirov boy would become an important influence in her life. She came to admire him a great deal, mainly because he was, as she is, a tireless worker. Having started late in his career, he felt he needed to train very hard to catch up on technique. Nureyev, like Hightower, was to Gielgud the ideal combination of talent and endless effort.

Gielgud had seen him dance with the Kirov in Paris, and was most impressed, though not so much that she did not see his little technical glitches. 'One had heard about this wonder dancer of huge personality. And we'd heard that he'd started dancing late, at seventeen or eighteen, and we thought, "Oh, yes," because there was something he did – a step – which wasn't quite clean. But there was no doubt about the striking personality and the enormous charisma. He was born with those, and used them wonderfully. He worked incessantly on the technical aspects and the cleanliness of the classical technique. He was clearly a great dancer.'

Nureyev, who joined the de Cuevas company after he sought asylum in the West in 1961, was gone from the company by the time Gielgud joined it. But she had often watched him from the wings, and she saw him dance *The Sleeping Beauty* with Hightower, with whom he performed many times. In Peter Watson's biography, *Nureyev*, he is reported as having regarded Hightower as a kindred spirit, the same expression Gielgud has used for her own relationship with Hightower.

She vividly remembers her first impression of Nureyev: 'Oh, that animal magnetism. He was fascinating to watch.' Although very few dancers have that quality, she believes the theatricality can often be found among Australian dancers.

When she was a young girl living in Paris, whenever the Russian companies – but not any others – came to town, she would always go and ask if she could take class with them. She has always admired the Russians as dancers, though more in the past than today.

'I always knew what my problems, my defects, were, as a dancer. But I was also very aware of what I could do, and what my strong points were. And I knew I had some qualities that even some of the Russian dancers didn't. And they had loads that I didn't. But it never occurred to me that this should make me feel shy or embarrassed. I suppose, having been brought up with Russians, I felt at home in those surroundings. The Russians were so inspiring. They seemed to have dance in their blood. Apart from the schooling being so wonderful, they really lived and breathed their dancing. It was something absolutely natural. It's contagious, the way they move. Even now, when I don't dance any more, I watch the old films and videos and feel I want to dance with them. When you saw their Corps de ballet at that time, it seemed like it was a uniformity, but of *individuals*, that everyone was dancing to the music, that they weren't being regimented, that the training and their dance instinct was so good that by simply dancing together to the music as individuals, it created a wonderful team. Whereas in America, England or Europe, in general a Corps de ballet was perhaps an extremely well-drilled one, but there didn't seem to be any individuality, and it seemed to be cutting down to the lowest common denominator.'

Sadly, she now feels that the Russians have changed quite a lot. With some exceptions, there is no longer that general feeling of spontaneity. It has become much more uniform; less individual. It has also become bogged down by the lack of choreographers. She believes this has been one of the main reasons for the defections of dancers, much more than the political aspect. The dancers, as artists, wanted more freedom and more vocabulary – more repertoire – to give them the wherewithal to express themselves. For some reason, choreographically, it became very stilted in Russia and in most of the cousin countries. 'It has taken a long time to show, because the method of training is still very good. But because it's not leading anywhere, perhaps the inspiration's gone.'

It is worth speculating about what her life might have been like had she grown up in Russia. 'I wonder whether I would have been accepted in the school, in terms of desired turnout. They try and find the ideal physiques for dance in the first audition process, at the age of nine or ten. And if the proportions aren't right, if the turnout isn't there, you're likely to be thrown out, without looking at what sense of movement or dance or musicality you might have. That is often the case in specialised schools, and it's probably so in France and Denmark and the other countries that now have schools that take students from a very young age.

'However, somewhere along the line in Russia there must have been people choosing students who did bypass that if they saw someone exceptional, such as Galina Ulanova. She had anything but the ideal physique for dance, and yet, perhaps for that very reason, became one of the greatest dancers. As I try to tell my dancers, almost all of those who've been the greatest artists have not had the ideal physiques, or strong techniques. They've had to fight all the way.' Nureyev was such a fighter, and because of this he developed a very strong technique.

But, impressed as she was by him, Gielgud had not even considered whether they would become partners. 'My ambitions were more in terms of the roles I would be dancing, rather than the people I would be dancing with, certainly at that stage.' But, even more basically, the notion of them being together never occurred to her, 'because – I was going to say, because he was too small; well, that's a terrible thing to say! – rather because I was too tall.'

In 1964, Nureyev made the first of several visits to Australia to dance with The Australian Ballet, with Fonteyn as his partner. His relationship with Australia would continue almost until his death.

Gielgud's first engagement with Nureyev came in May 1971. To add to the excitement of the occasion, it was also her first full-length ballet. She was with the Béjart company at their Brussels headquarters when Hightower contacted her to say that the Ballet of Marseille, of which she was Director, was due to tour Barcelona three weeks later. Noella Pontois from the Paris Opera, who was supposed to be dancing *The Sleeping Beauty* with Nureyev, was either ill or injured, and Hightower proposed Gielgud instead. In response, she received a telegram from Nureyev, which said simply, 'Gielgud okay.'

Nureyev had the sort of power which extended to the smallest detail. He insisted that the tutu Gielgud was to wear in the third act was to match exactly the costume worn by Fonteyn, with whom he was principal partner for many years. This caused a flurry, with Gielgud's mother trying without success to reach Fonteyn's tutu maker in London. She then sought photographs, also fruitlessly, until Hightower remembered a picture taken by a ballet photographer. Sutton contacted them in Paris, and they immediately sent her a negative. She then persuaded a shop to project it life-sized onto a wall, and copied it down, noting every detail. She then went to Hightower's husband, Jean Robier, a stage designer and painter, who was also very good at making tutus. He made a pattern from her sketch and notes while she went to find the necessary jewellery. The costume was completed in three days. Nureyev, fortunately, was delighted with it.

Gielgud, meanwhile, was hard at work preparing for the guesting role, which she did initially by herself. 'Béjart had given me permission, but the guesting may have been one of the reasons why he cooled off, because nobody from his company guested elsewhere. You either belonged to Béjart, or you didn't.

'I went to Barcelona, and rehearsed for two days with Rosella, and then just before the dress rehearsal, Rudi arrived. We went down to a little cellar place, down a tiny staircase, into a tiny studio, and we went through the pas de deux in Acts II and III. Then we did a dress rehearsal. Then we did five performances in a row, during which he was really, really nice and helpful, not only in his partnering, but with some coaching here and there, whenever he had a moment.'

They usually had dinner together after performance, with Hightower, Sutton and whoever was around Nureyev at the time. Lunch between rehearsals was on Las Ramblas in Barcelona, the famous street where there are many restaurants. That was where Gielgud first saw him mopping his steak with his napkin to remove all the fat. Like Gielgud, he was wary of oils and fats, which was quite a problem with the food served in Spain. Certain things with Nureyev had to be just so, down to the perpetual tea in his vacuum flask, served with enormous amounts of sugar.

'It struck me at that time, contrary to the legend, that he was actually very courteous with people bothering him, coming to him in restaurants, asking him to sign autographs by the dozen. I only saw him at his best. I think that much was made of the times when he was out of sorts, or when it became too much, rather than actually seeing how good he was most of the time. I mean, he *could* be pretty rude. Actually, I don't think he was too stressed in Barcelona, because he wasn't directing that production, just coming in to guest. He came in at the last minute and just danced his role.'

Nureyev drove himself after performance, too. Supper was taken after 2 a.m., since performances started at 10 p.m. He would then go out to clubs until all hours, drinking and carousing, turning up for class next morning, hangover and all, and pushing himself through the pain barrier, using his after-hours dissoluteness as a stimulant.

Gielgud's mother also formed a close relationship with him. In her biography, she recalls that on the first day of rehearsal in Barcelona he came into Gielgud's dressing room, and said, 'Mamachka, can you sew?' He then had her put the ribbons on a pair of ballet shoes, which were old, ghastly looking, and with the rubber holding the shoe around the ankle torn off. 'This is my best ballet shoe. Very important you sew it together so that it's not one millimetre shorter than before it ripped. You can do that?' Sutton said, 'Well, I'll try.' He said, 'If you don't succeed, you'll ruin my best shoe.' Sutton recalls, 'Then he left me. I was terrified lest I couldn't do the job properly, as I knew his reputation and thought he might retaliate by throwing Maina on her head. I delivered what I thought was a good job to his dressing room. He wasn't there but, when I went into Maina's room later, I saw six pairs of equally ghastly-looking shoes.' Her daughter said, 'Rudi left those for you.' Sutton asked, 'Did he say anything? Was he pleased with the other pair?' Gielgud replied, 'He must have been, otherwise he wouldn't have left these for you.' Sutton responded, 'Well, that's a great compliment. Thank him very much. Now I've got a week's work on this lot.' Sutton says, 'He never did say thank-you, but I saw he was pleased. I was happy to have been able to help him, and everything went smoothly. Maina said she learned more from him during that week than she had learned in all the years beforehand.'

Late in 1971, Nureyev and Gielgud again danced together, in *Don Quixote*, with the same Marseille company, this time in its home town. Nureyev, who had previously staged *Don Quixote* for The Australian Ballet in Melbourne, not only performed in the production, but also staged and produced it, and revised some of the choreography.

Gielgud, who by this stage was a Principal with the Deutsche Oper Ballet Berlin, was under the impression that she was to dance the main role, of Kitri, with Nureyev.

While in Berlin rehearsing, she heard just before leaving for Marseille that he was going to bring Lucette Aldous from Australia to do most of the Kitris.

'And so it turned out that I was to perform three of the leading soloist roles, one in each act, which normally would be done by three different dancers. But I was to do all three, at all performances when Lucette did Kitri. And then I was going to do one Kitri later on, with Rudi. So, he was going to switch partners, from this tiny thing [Lucette] to me. But it was still pretty exciting.'

They had three weeks of rehearsing in Marseille prior to the production opening, so Gielgud had the chance to be rehearsed by Nureyev and coached by him in all those roles. The performance also featured the Australian dancer Robert Helpmann as The Don. He had been a great star, too, as chief dancer and partner of Fonteyn at the Vic-Wells Ballet, a forerunner of the later Royal Ballet. Helpmann had returned home in 1965 to be joint Artistic Director of The Australian Ballet with Peggy van Praagh.

In Marseille, Nureyev did his class with the other dancers, and rehearsed his solos. Then he rehearsed the company, and in the evening he re-choreographed the Act II gypsy pas de deux, with which he was never pleased. He re-choreographed it everywhere he went. And because Aldous was arriving only a couple of days before the premiere, he re-choreographed it on Gielgud. It was supposedly the first time he actually created steps, as in re-choreographing something, because the version of *Don Quixote* prior to that was what he remembered from the Russian version.

Gielgud was greatly impressed by the dancing of

Aldous as Kitri. 'She was fantastic. Oh, yes, a wonderful dancer. And tiny, but she had such breadth of movement. She and Rudi got along very well. He respected her, and helped her a great deal. And of course he adored dancing with her, partly because she was tiny. I think she perhaps took to an extreme some of his things and lost a little bit of her innate sense of movement.'

Gielgud got to do only one rehearsal with Nureyev for her role as Kitri, and they performed the next day. In the last lift of the first act, 'he was supposed to carry me out, and as soon as he got to the wing, he just sort of pushed me off. Normally you take a bit of care as you put your female partner down, but he threw me. He was angry with me for something in the first mime scene. I was self-conscious during it, and I think it annoyed him.' She has a theory that part of how Nureyev functioned was to make himself angry, so it got his adrenaline pumping for his performance. But she could not afford the time or energy to be upset about it. She had two more acts to get through, including a very hard solo in the second act, which she 'adored'.

'The second act solo went really well. According to my mother, he was not happy about that, and showed it in the third act. But it did not occur to me at the time, and later, I would not want to believe it. Then there came the third act pas de deux, and it was conducted so slowly, but *so* slowly! It was like a double slow funeral march, during which Rudi swore like anything. I thought he was swearing at the conductor.' Later she found out it was at her.

The audience apparently missed the by-play. The critic John Percival, writing in the London *Times*, said:

It was interesting at a matinee, to see Maina Gielgud's debut in the same role [of Kitri]. Her interpretation is inevitably more subdued, although there are hints that with more experience of the part she might develop it rather individually. The vision scene especially suits her longer line and smooth style.

She is more impressive, however, in the other cast, when she plays three contrasted roles opposite Aldous's Kitri. In the vision scene, Gielgud is the Queen of the Dryads, very assured and authoritative. As Mercedes, the street dancer, she glows with sultry pride as she struts among the toreadors' daggers, and in the final wedding celebration she has a gorgeously soaring solo as a bridesmaid.

Nureyev worked himself from morning to night. 'But there were many entertaining meals with Helpmann, Rudi, Rosella, my mother – who also was with us for that season – and me. He was very, very curious. He wanted to know everything that was going on in the arts world. A favourite topic of his was film, because he loved going to the cinema. But he also had terrible stories to tell about people. Very witty, and a wonderful, absolutely incredible way with language. I don't just mean bad language, but language in general. He spoke very good French, but usually it was English. His rude language was also very much his own. He'd just find ways . . . and it would be exquisitely obscene, but also just dreadfully funny. And right on the mark.'

She found him to be a prankster and a great clown. He could be evil on stage, by upstaging other dancers, or throwing them off balance, or by not holding them properly. It could happen in anger, too. 'He left Makarova on the floor once, because he wouldn't move. There's a passage in *Black Swan* [the grand pas de deux in Act III of *Swan Lake*] where she comes towards him, and he's just standing there. Theoretically, the boy's not supposed to move, and the girl's supposed to go to him. It's better that way. But every gallant partner will always just move a step here, or a step back, or whatever it is, so that the next pirouette works really well. But apparently he'd warned her at rehearsal that he wasn't going to move. And he didn't. She slid to the floor, and he didn't help her up!'

Whenever Gielgud speaks of Nureyev, her voice takes on a special intimacy. 'He was just an extraordinary person, there was no doubt about it. As I talk about him, I can see his features and that scar on the lip, and it seems all the more amazing now to have worked with him, danced with him, talked to him. I mean, he was already a legend in his lifetime, but so much more now. The voice, the accent, as I say, the way of using language, it was so interesting, so individual. People like that are fascinating. They have an instinctive, acute intelligence, and a wonderful curiosity. I think that's always very attractive in people, when they're genuinely curious.'

She has said that he was not a gentle man. But did Nureyev have a good heart? 'I think it was probably killed off in some way. Perhaps by him.' Does she think he felt he had to become a killer? 'Oh yes, yes. You see, I think most of us have a sort of an awareness and a wish that other people might think well of one, that it would be nice to be thought of as a nice person, a person with a good heart. I don't think he had any hangups about that. That doesn't necessarily mean that he didn't . . . Who knows?'

She was not drawn to him as a male. 'I mean, I could see on stage the sex appeal. I could certainly feel that. But no, I had no wish to go to bed with him!'

She loved, although sometimes deploring, the way in which Nureyev would take huge risks in his work. 'It was dangerous in the sense that it was impossible for him to bring off what he was challenging himself with every time. So, he'd give himself a two in ten chance of really bringing it off. But it made it exciting, regardless, That was in the physical sense.

'Rudi had these very set ideas about classical dance, perhaps because he was labelled "*demi caractère*" back in Russia. He was the hardest working of all dancers. His theory was that he could only really perform when he was really tired. This meant his going through solos, for instance, several times before the actual performance. It would have taken a lot of drive to get himself into that tired state.

'Also, he made technical demands on himself that were beyond what is normally expected. But these were so great that often he would not totally achieve what he was trying for. It was sometimes clear to audiences that he was not technically always successful, and I found myself wishing he would confine those challenges to himself in the studio, as opposed to the stage. But it was what he considered an honesty towards his art form.'

A month after dancing with him this time, Gielgud told the *Guardian*:

> Nureyev was very sweet. One hears such hair-raising stories about how he treats some of his partners that one at first felt a little apprehensive. But it was just pure joy to work with him. I was so impressed with how he works on himself, how he constantly sets himself enormous problems. He taught me so much about how to 'present' myself – how to be effective on stage. You have to make the steps look as though you're telling the audience, 'Look, they are very difficult steps, but see how very easy they are for me.' It needs such a delicate balance.

Today, she says, 'His *dancing* in the classics often had little relationship to the actual *character* he was portraying. He was often wonderful in the *acting* and *mime* part of the portrayal of a character, although it was always unmistakably *Rudi* portraying that character, as it was in his inimitable walk and the way he partnered. But then he would enter the stage and dance an extraordinary solo, which didn't really seem to relate to the story.'

'It's very, very hard for male dancers in classical ballets. Their roles can be very ungrateful. They usually don't contain a lot of character and meat for interpretation. Their solos also usually contain much the same steps, and it's become "done" for each dancer to put in the steps he does best. There tend to be four or five different ways of combining certain steps. They're usually not choreographed in the same way as they are for females, in a style that appertains to that particular ballet.

'I got the impression that Rudi liked me . . . thought I was a bit strange. I think he respected me for being a hard worker, and questioning in terms of dance, and wanting to know as much as I could.' Was she in awe of him? 'Not overmuch, but enough. He wouldn't have liked it if I wasn't.' She calls him the Prince of Gypsies. Being a gypsy herself, she would have recognised another.

Sutton remembers Nureyev going off his face one day in a Marseille restaurant over a chicken dish, which he threw down the stairs because he was dissatisfied with it. Later, he told them apologetically, 'When a thing like that happens I get terribly angry. I get blood in my head. I don't know what I do. I once threw a gold watch from a skyscraper in New York, and regretted it very much afterwards.' On another occasion he spoke of how hard it was having to make conversation in public after a performance, 'when all you want to do is escape, eat your steak after hard work, and have fun.' He also shared the confession that when he was a child he was so poor that he had no shoes and had to walk barefoot in the snow. He never wanted to be poor again. He looked after money carefully, even after death, with the provision of two foundations: one for dancers and another for medical research.'

Suzanne Davidson knew Nureyev from the very early days. On his last visit to Australia, in 1991, despite being sick, he came to her house for a dinner party. There was a great sense of humour between them; they called each other Russian and Hungarian peasants.

Davidson says, 'Nureyev had an unerring taste, a sense of what was right on stage, not always for himself, perhaps, but certainly in a production. He would go around and talk with people, and had an unerring sense of quality, not just in dance, but in art in general. Look at what he left behind. It's a treasure trove of the best. There isn't a piece of rubbish in the whole thing. Yet he had no real education. He was seventeen when he went to the Kirov, as it was then, and he didn't get educated there. He danced like a mad thing to try and catch up. He did little bits and pieces [of dance] as a kid because he once saw some dancing when his mother took him to see a show. Then he really just joined a folk dance group, because in the Communist era there were a lot of folk dance groups everywhere.

'He had the good fortune [at the Kirov] of having Pushkin, who was his teacher, who was obviously a cultured, educated man, and who did influence him a lot. He certainly talked to me a lot about him.

'But his sense of right is something that was inborn. Of course, he was surrounded by a lot of good things, and, of course, he was also influenced. But it depends on what you pick up, what influences you allow to stick. 'And he *knew* – and this is what Maina has – this sense of what's right.'

Gielgud was in Paris one more time with Nureyev, in 1991, just a couple of years before he died. Although it was not generally known, he was very ill by then from the AIDS virus, which he had contracted several years before, but he asked her to give him a class. So the two of them and one of The Australian Ballet dancers, Andrew Murphy, who was also in Paris at the time, on a scholarship, went into a studio at the Paris Opera, where Gielgud gave the class to the 53-year-old who was at the end of his career, and the 18-year-old who was on the threshold of his. It was a remarkable experience for the three dancers, alone in the middle of that beautiful, bustling city where Gielgud and Nureyev had first met, thirty years before. To add to the poignancy of the occasion, it was Christmas Day. But that made no difference to a couple of devotees such as Nureyev and Gielgud. She says he probably asked her to come because he knew that she was one of the few ballet people obsessed enough to work on that day. But he also wanted it, she believes, simply because it was Christmas Day, and he, this idol of millions, was alone.

9

BEYOND BÉJART

In June 1971, a small article in the *Evening Standard* reported:

> Maina Gielgud, the young dancer who made such a brilliant impression here with the Béjart 20th Century Ballet, has decided to go to Berlin as the star of the Berlin Opera Ballet, at the State Theatre under the new artistic director, George Balanchine.

The move was also mentioned in the *Guardian*, which described it as her beginning a 'one year's concentration course on classical choreography'. It was said that her appetite had been whetted the previous month by dancing Princess Aurora with Prince Rudolf at Barcelona in the Marseille Ballet's full-length *The Sleeping Beauty*.

The move came about early in the London season with Béjart, when Gielgud was contacted by John Taras, who invited her to lunch. Taras, born in New York, has been a choreographer of note, having created his first ballet at thirteen. He had been ballet master of the New York City Ballet since 1959, at times taking leave of absence to work with other companies. When he met Gielgud, he was at that time Artistic Director of the Berlin Ballet. He told her that Balanchine would like her to work with the New York City Ballet, but she needed to get used to his style and repertoire, so Balanchine wanted her to spend a year with the Berlin Ballet, of which he was Artistic Advisor. She would have a contract, as a Principal, officially for the first time in her life.

'It sounded really exciting. I had no job from the next month because I had told Béjart I was going, with no thought of what I'd do. Having worked with a choreographer, in a choreographer's company, who was mainly focused on creating for male dancers, there now seemed the possibility of working with another very great man, whose company was considered to be the pinnacle of classical dance choreography. "Mr B", as he was generally known, was *the* creator for women. There are hundreds of Balanchine ballets. They tend on the whole to be abstract, as opposed to telling a story.

'It had always been the dramatic, acting, theatrical

side – as least as much as the dancing – that had appealed to me. So that was a minus. But on the plus side, ever since I can remember, people always told me, "Oh, you'd be such a wonderful New York City Ballet dancer, because you've got such long legs, and Balanchine loves long-legged girls, and he'd do wonderful things with you."

'I also thought, correctly, that it would be extremely difficult, after having worked for one person – for their vision – to then go into a repertory company, where you're on your own, where you perhaps have a variety of repertoire, but dancers in the company aren't all focussed towards one person.'

Gielgud, who had already had some experience doing summer classes with American Ballet Theatre and New York City Ballet, was happy to agree to what Taras and Balanchine suggested. As well as having the appeal of being a choreographer, Taras had worked with Hightower in the de Cuevas company, giving Gielgud a sense of connection.

Before leaving London, she appeared in a gala performance at the Coliseum, billed as 'The Greatest Show On Earth'. Organised by Richard Buckle, who was also its Artistic Director, it was in aid of the Save the Titian Fund and the Museum of Theatre Arts. It was a very grand affair, held in the presence of an historic gathering. The audience included M. Vaslav Nijinsky-Markevitch, the grandson of Vaslav Nijinsky, and his wife, Mme von Meck, the grand niece of Piotr Tchaikovsky, and her family, M. Jean Hugo, the grandson of Victor Hugo, his wife and family, and of Sir Michael Duff, grandson of the

Marchioness of Ripon, the first patroness of the Diaghilev Ballet in England, and his family. On stage it featured such outstanding dancers as Nureyev, Fonteyn, Pilar Lopez, Zizi Jeanmaire, André Prokovsky, Anton Dolin, Alexandra Danilova, Michael Somes, Desmond Kelly, Antoinette Sibley, Anthony Dowell, Stanislas Idzikowsky, Floris Alexander and Maina Gielgud, who danced the Rose Adagio from *The Sleeping Beauty*.

Gielgud went to Berlin full of high hopes. But to her great distress, she soon realised that she did not enjoy the experience. 'I just found it dry and square. It was a good company. They did a lot of Balanchine, yet I danced badly almost throughout the year. I worked terribly hard; I don't know what it was. There weren't many performances, and that was a big disadvantage. John was great to work with, but he didn't take rehearsals often. It was an atmosphere that I wasn't used to. I mean, I wasn't miserable, and I was getting roles. Maybe simply the Balanchine choreography didn't suit me. Certainly I was trying to do something with it, and you're not supposed to do that. You're supposed to let it speak for itself.'

At least during her stay in Berlin she finally got around to having her nose altered. She wanted to dance more romantic roles, and felt the bump from childhood was prejudicing her against being cast in them. For dancers, special care has to be taken with the surgery to keep their nostrils still wide enough so they can breathe properly. The new nose fulfilled its promise of allowing her subsequently to be cast in the leading roles in such ballets as *Les Sylphides*, *Giselle*, *The Sleeping Beauty*, and in the role of the Swan Queen in *Swan Lake*, and the pas de deux from *Suite en Blanc*, a ballet which followed her through her career.

During that difficult year, Gielgud did some guesting, including in Budapest in 1972 with Jorge Donn and Daniel Lommel. They performed a whole evening of Béjart works. Gielgud was also offered the chance to dance the full-length *Swan Lake* there, for the first time.

Her mother went with her, and so did Hightower, who helped her prepare for *Swan Lake* in just three days. It was just as well, because Gielgud had not realised that it was much more difficult than *The Sleeping Beauty*. She had learned the pas de deux and solos from the White Swan in Act II and the Black Swan in Act III, from when she was very young in Paris with Egorova and Goubé as her teachers. Act IV, however, is always very different in each production, and has to be learned on the spot.

When she arrived at the theatre, having to perform with hardly any rehearsal, she discovered that there was an unpainted canvas cloth on the floor, which caught under the dancers' feet. So any pirouettes were a nightmare. She got through the fouettés, because she was strong in that area. But she was disappointed in her first effort in such an important ballet as *Swan Lake*. 'I felt that it was pretty poor. But people seemed to like it, so it was okay.' She was not troubled by *Swan Lake* being the most famous ballet of all time, with such a history of having been performed by so many great dancers.

'No, I never had this worry about tradition, nor was I intimidated by all the great ones who came before me, while still having great respect for them. But it never made me scared of those roles. It always seemed to be pretty silly, just a waste of energy and nerves. There you've got the occasion of dancing these masterpieces, and it's just so exciting, and you just have to do what you can. You take note, and refer to what's been done before as much as you can, and use what works for you.'

She loved the leading role in *Swan Lake*, and this was a good production, whereas 'in some productions, the audience is just waiting for the Corps de ballet to finish, so as to get to the pas de deux. I've seen many productions, and one of those that to me made the most sense was Kenneth MacMillan's version, which I saw in Berlin. He interpreted the whole thing as the Prince's dream. That gave it far more sense.

'Even though the choreography for the Corps de ballet of *Swan Lake* is really good, and can be *very* beautiful, if you don't have a great Swan Queen then it eventually is just a bore. However, if you have a Prince who's an artist, who's able to put something of himself in it, as well as a great Swan Queen, then you see something that moves onto another plane altogether.

'I've been so deeply moved by some *Swan Lake*s, by Svetlana Beriosova, who brought me to tears as a child in London, Natalia Makarova, whose performance I saw in Washington, and Maya Plisetskaya, whose first *Swan Lake* I saw in Paris, when she danced with the Paris Opera. Plisetskaya wasn't necessarily as moving, but she was *extraordinary*. It was just like seeing Callas in dance. Immensely dramatic, and very exciting.'

Richard Buckle later wrote in *The Times* in London,

'Maina Gielgud is the most impressive Odette-Odile, in Swan Lake, to be seen in the Western World.'

But still not happy with her time in Berlin, Gielgud decided to go to New York and meet Balanchine to see if her planned engagement with New York City Ballet the following season was really going to happen, as 'Mr B.' had advised. In one of those turns of good fortune, when she passed through London on her way, she met Beryl Grey, the Artistic Director of London Festival Ballet, who offered her a guesting engagement in *Swan Lake*. They were introduced by Peter Williams, the editor of *Dance and Dancers*, whom Gielgud says 'was a wonderful supporter and friend, often most helpful with advice and contacts in my career. He was often referred to in the British ballet world as "The Godfather" of dancers. He also started the Resettlement Fund for dancers in the UK.'

With this contract giving her extra confidence, she approached Balanchine in his office and asked about being accepted into the American company. 'He was very nice, and I was very forceful. He just kept on saying that I was too big a fish, and New York City Ballet was a no-stars company. He said I had a big name, and a lot of personality, and he thought I'd find it very difficult.' She did not agree with this image of herself. 'Sometimes I dress up, but ...' she laughs, 'I don't give myself airs and graces or act a part.' In fact, she believes Balanchine apparently had said the same thing to a number of other principals when they wanted to join his company.

Persistently, she requested a second interview, 'to tell him, "really, I don't want to be a star. That's not my intention. I have enormous respect for what you do, and I would just love to be part of your company, for no other reason." I told him I was not searching for my name in lights, or any of that. I said I would be happy to come into the Corps de ballet. But he said, "No, no, no. I just know it wouldn't be right, and it wouldn't work out."'

She was not as devastated as she might have been, because she had the Festival Ballet guesting contract. It was only for three performances, but it was 'interesting'. She went to Newcastle, did *Swan Lake* well, after which Grey said they needed someone to do *Nutcracker* the following week, and asked if she had ever danced it before. 'I said, "Oh, yes." In fact, I'd never done it!' The admission is made without any sense of remorse. 'I wanted to do it. I knew it, anyway, so I suppose it was a way of giving both Beryl and me confidence. And I had to live up to it.'

Gielgud's bold bluff with London Festival Ballet paid off, because after she did *Nutcracker* with them, she was given the best news of being asked to join the company permanently as a Principal from the next season. She had been keen to work in choreographers' companies, but because she had now done *The Sleeping Beauty*, *Swan Lake* and *Nutcracker*, she was also very interested in developing further in full-length classics. London Festival Ballet, which functioned as repertory companies had back in the time of Diaghilev, the Ballets Russes de Monte Carlo, and the Marquis de Cuevas company, would certainly give her that opportunity, while New York City Ballet would not have done so. Also, she had permission from Béjart to dance *Bhakti*, *Squeaky Door* and the *Webern Opus 5* pas de deux, giving her a special little repertoire of her own that not many other dancers had.

Gielgud stayed with London Festival Ballet from 1972 to 1976, which meant that she was with them in the critical years for a dancer, when they typically reach their peak, coming into their early thirties. But it also gave her a chance to guest with other companies, as well as appear in galas. She came to meet people from all over the world, which would be good not just for her dancing, but also later as an artistic director. For instance, she met Yekaterina Maximova and Vladimir Vasiliev, the famous Bolshoi Ballet couple, whom she got to know when they often danced in the same summer galas in Europe. 'And, later on, when I was here [at The Australian Ballet], I invited Maximova to come and dance in *Onegin* with us. And Vasiliev is now actually *the* Director of the Bolshoi, after Grigorovich was pushed out. He is not just the ballet Artistic Director, but the Director of the opera and the orchestra – the lot. What a job!'

Ronald Hynd, the British dancer, choreographer and ballet director, who had studied with Rambert, created a ballet on her, called *Le Baiser de la Fée* (The Fairy's Kiss), with her in the main role of the Fairy. 'Ronnie had just come from that curious land, Australia, where he'd just created *The Merry Widow*, and he came back very excited because he felt it had been very successful. He told her that while working on the role of the Widow, 'I was thinking of you so much. You really must do it one day.' As much as she has wanted to, somehow she never has.

For Gielgud's first London Festival Ballet season, Grey brought Peter Martins as a guest especially to partner her in *Swan Lake*. Danish-born Martins had become the leading dancer with New York City Ballet, and Gielgud considered him to be 'one of the best partners in the world. Very tall, very elegant, beautiful technique.'

Gielgud worked a lot, too, with Leonide Massine, the world-esteemed Russian-American dancer, choreographer, ballet master and teacher, who was a very great choreographer in the 1930s and 1940s, and became Diaghilev's favourite. Massine worked on film as well, including *The Red Shoes*, and *Tales of Hoffman*. Roles in his ballets which Gielgud performed included the flirtatious Glove Seller in *Gâité Parisienne*, and the Street Dancer in *Le Beau Danube*.

'A lot of the things that he said, I only understood much, much later: style things such as "divorcing from the waist down, like the bass on the piano, and the melody upstairs." I couldn't comprehend what he was saying. I couldn't do this "divorce" as much as he wanted it.'

Studio space was limited, which meant that Gielgud and the other dancers had to dash from one place to another, and quickly do their precious rehearsals. While they found the lack of rehearsal time frustrating, at the same time it kept people on their mettle, and got the adrenaline flowing in far greater quantities. It was really a case of 'sink or swim'. There were certainly no roles for dancers unless they could deal with those circumstances and do a good, or at least presentable, performance.

On tour in the provinces, they would go into a theatre

in the morning, do a class, or perhaps only exercises at the barre, and go straight into a dress rehearsal, with the technical side put together in as short a time as possible because of the cost of the theatre, particularly the staff and the rent. The lighting would be more or less there. And it would be a Monday, with the person having to do the first performance, often Gielgud, going on that same night.

These days, at the English National Ballet, as it is now called, dancers do a dress rehearsal on the Monday night and then perform on the Tuesday. Back then, the dress rehearsal was the only way to get used to the stage, where the variations of size, gradient and condition of the floor would be enormous. They had no floor cloths, no linoleum. Some had a good surface that was very smooth, while others were rough and gnarled and knobby. Sometimes the floors had little holes here and there, and even trapdoors. All that investigation had to be done so that the dancers could get a good understanding of where they were going to put their feet at any given time in the ballet.

On tour, Gielgud usually arrived the night before the first performance so that she could get a good night's sleep. She always spent her salary on good hotels and meals. Soon after joining London Festival Ballet, she made friends with Jimmie Slater, accompanist and assistant conductor, who often went to the same hotels and shared her love of good and healthy food. Slater, who was first drawn to Gielgud when she thanked him on her first day of rehearsal, was to become a lifelong friend, one of the few in the ballet world who kept in contact with her, wherever life took them both. He and Gielgud had a similar sense of humour, and Slater teased her mercilessly, which she found healthy, and important. 'I've always needed people around me who pull my leg.' In her first years at The Australian Ballet, she brought him out as visiting conductor, and their friendship continued until his recent death.

Habitually, Gielgud would go to the theatre, probably earlier than anybody else, and have a good look around. This 'made the stage technicians furious, and rightly so, because it was dangerous, with me getting in the way.'

Was she seen as an industrial renegade? 'Dancers weren't very into that.' She never felt badly treated. Besides, she would never have sought out the union representative. Her voice takes on an edge. 'Oh, God, no. You had only to hear a whisper of a company meeting, and I was somewhere else. I couldn't bear that; couldn't bear that!' She shudders. 'Waste of time. Life's too short. Get on with what's there. There's not enough time as it is to think about what one's doing, and try to do it as best as possible. To this day, I don't know whether Festival Ballet owes me huge amounts of overtime, or not. I never enquired. It never occurred to me, literally. I only realise about it now because the dancers are handing in their overtime sheets. We also paid for our own shoes, while these days the companies do that.'

When performing, it is always a challenge to work out how much to do full out in class and rehearsal. 'One needs to keep energy for the performance that night, while at the same time using the day's rehearsal to develop the role from the previous week. I looked for ways of using the rehearsal without expending too much energy on the actual *dancing* – for instance, concentrating on the style, musicality and acting.' She was always looking for 'the trick' that would solve everything, while knowing that it did not really exist. Then there was the question of how much to interpret in rehearsal, 'because one goes through stages of trying to develop a role, and feeling that you need to use every rehearsal for the acting as near to a performance level as you can. But at the same time you can go stale on it. And you get the feeling, especially on the same day as a performance, that if you give of yourself emotionally in the rehearsal beforehand, you may have less to give in the evening. So you learn, and you draw conclusions. They might not be the right ones. But, like everything else, you have to question all the time.'

Her routine was very routine, indeed: get to the theatre for a 10.30 a.m. class, then rehearse, and then stay there all day, sometimes rehearsing right up to an hour before performance, working on five ballets, while that night she might dance three others in a triple bill. If dancing a full-length ballet, she might go out for a meal after 3 p.m., after rehearsal. In England, she always went to a Chinese restaurant where there was an English menu. She would order a steak and plain boiled rice, and some tinned fruit. English restaurants were disastrous, and, besides, they were always closed at that hour, while the Chinese restaurants stayed open right through the day. If, 'by some miracle', she had some free time, she would go for a little walk, think about what she was doing, and then return to the theatre by about 4.30 to do her make-up, warm up, and spend some time on the empty stage, before the 7.30 show. When she had time before a full-length performance, she would lie down on her dressing-room floor, listen to the music of the ballet, and run the sequence of steps through in her head, visualising her ideal interpretation to the music and the role. Generally, though, rehearsals kept going close to curtain time, causing her to panic about not being ready. It always took her a long time to put on her make-up. She solved this by working out a system of arranging all her make-up at the edge of the stage, so she could start applying it whenever there was a section of rehearsal that she was not in. She hated getting on stage at the last minute. 'As late as I am for everything, that's one place I could never be late for.'

On the tours, despite difficult conditions, rehearsals in draughty church halls with broken windows, and slippery floors, having to find the right food, the financial expense – in spite of everything – it was her whole life, and, certainly for some time, 'I loved it. I was dancing really well, and I was very excited at doing all these roles.'

But after a couple of years with the company she found a major frustration was the lack of rehearsal time. 'I was not going anywhere, not developing the roles, and needed time, coaching, help and guidance.' Knowing that Vera Volkova, a great Russian teacher, who had taught Fonteyn in London, was now in Copenhagen, she went there on her holiday to study. 'I have really wonderful memories of that time, with her coaching every day. As the Russians tend to do, she had the most wonderful imagery to explain how things should look. She'd just draw you a picture in words. For instance, in trying to make use of the hands and wrists, she would say, "Just imagine you've got these little baby lungs on your wrists, so that your arms and your hands are breathing."'

Volkova became a confidante, and Gielgud told her about the problems with the company. 'I didn't know what to do next. I seemed to be going around in circles.' Volkova suggested she find out if there was a chance to get into The Royal Ballet, because there was more rehearsal space, good studios, and more time to work.

Gielgud strenuously denies any suggestion that this constant moving around in her life indicated a restless nature, but acknowledges that she probably was, and still is, a free spirit. The journeying from company to company, she says, had solid reasons.

Life became better at London Festival Ballet with the arrival of new partners. One was the Danish-born Adam Luders, who later moved as Principal to the New York City Ballet. Another was English-born Jonathan Kelly, who would go on to dance with The Australian Ballet, and now lives in Australia. He and Gielgud danced much classical and Béjart repertoire together. A third partner was the German, Peter Breuer, with whom she danced countless performances of *Swan Lake* and *The Sleeping Beauty*, and some Béjart. She had other excellent partners, such as Alain Dubreuil and Dudley van Loggenburg.

Kelly 'became a most wonderful actor and artist as

well as a very, very fine dancer, and made a big name for himself, both in England, and here at The Australian Ballet. He was a very serious young man, who looked very promising, as well as being tall. He used to be very earnest, and come in very early and do a lot of work by himself, and I took notice of that. We were in Venice one year. It was the only place in the world where I'd go for long walks. I used to purposely get lost, and have great fun doing that, and sit down in cafes, and I kept coming across Jonathan doing exactly the same thing. He had his books, and I had mine. We got talking and got to know each other, and that's when our friendship started.'

Gielgud and Beryl Grey occasionally had lunch and talked about how various dancers in the company were progressing. Gielgud had asked to dance with both Luders and Kelly. When repertoire was discussed, Gielgud sometimes made suggestions about ballets. Although it was not unusual for artistic directors to take out their top principals, or guest artists, for a meal, it was uncommon for such an interest to be taken by a dancer in the artistic management of the company.

She also became great friends with Luders. 'He was a good partner. He was very tall and very thin, with a very small head on top of this long, long body. He was very talented – a lovely artist in a slightly cool sort of Danish way, and also very elegant. Jonathan, Adam and I talked a lot about what we should do with our careers from then on, and where we would be in twenty years' time. Jonathan and I often discussed how great it would be to have and direct our own company, which is funny now.'

It was around then that Gielgud started showing an interest in other dancers' careers. Once, while she, Sutton and Luders were on holiday together, they worked out that he should really go to the New York City Ballet because they felt he was their type of dancer. They had a lot of tall girls, and the proportions would look right. Eventually Luders did just that, and became a very well established Principal there.

'I'd started already keeping an eye out for talent, and always trying to work out where it should be placed, and how it could develop best. I was always interested in how people worked – their attitude, talent, artistry, how they rehearsed – as compared to how they performed.' This gradually grew into even more definite signs of the director in her beginning to assert itself.

In performance, she used to 'get annoyed about the lighting, which was most often not putting the dancers "in value", or enhancing what they were trying to express, or the emotion of the moment. It needled me. So, somewhere without actually formulating it, I wanted to get my hands onto all of that.' She never had much contact with the girls in the company. 'I don't know how to be with girls, most of them.' At the same time, she respected them, and watched them work, as well as the men, with a keen eye.

She continued to work very hard. Sometimes, when others were injured, she danced up to seven full-length ballet performances in ten days, which was remarkable. On triple bills, she would probably appear every night in two ballets. On occasion in London, at the Coliseum, the program would change every night of the week. She would be exhausted afterwards, but, like the others, so wound up that it would be hard to sleep, sometimes still awake at 3 a.m. Then, like all dancers, she had to get up early the next day, crawl out of bed, hardly able to put one foot in front of the other until she had done her barre, at least, and then start the whole thing all over again.

The reviews were usually favourable, especially in the provinces, with a few 'vile' ones in London. These did not bother her because she felt she knew when she had danced well, and when she had danced badly. Some reviews said she was among the best, enjoying her most in Béjart ballets, calling her exotic, noting her look of 'faint surprise' on stage, observing her classical virtuosity, or saying she had too limited a turnout ever to become a great classical dancer.

Others, such as the Bolton *Evening News* in October 1973, were mixed:

> Maina Gielgud danced *Aurora* last night with a precision which gave her performance a cold beauty. She acted as one would expect from anyone who bears so distinguished a name. She danced faultlessly with a fine long line and an awareness of the music. But she lacked warmth. I could not feel that I would brave a haunted wood for her . . .

One critic went so far as to suggest she might become a successor to Fonteyn.

Richard Buckle, writing in the *Sunday Times* in

September 1973 about Gielgud and Breuer in *Webern, Op. 5*, described them as breathtaking. Earlier, in April the same year, writing about her as the Queen of the Wilis in *Giselle*, he said:

> Gielgud as Myrtha was a revelation – so extraordinary that I could not wish to transfer her to the principal role. Such soaring grace, such baleful potency of gesture, such possession by dark powers! I thought of her Uncle John speaking: 'Ye Elves of the hills, brooks, standing lakes and groves': the most musical and magical incantation of our century.

While she chooses not to make very much of it, in 1975 she also did her own production, in workshop, of a ballet based on *The Little Prince*, the beautiful allegorical story by Antoine de Saint-Exupéry. It had been one of her favourite stories as a young girl. 'I'd never tried to choreograph it, so I thought, "Why not?"' She cast Luders as the Little Prince. Being so tall, he was hardly 'little', but she chose him because 'I could just see him in the role with that scarf, so I dressed him up in it.'

Creating the work was hard, but exciting. Just before *The Little Prince* opened, she suddenly realised how different it was from when she herself was performing, 'because now it's theirs'. Beforehand, though, 'There was lots of fiddling, lots of annoying my dancers, simply by wanting to get it right.' In what was becoming a familiar pattern for her, which sometimes annoyed people intensely, she approached them while they were having a break, or even while they were having a smoke outside, to tell them she had an idea, that she had solved the problem, and could they just try it. 'People say that I'm like a dog with a bone!'

23 Black Swan, *Swan Lake*, London Festival Ballet (1974)

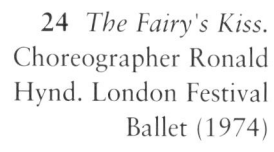

24 *The Fairy's Kiss*. Choreographer Ronald Hynd. London Festival Ballet (1974)

25 *La Sylphide* with Adam Luders, on the Ile St Marguerite, near Cannes, for Rosella Hightower's 1976 production

26 In Rosella Hightower's 1974 production of *Giselle* on the Ile St Marguerite, near Cannes. The Man in the Iron Mask was said to have been imprisoned on the island. The prison cells were used as dressing rooms.

27 Guesting in *La Fille mal gardée*, Budapest (1977)

28 *La Fille mal gardée*, Budapest (1977)

29 *La Fille mal gardée*, Budapest (1977)

30 Summer at Rosella Hightower's Centre in Cannes, 1966. Béjart gave classes for fourteen days. He told Gielgud then that he would take her into his Ballet of the Twentieth Century as soon as he had a vacancy. He engaged her in spring 1967 to start at the Avignon Festival in July.

31 Rehearsal of *Tchaikovsky pas de deux* with George Balanchine at the Grand Theatre, Geneva (early 1970s)

32 Anton Dolin coaching in *Steps, Notes and Squeaks* at The Old Vic (1979)

33 With Dame Peggy van Praagh (1984)

34 With Jiri Kylián. His first visit, to stage an evening of his works, with The Australian Ballet (1993)

35 Leaflet for *Steps, Notes and Squeaks*, 3–21 June, 1980

Steps, Notes and Squeaks

36 James Slater; Festival of Perth (1980). Jimmie – a very great friend. 'We laughed so much!'

37 Open Space Theatre (1978)

38 With Jonathan Kelly and Svetlana Beriosova, Open Space Theatre (1978)

39 With Jonathan Kelly; pas de deux from *The Sleeping Beauty*, Old Vic Season (1980)

40   Steven Heathcote and Lisa Bolte in Gielgud's production of *The Sleeping Beauty* (1988)

41   Paul De Masson (Principal dancer and later Ballet Master of The Australian Ballet) and his dog, 'Boyo', 1987. The dog later appeared in the hunting scene of *Giselle* – and stole the show.

10

PARTNERS

The best people to convey what Gielgud was like when she was dancing are those who performed with her. Two of them, one of whom danced with her a great deal, were able to be interviewed in Melbourne. While their views are well disposed towards her, they also have the quality of being dispassionate.

The first, Jonathan Kelly, was a Soloist with London Festival Ballet (now named the English National Ballet) when Gielgud joined it as a Principal in 1972. They became very close friends as well as very successful dance partners. They still have a high regard for each other, and still meet in Melbourne.

Kelly now has a farm north of the city, at Macedon. He is a strong, healthy-looking man, still with much of the poise and sensitive manner of a dancer, tempered now by the strength and earthiness of a man working on the land.

'I remember when Maina auditioned for the company. She had just left Maurice Béjart, and she was something different and extraordinary, and not your average classical ballerina by any means, because she had been brought up in the Béjart milieu. She was something very exotic, extremely thin and phenomenally self-disciplined. Different from the rest of us. Never a member of the group as far as Festival went. I don't like to use the word "oddity", but not in the swim.

'Maina was trying to get her career as a classical ballerina up and running, and Festival was a good avenue for that, because the company had such a large classical repertoire, and they performed rather like a sort of gypsy company all the time.

'She wasn't accepted immediately, but very quickly one realised that she was an exceptional artist, with an incredibly broad technique. I think Maina still tends to be undervalued to a certain degree as a dancer, because she was different. I don't think people quite realised just how much she could form her way of working and dancing. She wasn't the average pretty little romantic ballerina. She was something more exotic than that.

'It took a while for her to be accepted in England by the British press – ultimately they did – and by different dance managements and companies. But she's very strong-willed, and eventually she turned them around.

'Maina spotted me as a potential partner, and asked me if I would work with her on a piece that she wanted to introduce to the repertoire. One of her draw cards was that she could use some of the Béjart pieces in Festival Ballet, and they wanted to use them for touring, because Béjart has such a large name in Europe, and Maina knew that. She could promote herself, as well as increase the company's repertoire.

'She wanted to do *Webern Opus 5*, and was interested in me doing it. She started to do the negotiations as to how we'd get over to Brussels, where we would rehearse, how we would work, and coached me in the orchestra pits down underneath the various regional theatres. It was absolutely extraordinary for a dancer, because they're not normally like that; [they're usually] far more interested in their own narrow framework, and never step out of that.

'I think Maina already had the touch of the director and the impresario in her, right from that age. She was enormously supportive of me. We went over to Brussels, and were rehearsed by Béjart, and she started to push for me – for my development in working with her – where it was possible to push through management.

'My best dancing has always been with partners that I have enjoyed working with, and generally nearly always liked as a person, maybe not the whole way through our relationship, but certainly for the majority of it. You have to be able to feel at ease with the other person, and comfortable.

'Maina had an enormous presence, an enormous sense of something. It's hard for me to say when I was dancing with her, because I was involved, but I can certainly say it from watching her perform. She had the capacity to take a production and make it her own, even one that wasn't particularly good.

'Without doubt, Maina was one of the most formative elements in my career. After I left Festival, I came here in 1975, and between then and 1978 I had the same thing with Marilyn Jones.' He did not dance all the roles with Gielgud, because 'she had far more high-powered partners at that stage than myself, such as Peter Breuer'.

After Australia, he returned to England and ended up joining Gielgud in her own production, *Steps, Notes and Squeaks*. As a result, they were launched together in a long partnership. They were both free – by this time, Gielgud had gone freelance – and both Principals, and suited each other very well, working together as a unit. They had many seasons in London with *Steps, Notes and Squeaks*, at Festival Hall, Sadler's Wells and the Old Vic. They also toured widely, to places such as Romania, Yugoslavia, Cuba, France, Spain, Italy and South Africa, dancing mainly the major classics.

Although she was one of the great prima ballerinas of the Western world, it is interesting to speculate on whether Gielgud's career as a dancer might have gone even further if she had stayed more with one company.

'It's a good question. I'm very similar to Maina, in that in my career I've been a gypsy, so I can only relate your question to myself. I think that that may have been the case. But I think what happens with people's careers, as in life, is that most things are a question of timing. And probably by the time Maina was ready to settle down with one company, she was no longer at her best, and it just wouldn't have worked. If it had occurred in a classical company much earlier, it may have been the case. But I think Maina was always a very intelligent, independent spirit, and that doesn't always become the most malleable material.'

Asked as well to recall their off-stage times together, and what she was like as a woman then, he says, 'I was a very close friend of Maina. I often stayed in her apartment. Look, it's very difficult to say, but definitely in my life Maina has been one of the most constant associates, in terms of time and our experiences. To be honest, Maina, like a lot of people, is one of those people who, when she was at her thinnest and most "together" as a dancer, was not very accessible because of the strains involved. And probably part of the reason why we got on is that, in that sense, we were both quite similar.

'I liked Maina best when she was down, because she was at her warmest, because she had time, because she wasn't living for ballet alone, and could afford to relax. There's no doubt Maina herself would admit that she's an obsessive worker, covering all the angles of any project that she gets into. That's what's made her a very unique director. She's in every area: the wardrobe, orchestra, press, photos, programs, let alone the casting, scheduling, rehearsing and organising. Now, that puts a lot of people's noses up after a while. But it's no doubt that part of the reason for what makes a team function is that attention to detail.'

At the same time, he admits, 'Maina's company's not easy.' We discuss what can be seen as impatience on her part at times; her urging others to get on with it. 'Yes, yes. It's one of the hardest things for Maina. It's also part of this self-willed, slightly isolated person, as a dancer, who was never one of the mob, never one of those who would go out, boozing and the rest of it, because it was not her style. And that inability – and probably her childhood, too – didn't enable her to get the sort of people skills – human skills – that would have been very useful as a director. I think that's an area that was not developed, and one that Maina has found difficulty coming to terms with, but has sort of managed over the thirteen years she has been here. [Kelly was interviewed in 1995.] She's gotten better in the last few years, and people have come to know her, and think, "Oh, well, that's just Maina."'

Paul De Masson also first met Gielgud at Festival Ballet in 1972. He was born in Perth, and has been a dancer all his life, starting when he was eight. He is presently a Principal Artist with The Australian Ballet, who does character roles. He is also on staff as Ballet Master.

A lean, softly spoken man, with very fine features, he is still every bit the dancer. He works closely with Gielgud, and they seem to have a rapport. De Masson's career started in Europe, travelling around and ending up with the Roland Petit company in Marseilles. He went with them to Paris, then on to London, where he stayed. He sold ice creams in the theatres while doing the round of the auditions, and eventually joined Festival Ballet. He stayed with them until 1975, toured Australia with the company in the Nureyev production of *The Sleeping Beauty*, when he and his future wife were both offered positions with The Australian Ballet from the then joint Artistic Director, Robert Helpmann. In 1976 he left London and came back to Australia. He danced with the company from then until 1988, when he went freelance for four years, sometimes returning to guest in Australia. As he says, he pushed and pushed to get on The Australian Ballet staff, until in 1992 he was appointed Ballet Master by Gielgud.

There are very few of the great full-length classical ballets that he has not danced. He believes himself to have been successful as a performer, though not so sure of achieving any great fame. Apart from his qualities and talents, he has a very natural theatrical side with which people like to work.

Of that first meeting with Gielgud at Festival Ballet, he remembers 'her being very tall. Well, I thought she was tall, then, for a dancer, but when you look at dancers, they're on pointe, and of course they look taller – and very slim. Incredibly toned. [She was] very different as a dancer, because she'd been with Béjart for a long time. Not like the sort of classical dancers that I was used to seeing.' Béjart was then considered in Europe to be the top company in which to work.

Apart from the classics such as *Swan Lake*, he remembers seeing her as a poisonous butterfly in the John Taras choreography of a ballet called *Piège de Lumière*. The lead convict falls in love with her, and they do a pas de deux together, and then she puts her pollen on him and he goes crazy. 'Maina was outstanding in that; she was just the most amazing character. Obviously, through her Béjart training and dancing, she just put an edge on it that no one else could.

'She was outrageous in a lot of ways because she was so different to what we were used to. Festival Ballet was a very old-fashioned company. She did very strange things sometimes. When she was doing *Nutcracker*, for instance, in Festival Hall in London, she once came in wearing big plastic ears, like Clark Gable ears. This was in the dressing room, backstage. She was just walking around with big plastic ears, for no reason. And she'd just wander about, I suppose, until someone would notice, and people would turn around and say, "Do you see what she's wearing?" And there she is, in full costume, with these big plastic ears. I think it was somehow her way of cutting off from everyone else.'

He agrees with the observation that Gielgud is eccentric, 'but also bohemian. But then, she was very French. It was the 1970s and 1980s.' He has always remembered a remark once made by Anne Woolliams, who was Artistic Director of The Australian Ballet from 1976 to 1977: 'There's no point having all that eccentricity if you can't take it on the stage.'

De Masson agrees. 'And it's quite true. A lot of people – not just dancers, but a lot of actors – would be outrageous in public, "Oh, darling", and all that sort of stuff, and when they get on stage, they go back into themselves. I see it a lot with dancers: outrageous in public, at parties and things, and then they go on stage, and they get nervous. Maina was different. Her eccentricity was very controlled, but when she went on stage, she was outrageous. Her performance went further than anyone else I'd seen at that time.

'I think she was strangely regarded. People were suspicious because they didn't know her, because she was very much to herself. That's probably where people think she was mothered to death, because she used to sweep into the theatre, and you wouldn't see her afterwards. Always looked like she had a lot of money, even though she might not have, I don't know. But people thought, "Oh well, Mummy's pushed her", or something. And that's probably where it came from, because I saw other dancers whose mothers were on their backs constantly. Mind you, I never saw Maina's mother at all in Festival days.' Gielgud herself says her mother's visits were quite rare.

De Masson does not believe Gielgud was popular in those days, but nor was she necessarily unpopular. 'In lots of ways, she was almost a comic figure for people; they used to send her up a lot. She was so serious in her work. The English noticed her very much because she was so different. It was, like: "There's Maina Gielgud..." There was always a gossip story around – not gossip, because Maina never did anything to create gossip, not that anybody knew – but more so, I think, because they *didn't* know her.

'I remember once touring to Granada, and Maina wore the shortest mini skirt I've ever seen. I mean, it was almost a belt. And then she had a belt over that, raffia or something. She was very, very slender, and very tall, and had sandals on.

I'd never socialised with Maina at all, but Jonathan Kelly and she were partners, and I was friends with him, and with Abby, who became my wife, and so we ended up, strangely enough, the four of us, on a Sunday going to see the palace with all the water. It was very hot weather, and Maina had this short T-shirt on, and she was just this outrageous, tall ballet creature. Her hair was all out, which is probably why I thought she was bohemian. And she dropped the belt, and didn't even notice. It was on the path somewhere. I was so in awe, I ran all the way back to get it.'

De Masson and Gielgud danced a little together, including Béjart's *Rose Variations*, based on the Rose Adagio from *The Sleeping Beauty*, which she chose him to do. 'It was a great opportunity. I was quite young, about eighteen or nineteen. I've since realised that she instigated my doing it. I was dancing with three other principal dancers, and I was Corps de ballet, and so she gave me an opportunity to go there.'

He found her, as a dance partner, to be very responsive and collaborative. 'I always felt very green, [coming] from Australia, and so I looked at her in awe all the time. Anything that she wanted, I'd be there, I'd hop to it. We never really had a working relationship, because I was always that person who happened to come in and do things with her. Another time I danced with her – again, not really dancing – was in Massine's *Gâité Parisienne*. We were the billiard players and she was in a red flashing dress, and we just danced around her, and she was gay, and it was all different. She's very different in everything that I've seen her dance in.'

De Masson once dropped Gielgud in *Nutcracker*, and she broke her toe. He could not believe it had happened, because the company had done the ballet so many times. 'I didn't drop her; I just didn't catch her.' He says there are a couple of versions of the ballet, and Gielgud had done a different one. 'When she came along, she was with Adam Luders, who's very, very tall. We had a quick run before the curtain went up on the second act. Adam looked at me, and said, "Are you ready, Paul?", and I said, "Yes", not expecting anything different.' Next minute, she was thrown into a fish dive, instead of just a carry jeté, and he was meant to catch her. 'Instead, she just went hurtling through the air, and no one advised me that it was different. It was like this great big Jumbo jet coming towards me. I just stepped out of the way, and she went *crash*!' De Masson says Gielgud never knew afterwards that it was he who was responsible for her broken toe, 'because I ran out of the theatre.'

11

A GUEST IN OZ

Just after Gielgud broke her toe in 1975 in London, she was recovering in Cannes when she received an urgent telephone call asking if she would come to Melbourne immediately to be an emergency guest in *The Sleeping Beauty* with The Australian Ballet, because Lucette Aldous was ill. Telling Grey that her foot was much better, which it was, she obtained permission to go, and rang back to say that of course she would accept the Australian role. She said nothing to them about her foot.

It turned out to be not an easy time. She had been looking forward to being coached by Peggy van Praagh, the company's founder, and original Artistic Director, a position she was now sharing with Robert Helpmann, who had staged the ballet. Gielgud liked his ideas for the work very much, but van Praagh was in hospital, having a hip operation.

Then there was the broken toe, about which she 'was keeping very quiet'. Helpmann made much of her being there, which compounded her discomfort, because she could not do the rehearsals in her usual total way, 'and all eyes were on me. And I was the person who always did every rehearsal full out.' But her overall experience of the company impressed her very much, and deeply influenced her applying for the Artistic Director's job seven years later.

The ballet opened in Melbourne at the Princess Theatre, which is one of the last of the great classical theatres left in Australia, occupying a place of honour in Spring Street, at the east end of the city.

Preparations were intense, and Gielgud found the most nerve-wracking aspect was not new ballet steps, but getting used to a tricky scene in a big revolving bed, with her not knowing when to press the button to make it move. 'Having arrived at the last minute, I was terrified.'

However, she says, 'It was great dancing with the company. The dancers were so friendly, and always having parties, and when I left they gave me a most beautiful book, signed by everybody. They're still like that. They were very good dancers, and I got to know a few of them who later came back into my career or my life.'

Prior to that, she had heard much about The Australian Ballet, and had once rushed in from the provinces with her friend Slater to see them dance *Don Quixote* in London, watching them from the back of the Coliseum Theatre, because there was standing room only. 'I thought they were terrific. They were so full of energy and vitality, and really seemed to be 100 per cent into what they were doing; remarkably so, in a way that you don't see elsewhere.' That impression has since been sustained. 'Absolutely. Yes. That's Australian dancers.'

While in Melbourne, she achieved her wish to be coached by van Praagh – in a way – because when she visited her in hospital, they had long talks about technique. It would have been a remarkable scene with the two women together, as van Praagh gave her hints from her bed on the use of her hands and arms. Gielgud needed this, because having been coached earlier by Volkova, she had followed some dancers' habits of taking corrections too far, and now van Praagh was restoring the balance. There was a great affinity between them, with the common interest being ballet, 'and just wanting to know more about it. I wanted to learn, and she wanted to teach, and I respected her.' Van Praagh got to see one of the performances of *The Sleeping Beauty*, and approved, watching from her wheelchair.

It is unusual to hear Gielgud talking about having an affinity with van Praagh, because there are very few people with whom she seems to have such intimacy. 'Yes. That's what I call the snob part of me. It has nothing to do with wealth, nor for that matter status. I am just fascinated by extraordinary people.'

Van Praagh, like the younger woman, was also a fighter. 'But she was very fierce. People were in awe of her.

If dancers came knocking at her door and asked why they weren't cast in something, she'd say, "Your neck's too short," or "Your legs are bowed." It was often things that you couldn't do anything about.'

Gielgud got along well, too, with Helpmann, whom she had known back in Marseille when they both did *Don Quixote* with Nureyev. 'He was such an outrageous personality.' He died ten years later, in Sydney, soon after he performed his created role of the Red King as a guest in The Australian Ballet's production of *Checkmate*, on Gielgud's invitation. In his earlier, wilder days, he loved having an effect, a characteristic he never really lost. Gielgud says, 'He was very aware of how he was affecting people and getting across a certain image of himself. He built this personality, this character, and it certainly worked wonderfully for him. He was fabulous on stage in his roles, and also off!'

Gielgud was in Australia for just a few weeks, dancing only in Melbourne. But Helpmann, obviously much impressed, immediately invited her to come back, and she returned later in the year, for two and a half months.

She got to know a lot of Australians in those early days, including Gary Norman. His wife, Gailene Stock, had also been studying with Hightower when Gielgud was in Cannes. Norman and Stock are now running The Australian Ballet School. Another dancer there at the time was Wendy Walker, who is now the Ballet Mistress with the company after many years away, dancing with Festival Ballet, and then on the staff of American Ballet Theatre. Gielgud got to know William Akers, too, the lighting designer, whom she brought back into the company when she joined it in 1983.

'It was like my dream company. I thought, "If only it could be like this everywhere!" They had time to rehearse. They had what seemed to me wonderful studios [the old premises in Flemington] compared to what we had in Europe.' As Gielgud says, it had a lot more facilities than most other companies. This was improved even more when they moved in 1988 to their new headquarters in the huge arts precinct beside the Yarra River, in the heart of Melbourne.

Gielgud was thirty and in her dancer's prime when she returned to England from Australia early in 1975. She resumed with Festival Ballet, and had a long season of many roles, as well as doing guest performances with companies in other countries, again including Australia.

Back in Australia in September 1975, she experienced even more of the friendliness which she found last time in The Australian Ballet, which endeared her even more to the place.

She brought with her the Béjart *Squeaky Door*, which did very well. She also danced for the first time the famous *La Fille mal gardée* in Sir Frederick Ashton's version. This ballet, choreographed by Jean Dauberval, was first produced in Bordeaux in 1789. Translated as 'Vain Precautions', or 'The Unchaperoned Daughter', its popularity extended to Russia in the following century.

La Fille mal gardée featured in a quaint little story involving Gielgud, her mother and a French fortune teller. Mother and daughter had already been to consult Mme Pierre, as she was called, a few times and were most impressed by her powers. They used to take the train to see her, in an outer Paris suburb, in a little street in a little house, up a winding staircase. 'What we liked about her was that she was very normal. She wasn't very mysterious and gypsy. She was just a little bourgeois Frenchwoman. You'd go up, and she'd open the door, and she'd say, "Oh, yes, bonjour Madame... Oh, do forgive me a moment; I have to go downstairs and fetch the bread." We thought that was great, because she wasn't spooky. I think she had a crystal ball, but she mainly used the cards. Mummy went to see her while I was in Australia, because, as she so sweetly put it, "I hadn't heard from you, darling, for so long, that I had to go to a fortune teller to find out how you were doing." Then I got a letter from her, saying that Madame Pierre – who's since died, I'm afraid – told her that I was about as far as I could possibly be from Europe, and I was doing something with pink ribbons and ladders. This led Mummy to ask, "What on earth are you doing?" Mummy didn't know I was doing *La Fille mal gardée* – and hadn't ever seen it – nor had Madame Pierre. And, of course, the ballet is full of pink ribbons that you tie into knots, and you climb a ladder in and out of a loft. It was pretty extraordinary.'

While Gielgud was still guesting in Australia, Anne Woolliams came out from England to stage *Romeo and Juliet*, by John Cranko, which Gielgud had always dreamed of dancing. 'I think she wasn't at all sure initially whether I would be suitable or not for Juliet.'

Gielgud and Gary Norman worked very hard together on preparing for the production. Their rapport was reinforced when they went up to Sydney to see the Stuttgart Ballet perform *Voluntaries*, a tribute to Cranko, with choreography by the great Glen Tetley. South African-born Cranko, who died in 1973, developed tremendous skill as a choreographer, and built the Stuttgart Ballet into one of the world's great companies. After the performance Gielgud and Norman, overcome with emotion, could not move from their seats.

For Gielgud, it was ideal to be working with the company where she wanted to dance, having five weeks' rehearsal and having such a greatly talented coach as Anne Woolliams. As Artistic Director herself, Gielgud later invited Woolliams to coach and stage the company's Cranko works, as she did Reid Anderson, another superlative coach. Both of them worked closely with Cranko. Gielgud says this was part of her policy: to have the best possible people from around the world coaching the repertoire in which they specialised.

She was very impressed also by Norman's acting ability. Aldous and Jones were dancing the role of Juliet as well as Gielgud, which was a usual rotation. Apart from Nureyev, most dancers would simply not have the stamina to be able to do a full-length ballet every night.

There were three dress rehearsals, with the full orchestra, and Gielgud was amazed at how close they were to the finished product, a rare event in Europe and

America, where there is usually only one dress rehearsal and that is usually chaotic. She has continued the tradition, having at least two dress rehearsals for the company. 'I think it's one of the most important things. It means that the standard of the performances of The Australian Ballet is that much higher on the technical side, lighting side, the whole "look" of a production.'

But then Norman sprained his ankle at class, holding them up for a fortnight. After all the build-up, she danced Juliet only five times. Sadly, she never danced it again.

While waiting for Norman to recover from his injury, Gielgud unofficially rehearsed the understudy cast, which included Alida Chase and, interestingly, Ross Stretton, who at the end of 1995 would be appointed to succeed her as Artistic Director of The Australian Ballet.

Having all that rehearsal time in Australia, in contrast to the practice at London Festival Ballet, impressed Gielgud so much that while in Australia she started thinking seriously that perhaps she should look for a company which provided this possibility.

Somewhat prophetically, while she was guesting in Australia, the then Administrator of The Australian Ballet, Peter Bahen, told her while she was visiting his home in Melbourne, that one day she would make a really good artistic director. At the time, it raised questions in her mind. 'Perhaps this is why I'm interested in all these things, why I go to performance after performance when I'm not on, why I worry about the lighting and the costumes, why I am always so concerned about the repertoire and the dancers. He started the brain going, with me thinking that perhaps that was what I was building up to.'

In late 1975, on her return to Festival Ballet, she was told that Nureyev wanted her to dance in his production with Festival Ballet of *The Sleeping Beauty*, which they had danced together in Barcelona some years before. But, instead of her again doing the lead role of Aurora with him, she was cast on the first night as the Blue Bird and the Lilac Fairy, and Aurora only later, with Peter Breuer. She tried to talk to both Nureyev and Grey about it, but each referred her to the other one. 'It's typical of what happens. When I knew that I was going to direct a company, I vowed that I would do everything I could not to put dancers in that silly position.'

Gielgud's reaction to missing out on the lead role with Nureyev on opening night was typical. She determined to do the lesser roles, 'and show the world that I should be doing Aurora because I was going to be so good in those.'

But her mother was horrified, saying she had received rave reviews last time, and Nureyev had been so happy with her, but suddenly now this. Sutton felt she should refuse. 'Actually, I'm still sorry that I didn't do the lesser roles. I allowed myself this time to be influenced – by my mother – which didn't happen very often. And, basically, that led to my departure from Festival.'

During that season, she was invited to guest at a gala with The Scottish Ballet, and went, even though it was the night before her dancing *Swan Lake* in London. She never took tablets – except once when she tried slimming pills, for only three days – but coming back on the train from Glasgow she needed to sleep, and took something herbal. It wrecked her, and she felt she danced *Swan Lake* badly.

Back in London, she received a message to go and see the Director, Kenneth MacMillan, at The Royal Ballet, which excited her, because she had been hoping to move there, or to the Sadler's Wells Royal Ballet, as discussed with Volkova. Both companies had rehearsal time and space, as well as good coaches.

'MacMillan was quite a shy man, not very sociable. I'd never worked with him, or done a choreography of his. He and Ashton were both chief choreographers. He was very apologetic, and said, "Look, I don't know what you're hoping, but I really can't do much for you." McMillan suggested that, as de Valois was keen for Gielgud to play the part of the Black Queen in her ballet, *Checkmate*, which she was staging for Sadler's Wells Ballet (now the Birmingham Royal Ballet), Gielgud guest with that company. Gielgud was delighted.

The company's usual program was to do several seasons at Sadler's Wells in London, and the rest of the year tour the provinces and overseas. Being smaller than the main company, they danced a lot, and had longer rehearsal periods, and good studio facilities. Peter Wright, the Director, was considered by Gielgud to be one of the best in the world.

De Valois, who founded The Royal Ballet as the Vic-Wells Ballet in 1931, and started the Sadler's Wells company in 1947, was there for thirty years. Celia Franca, who founded the Canadian National Ballet in 1951, stayed for almost twenty-five years. Some of the directors of the Paris Opera before the 1960s stayed for ten to twenty years. But nowadays artistic directors do not have a history as well as a tradition of longevity in their jobs. Gielgud stayed with The Australian Ballet for fourteen years.

As well as *Checkmate*, there was further possible work at Sadler's Wells for Gielgud. She could dance the third act of *Raymonda* and in Balanchine's *The Prodigal Son*. 'I just thought this was fantastic, because to get one toe in the door would let me prove myself.'

She resigned from Festival Ballet, and sought out people to help her with the unknown work ahead, including Nureyev, who knew so much about *Raymonda*.

About that time, she taught her first class. 'This was an amazing experience, and happened quite by accident. I had gone to The Royal Ballet's studios, where they very kindly always allowed me to take class. It was a Saturday, and the teacher didn't turn up. There were only a few of us there, and the others happened to be Margot Fonteyn, Natalia Makarova, and Lynn Seymour. They all turned to me and said, "Oh, Maina, you give this class." So I did.'

She loved working with de Valois on *Checkmate*, together with the Soviet-born Makarova, learning the same role of the Black Queen, which she would dance later. Gielgud remembers Makarova chain-smoking during both rehearsal and class itself, even puffing away while doing her barre. A lot of dancers did that in those days. Gielgud also danced the Queen of the Wilis in *Giselle* with them, and the season ended with talk of doing a Tetley piece, *Gemini*, which he had created for The Australian Ballet.

Gielgud travelled with the company as a guest for a while, and then was invited to join them as a Principal in 1977. She was thirty-two.

In terms of her whole career, she believes that by then she was not dancing at her best. 'This had nothing to do with the physical age. It was because of the kind of roles I did, and the life as a freelance, which wasn't really particularly good for developing further. I agreed to do a little bit less than I had been doing, because it was great to be with Sadler's Wells.'

She felt her peak years were at Festival Ballet, when she was doing three, or sometimes up to five, full-length ballets a week.

'Going to Sadler's Wells was a move which could have worked, or not, and it didn't, really. I danced well, but it didn't take off.' But it led to her being with Tetley, which was 'thoroughly enjoyable, although murderously difficult. I loved working with him, and I loved the ballet [*Gemini*], although I found the music very hard. I was partnered by Desmond Kelly, who was their top dancer, and a terrific partner. But I was black and blue all over. I did a pretty good job in rehearsals, but when I got to performing it, I knew I'd disappointed Glen, and myself. It just wasn't "it".' Gielgud was given more new roles as the company toured. But again, she found it hard going.

At the end of the year, just before her contract finished, she was asked to come and dance again with The Australian Ballet, because they were desperately in need of a Swan Queen. She was refused permission to go. Breaking a contract was not an option. But in retrospect, she believes that perhaps she should have left and taken the Australian offer.

'It's funny, because had I gone, I might have been in a different function in Australia. Perhaps after guesting again with The Australian Ballet, they might have asked me to stay permanently. So that would have been the company that I could have joined. I knew that everything was there that, as a dancer, I'd dreamed of developing.'

12

FREELANCE AND FINALE

By 1978, Gielgud was now free to fly, except that she found the new life had its limitations. Freelancing was both fascinating and frustrating. And she was probably more alone than ever, despite finding at last a home for herself, an apartment in Soho, which she still has. The fun came from working in so many different companies, and countries. She would now visit places such as South Africa, which she did three times, Hungary, Romania, Czechoslovakia and Australia again. She also guested at the Festival of Cuba twice, once with Jonathan Kelly as her partner. The frustration came from not knowing when or where the work would be next, while at the same time having to stay ready. She usually did not have the time to prepare for her roles, and this had theoretically been one of the attractions of the freelance life. While at least she got to do more of the full-length ballets, she also missed out on having new roles created on her by choreographers.

In South Africa, she danced with CAPAB Ballet in Cape Town, and PACT in Johannesburg, where she was again partnered by Jonathan Kelly in *Swan Lake*, *Bhakti*, and the amusing John Taras pas de deux, *Soirée Musicale*.

Freely translated, a review by Victor Holloway in *Die Burger* (Cape Town) in September 1989, while having some reservations overall about performances, praised the unfamiliar works. Giving Kelly, whose work was already known there, mostly high accolades, it said Gielgud was the best, because she 'charmed the audience with her technical ability, her perfect timing and her total involvement. In *Soirée Musicale*, but especially in *Bhakti*,' of which they did the third part, 'Miss Gielgud and Kelly brought to life the Indian gods Shiva and Shakti in a sensuous love poem.' The many beautiful moments perceived in their *Swan Lake* also received very good reviews, with the exception of one critic who, after writing, 'As a dancer Maina Gielgud is superb, with breathtaking technique, complete and absolute control, and uncommon strength,' then went on to say there was something missing in her interpretation of Odette-Odile.

This opinion was not shared in *Dance News* the previous February, where Wilfred Hoffman said the guesting by her and the Hungarian dancer Imre Dózsa in *Swan Lake*, 'showed the best dancing that Belgrade has seen in years.'

Back in London, in August, the *Daily Telegraph*, writing about a gala ballet season at Royal Festival Hall, says, 'Things brighten up to some extent when Maina Gielgud and Jonathan Kelly manage to do what is possible with the rather heavy-handed humour' of *Soirée Musicale*. *Stage and Television Today* described them both as 'delightful ... his cheery demeanour served as an admirable foil for her sophisticated sense of chic.'

That chic is not just confined to the stage. In that year, Gielgud was featured in several magazine and journals, and sometimes looking very glamorous indeed. She was photographed on a boat with Pierre Cardin and other dancers and models, and in her case, it was hard to tell the difference. On another occasion, she featured in a cover story in the London *Telegraph*'s *Sunday Magazine*, in blazing red and black tights and various other exotic costumes, as she posed for an article on the coming of the 'Russian look' for next winter.

While in Cape Town, she came to learn about the *I Ching*, the Chinese book of changes. She says that when she joined The Australian Ballet, she mentioned the book to a few people, trying to find some common ground with them in conversation, because there were some communication difficulties, and there was 'this feeling that the boss was out up there somewhere'. She was not very good at small talk, anyway, preferring to find challenging subjects. So the *I Ching* was brought out during plane trips on tour.

When one of the dancers went away on a scholarship to Canada, people there asked him whether it was true that Gielgud consulted the *I Ching* to cast the dancers. She laughs, and asserts, 'I can assure you that this director does *not* do the casting by the *I Ching*!'

While waiting for the next role as a freelance created a certain tension for Gielgud, it also kept her, as it were, on her toes with anticipation. 'I'm someone who always gets excited at what might happen.' Then, while visiting Paris with her mother, she was rung from London by an antique carpet dealer, Robert Chenciner, who wanted to know if she would be interested in doing a one-woman show in a small fringe theatre in London called the Open Space. He had rented it as a birthday present for a dancer friend to do her own show there, but she had left and gone back to Australia.

Chenciner had obtained Gielgud's name from someone at London Festival Ballet, who said she 'might be crazy enough to do something'. Gielgud had a good laugh, thanked him anyway, and went off on holiday to Brittany, where he continued to pursue her. Finally, in the middle of lunch one day, she realised it might be worth doing. She started to jot down a few ideas, and out of this was born *Steps, Notes and Squeaks*. It was to become a huge success, and the high point of the last years of her dancing life. It occupied much of her time as director, producer and dancer from 1978 to 1981.

The idea of *Steps* was to portray a day in the life of two dancers during the lead-up to a gala, with the different people involved: the partner, the pianist, the coach. The importance of coaching was a big theme, as was the role of the choreographer creating new work, all leading up to a performance. Gielgud drew on her experience of working alone with a rehearsal pianist, who contributed much to the work; for this she used her old friend, Jimmie Slater. She was inspired by her time in a *Swan Lake* rehearsal with Svetlana Beriosova, whom she realised had so much to give to younger dancers. At the time, Beriosova was not in work, which Gielgud thought was unfortunate. 'This amazing woman's knowledge was not being used. What better thing to do than to draw her to the attention of the very big public that she still had in London? Perhaps it would help her for the future, but, anyway, to watch her coaching was so beautiful.'

The show, the text of which was largely improvised, showed the themes of the glamour of ballet and the hard times, and some contemporary dance as well as classical ballet. Set in rehearsal, it revealed the rigours, but also the humour, in preparing a role with everybody involved – coach, choreographer, accompanist, wardrobe mistress, lighting expert and performers.

Gielgud chose *The Sleeping Beauty* as the centrepiece, and went to London to start. The Open Space theatre was very small and had a concrete floor. Chenciner said there was no money to pay anybody, but as it turned out, people were prepared to do it just for fun, and so it was launched. Jonathan Kelly turned up and became Gielgud's partner for most of the seasons after the first one, which he shared with the English dancer Piers Beaumont. Marjorie Slasky, famous for her tutus, played her own role of wardrobe mistress and costume designer. Gielgud did much of the promotion, too. She even went around London with

Chenciner putting up posters illegally. Someone offered their printing press to do the programs. Everyone got into the spirit of it.

The first season ran for seven performances. The theatre had only a hundred seats, and people had to be turned away in droves. Some came out of morbid curiosity, because the place was so small, and the audience could see everything of the dancers up close. Indeed, the ceiling was so low that high lifts or jumps were almost impossible. From watching a film of it, the show seemed to be very entertaining, with the cast members taking the mickey out of each other and themselves. There was a great deal of friendly laughter from the audience, who loved it. So did the critics. It received an enormous amount of publicity.

'It was just a most amazing story,' says Gielgud, 'because nothing like that had been done before. And it was also using big names of the ballet world, but in a different way from how they're normally seen in public. It was like looking through the keyhole.'

They moved to the Royal Court Theatre, and by this time the performers were even being paid expenses. Then it went to The Ambassadors in the West End, still with full houses, and so it went on. Cast members came and went, and over the succeeding years the show toured overseas to countries such as South Africa, Australia and New Zealand. It also went to the Éspace Cardin in Paris, and to Greece. The seasons were not consecutive, but there always seemed to be fresh interest in the program.

Different versions were done, based on *Swan Lake* and *Giselle*, and other artists took the roles of coach, partner, pianist and choreographer. Some of these included Dolin, Helpmann, Hightower, the French dancer and teacher Yvette Chauvire, and the British dancer Barry McGrath and choreographer Peter Darrell.

Many of these appeared in an extraordinary season at the Old Vic, during which de Valois agreed to coach Gielgud and Kelly in *Checkmate*, with Helpmann in his created role of the Red King. That was the premiere performance of that season, in the first part of which Helpmann coached Gielgud and Kelly in the Black Swan pas de deux.

But by 1981 Gielgud's career was beginning to go flat again. She returned to Australia with a 'Stars of World Ballet' tour staged by Michael Edgley, which included Fonteyn. Gielgud was supposed to do the Tchaikovsky pas de deux, Black Swan and *Squeaky Door*, but by then she was not in her best shape, and ended up often only dancing *Squeaky Door*, and wondering why she was not doing more.

She tried to get back into London Festival Ballet, having been assured by the new Director, John Field, that he would do everything possible to get her in. But it did not eventuate. Finally, through the choreographer Ronald Hynd, she was able to guest with London Festival as the Snow Queen in *Nutcracker*. But basically she was still out in the cold.

She says every dancer goes through times of self doubt. Indeed, from her descriptions, they suffer from an extraordinary mix of the narcissism that comes from watching themselves in the mirror at class every day, along with never being satisfied with themselves, physically, or otherwise, which is remarkable considering their splendid appearance. Behind those smiles on stage during performance is the constant fear of not being good enough. Each dancer believes their lapse of self-esteem is unique to them.

She would never have dreamed of discussing her problems with anybody. Once or twice she raised with her mother the possibility of abandoning it, but soon stopped that. 'I knew that what I wanted above all was dance, and this [problem] was transitory, not deep, stuff. I think as soon as you start talking about things, they become bigger. I might have ended up not knowing my own mind. I did spend a lot of time on the telephone with Jimmie during that period – hilarious conversations, and depressed ones when neither of us had much to do.'

She went on a luxury music cruise on the 'Mermoz', and danced with Derek Deane, now the Artistic Director of the English National Ballet, and had a great time because of his ascerbic sense of humour, including his acid comments about the behaviour of other people.

But she was still having thoughts about stopping dancing. 'I think I could have continued dancing, but I had been having problems keeping my weight down. It was perhaps to do with just not feeling that I was in circumstances that would help me develop further.' She is talking about only one or two kilograms, but in the ballet world that is a worry. 'It is such a fine line. It would have started because of performing less regularly. And of course, the more conscious you are about it, the more difficult it is.

You leap off the deep end and eat a bit more, and fool yourself that it's because you need the energy to do the work.' These days dancers with problems about their weight can go to dieticians and therapists, but Gielgud does not believe it usually helps much.

Indeed, this was one of those occasions when Gielgud, for some hidden reason, did not like being questioned too closely. Any attempt by the biographer at trying to initiate analysis of her feelings as she approached the drastic step of giving up dancing was met with impatience and icy bluster. It must have been a very painful period for her, surely, but she would talk about it strictly on her terms only. The story is fascinating, nonetheless.

Of her eating problem she says, 'I honestly don't think it was too bad. But then, it's hard to say, because dancers rationalise. You have to, because you have to get on stage and still need to feel confident when you are performing.'

In what she describes as rare moments of insomnia, she even half-heartedly considered working at a health food shop next to her Soho flat, 'getting a nine-to-six job!'

Instead, she choreographed *The Soldier's Tale* (L'Histoire du Soldat) in Festival Hall, in 1980. It is a narrative ballet, to be read and played as well as danced, to the music of Stravinsky. Gielgud danced in it with Wayne Sleep, as well as creating the choreography. She enjoyed it, but it led her to think that doing some more choreography would be interesting. She decided to be careful, though, with making a final, drastic decision to hang up her shoes.

'I thought to myself, why not take on a project which

is going to be really engrossing – like creating a ballet – stop dancing for, say, six months, and see what happens – see if I *have* to dance again? If that's the case, it doesn't matter that I will have got out of shape and put on weight, because if one *really* wants to do something, one gets oneself back into shape. On the other hand, if I find life is just as interesting doing things on the other side, then I'll know that that's the right decision to make.'

She knew that stopping dancing for six months was a major decision. 'But part of it was that I didn't want to be looking after myself any more. I wanted to get away from this total concentration on the self, and have more communication with others, and be doing things more directly with people, which choreographing and teaching and coaching is. When you're a performer, the ultimate goal is, yes, of course, communicating, but with a huge number of people you actually don't know. So it's in the abstract, and to be able to do it, you need to be so self-centred, thinking about what you eat, how many hours you sleep – everything on keeping yourself together, mind and body, for that purpose. I thought it would be very nice to get off me–me–me, and not have that at the back of one's mind, almost all the time; to communicate with people in life, in the studio, and pass on as much as one can of my experience, and what I was lucky enough to be taught.'

She proceeded with choreography. For London City Ballet in 1981 she created and staged *Ghosties and Ghoulies* on Jeremy James and Nicola Lawson, his wife-to-be, who, together with James' cousin Julian Stein, Gielgud says became some of her greatest friends, and stayed in her

London flat for a number of years when she went to Australia. As our interviews progressed, she seemed to want to make the point more and more that she had some very close friends, as though all the talk of her being such a solitary figure might create the impression that she was isolated. Since childhood she had always loved Lewis Carroll, and *Ghosties and Ghoulies* went well, though she swore she would never do a voice and music collage again, as it was so tricky and time-consuming.

She began giving class for the company, conducting occasional rehearsals, and later in 1981 was offered a full-time position as Rehearsal Director. She enjoyed the new life of teaching. They toured to Scandinavia, and she even tried to ski, something she would never do while a dancer, and ended up wrapped around a tree. They toured the English provinces, and went to the Arab states. She relished her new found proximity with other people, and found she enjoyed letting go 'of the responsibility of having to get up on stage and produce the goods at 7.30.'

She even started to realise the type of politics that go on in all companies. 'When I was dancing, I thought my mother was inventing all that.'

The satisfaction of the new life was enough to answer the final test of asking herself how she could have given away all the dancing, and she discovered she did not want to be out there, on stage, doing all the roles. There was no palpable moment when she actually decided to stop dancing. 'It was just a slow evolution. You read about how awful it is, but I think I must have had one of the smoothest transitions possible.'

Very significantly, Gielgud did not inform her mother of her decision. 'I told her that I was choreographing *Ghosties and Ghoulies* and she was very pro that. But I didn't say a word about not dancing any more.' Why not?

She laughs. 'Because I knew she would just make me feel terrible, and try to dissuade me – you know that particular way that mothers have – and I just didn't want to deal with that. I'm sure I intended to tell her at the end of six months, when I would know for sure. But I didn't want to go through the "I'll see how it feels, and then decide" routine.'

Gielgud had been with her mother in Cannes and was back in London when Sutton read about the decision the next day in the Peterborough gossip column in the *Daily Telegraph*. 'Of course,' says Sutton, 'I almost fell off my chair.' Her daughter telephoned her, but still said nothing about it. Finally, Sutton rang her and raised the matter. A long silence followed. Then Gielgud said she had not known how to tell her, and thought her mother would try to talk her out of it. 'So I thought it better to say nothing.'

When asked if she was actually afraid to tell her mother the news, she pauses, and says, 'I know it was very cowardly of me.'

Sutton, no doubt still in shock, then asked her daughter — 'not very amiably' – about what she was going to do. Gielgud told her about London City Ballet taking her on tour, which meant she would be learning something about running a company, as their Rehearsal Director, and would be giving classes. She concluded with, 'I hope you understand.' Sutton says that, after all those years of work, she was shattered, but she simply told her daughter to let her know if she wanted any help.

'However, I couldn't get over the fact that what we had worked together to achieve was finished. Of course, I knew in the back of my mind that she would eventually stop dancing, and perhaps turn to acting. I never thought for a moment that she would tend towards ballet direction.

'I talked to God, as always when I am down, about how things looked for her. I asked whether something could be done.' She also talked to her deceased husband, Lewis, saying, "You can't let your daughter go on like this; maybe she'll get a better job, maybe she'll coach people, maybe she's going to give classes – but where is all this after the big career she made and was at the top?" I then sat back and waited.'

Gielgud was riding in the London tube in February 1982 when she read an advertisement in *Dance and Dancers* calling for applications for Artistic Director of The Australian Ballet. She wondered about it, recalling Peter Bahen's remark back in 1975.

She thought it would be a big job; and there had been the dreadful strike at the Australian Ballet in 1981. But two very good friends, Peter Williams, the editor of *Dance and Dancers*, and David Palmer, the London representative of The Australian Ballet, rang her that same day and persuaded her to apply. She received a reply from the designated headhunter, Lindsay Moore, saying they were interested in her. Meanwhile, she heard they were interviewing a huge field of people, but the references about her were good.

The Chairman of The Australian Ballet board, Sir Robert Southey, met her in London in the middle of 1982 and asked her many questions. Then, in October, she was flown to Australia to meet the board and the company. Marilyn Rowe was Ballet Director in the year after the strike, and Gielgud's old partner and friend, Jonathan Kelly, was dancing with the company.

Gielgud arrived on a Saturday morning, and went to the matinee performance, and to another performance that night. She also travelled with them from Melbourne to Brisbane to see some more performances and she was very impressed with the talent. She met the board, taught a couple of classes, then went back to London. She was finally given the news of her appointment by Southey, who rang her from Melbourne a few weeks later.

As she described this, her eyes filled with tears. It was clear that she was reliving the joy of the news, while at the same moment feeling the pain of knowing that soon it would all be over.

13

DIRECTIONS

The first real sign that life in the company was going to be different for Gielgud presented itself the very day she started at The Australian Ballet. Arriving in Melbourne in the middle of January 1983, she went immediately to the old headquarters in the inner suburb of Flemington to find that the dancers had just finished class. She spoke to them briefly, saying she was happy to be there and, while she realised that it was impossible to keep everybody happy, she hoped to keep as many dancers as she could interested and inspired for as much of the time as possible. She later told the ballet staff she would like to watch class the next day, and on the following day,

Saturday, she would teach one herself. She says this news was received in silence.

Southey, who had met her at the airport, told her that the news of her appointment had been very well received in the company. On a broader base, it was given friendly, if fairly matter-of-fact press, with the announcement of it a bit on the bald side, as if they did not know much about her, or quite what to make of her. Certainly, she felt she was made 'most welcome, which is typical of Australia, and The Australian Ballet'. But the reception of her statement about taking the Saturday class was a surprise. Saturday is not a normal working day in rehearsal period, but there is an optional class. Gielgud later learned that under their contracts, the dancers had to do only four classes a week, which were counted as hours worked. Some chose to do even less, happy to suffer the penalty of having their pay docked. Not yet knowing this, she watched the first class. 'It just confirmed what I'd seen before: what hugely talented dancers there were. Many directors walk into a company and there's a lot of dead wood. But there just wasn't any of that here. It was extraordinary... as well as having all that talent.' However, there were very few soloists, especially males, and not many principals.

When Gielgud arrived to take the Saturday class, she found that out of fifty-five dancers, only seven had come: five girls and two boys. 'That was a little bit of a shock. It felt to me that they were saying, "We don't care if you're the new Artistic Director or not; we're going to show you that you're not going to change these kinds of things. We've heard you're a workaholic."'

Gielgud says, 'Dancers all over the world do six classes a week – they have to – to develop and have lasting careers. So here *was* a challenge.'

She was perplexed. 'It was just a completely different situation, because in the companies where I had been, first of all, you weren't paid for class. It was a gift, and you had to do it every day; that went without saying. People who didn't go were branded as very lazy. Some companies, such as the Grand Ballet Classique de France, didn't give any classes at all, so you had to do your own training, which was very, very difficult.

'So the whole thing was completely upside down. But, I thought, "Well, it's Australia, so that's why."' It would be an ongoing problem. 'I also realised that a carrot in Australia is not necessarily the same as in Europe, and as time went on I realised I didn't know what a carrot is here. It's very difficult to run something unless you know what the carrots and the sticks are!'

After being told about Australians having a more take-it-easy attitude than she had known, she began a long campaign among the dancers to turn the energy around. 'I thought I could do it by being an example. I had a strange idea that what happens at the top permeates down in some way. And I suppose it did, but, it took about twelve years.' She laughs.

Gielgud then met with Colin Peasley, the Ballet Master, and Marilyn Rowe, the Ballet Director. They discussed the year's schedule, and Gielgud found it on the whole very organised, except that many of the people who were needed to stage the ballets had not been approached.

Even prior to her arrival, Gielgud had already made her presence felt by cancelling a plan for the company to do the Kenneth MacMillan ballet *Mayerling*. 'It seems that nobody had realised that there was neither the number of dancers, nor, at that stage, the quality of principals, to stage it.' Then in March of her first year she caused a fuss by cancelling a proposed season by The Australian Ballet at Covent Garden and in Italy.

Noël Pelly has been involved with The Australian Ballet from its inception in 1962, and is currently a board member. He was Deputy Administrator when Gielgud arrived, and a few months later became Administrator. They developed a remarkable partnership.

Pelly says that the cancellation of the overseas tour caused much consternation. 'Covent Garden became very upset, as did the organisers in Italy, because it was to have been part of the Spoleto Festival. Both gave The Australian Ballet a very black mark. The [Arts] Ministry here really had it in for us. But Maina stuck to her guns, and said, "No, we're not ready."' Gielgud says she only knew what the Administrator, Peter Bahen, told her at the time, that the dancers were likely to be distressed if the tour was cancelled, and many would probably leave. She knew the tour would incur a half million dollar loss, which was not worth it in those circumstances, and that was her main concern. The board backed her, showing faith in her integrity and artistic judgment.

According to Pelly, it was not until 1986 that Gielgud felt the company was ready to go overseas. They went to

Japan in 1987, and the following year did an 'Australia to the World' tour to the USSR, London and Athens. They have done an overseas tour virtually every year since then and received much praise and publicity. But back in 1983, when the dancers heard about it, there was an impression that Gielgud had not thought them ready, that the dancing was sub-standard. Gielgud's response was, 'If there would have been time to get a repertoire together that showed off the existing dancers, I think I'd have been pretty happy to present them, but there was no way of showing them off with the planned repertoire.'

For their part, some dancers were suspicious about whether she was going to try to change them. Was she, they wondered, going to expect them to work extra hours? Gielgud, who saw some of them watching the clock, with their bags by the door, ready to go right on the dot, says, 'That was regardless of why that might be. In fact, I was not intending to. I actually thought, and still feel, that the award conditions, including hours of work, are sensible: not too little, not too much. Rehearsals for those performing have to stop three hours before a show starts – a far cry from making up on stage in London Festival Ballet!'

Some of the Australian attitude back then was no doubt an inheritance from the dancers' strike in 1981, which came about over what was perceived as too much artistic interference by the administration. It sent shock waves around the ballet world because it was such a drastic event.

Gary Norman says the strike was also about better wages and conditions, including better hours. 'We didn't want to be working all the time, although now, they are working constantly, all the time.'

Norman says that Gielgud had established a good rapport with the company previously when she was a guest dancer. At that time, 'It was a much more mature company, because you had artists who were much older in the positions of Principals, Soloists and Corps de ballet – more mature people as well as artists.' This meant there were different stimuli then to when Gielgud came back as Artistic Director. People had moved on in their careers, some had stopped dancing, and the company as such was much more youth-oriented. As well, there had been the strike, though people were getting over it when Gielgud arrived. There was a feeling among the dancers that she would mean a new beginning. She inherited a new group of people who had just come into the company, and Gielgud, whom Norman found to be very pleasant in her manner, got to know them fully. 'Straight away, she was there all the time. As she was as a dancer, it was now going to continue on, as a director.'

Adelaide-born, Norman came to The Australian Ballet School in 1967, and three years later joined the company. He had what can only be called a meteoric rise. He was a member of the Corps de ballet for only one year, a Soloist the next, and a Principal the next, at twenty. He had danced with Gielgud when she guested in *The Sleeping Beauty* in 1972, and again in *Romeo and Juliet* in 1974. He danced in Canada, and came back in 1977 because he wanted to work with Anne Woolliams. Norman is an intense, athletic man, who still keeps in very good shape.

His first memory of Gielgud was of 'a very dedicated, very directed person. Her mind was totally on ballet... and she hasn't changed since. She's wed to dance. Sometimes I feel a bit sorry, because she hasn't tried to have an outside existence.' At the same time, he believes the position she has maintained, because of being a director, was probably just as well. 'A funny mix, isn't it?'

Initially, he thought her way was fine, because she was a solo person, and that was her life, 'to what extreme, I wasn't to know that, until later on. She just became more and more involved in the work, maybe to a point where it almost became destructive after a while.' At the same time, he says he did not have misgivings with her as a director. He says Gielgud tried to listen to people, but because she was so involved in everything, perhaps she thought that her direction – which had been so continuously successful over time – was the only way it should go, boosted by the belief that she was obviously doing the right thing. 'She just couldn't see... past the mirror, almost.' If Gielgud had been able to see, she might have noticed warning signs from people, such as why dancers wanted to leave the company, 'why it was built up to the point where dancers eventually felt that they had to make communication stronger to make their voices heard.'

Gielgud says, 'I knew I was coming into a company that had a union. I'd worked in a lot of countries where there wasn't one, so I knew it would be different. I thought it would be a challenge. I tend to see the similarities first in many situations, rather than the differences. My early impression was that there was a balance here.'

But troubles began surfacing fairly soon between Gielgud and the Administrator, Peter Bahen, who reportedly had been used to having a fair amount of authority in artistic decisions. It began after the first week; there was a personality clash as well as problems with general communication difficulties such as Gielgud not being given her own outside international telephone line. She says she and Bahen were already starting to have their differences over her wanting to meet the heads of the various departments when she came to Australia to be interviewed for the job. Then, after she started, she asked to see people's job descriptions, so she would know who was responsible for which areas, only to find these did not exist. She says she was refused access to artists' contracts. She had also sought details of the artistic budget, but one did not formally exist. She and Bahen were very soon arguing. 'Yet here was the man who first said to me, "Oh, Maina, you'd make a great artistic director one day."' She laughs, 'He must have rued the day, if he remembered it.'

Pelly was not going to take the Administrator's job at first because of the strain of the strike and his having to work as Bahen's deputy and be the problem-solver in the background.

'But then I thought about it, and I was very impressed with Maina's mode of operation – what her goals were, and the way she attacked the job.' He thought, 'Here's a woman who knows what she wants to do, and it's my job to help her with it. And that was my philosophy right through the time. I can honestly say, without equivocation, that Maina and I really never had a difference of opinion, which, over nine years, was something I was very proud of. And, you know, she always asked one's opinion. She had some strange habits as well. If you were saying to her, "Well, we can't afford that" – and her mother often talks about this – she would just look out the window and pretend she didn't hear. On the whole, she got what she wanted.'

Between them, they did much rebuilding of the company, which at the beginning of the 1980s was not in good shape. Pelly says, 'Morale was not too flash. The principal line was thin. It was an ailing company. Maina had the job of producing a new generation of dancers, and that she did.'

Former dancer Suzanne Davidson runs The Australian Ballet in Sydney, and has been with them for a long time. She was brought in from London as a Senior Soloist by Peggy van Praagh when the company started in 1962. Later, she taught at the company's school, and did educational programs. She went to Sydney and toured the high schools, 'because that's our next audience,' putting on lecture demonstrations of dance. She used to travel around in a big station wagon, loaded up with dancers, musical equipment, costumes, even barres. 'We'd arrive in a school, and all the kids would be sitting on the fence, yelling out, "Here come the poofters!!" They used to come because it wasn't geography or science, and anything was better than that. It was taken for granted that the girls would like it, but actually the boys used to just love it. They couldn't believe that dancers worked as hard as they did.'

Davidson is a frankly spoken person, who knows

dance very well. She founded the Sydney Dance Company in 1967, and ran it for ten years. She is also very close to Gielgud. They first met when Gielgud was guesting at The Australian Ballet. 'I don't support her because I'm a friend of hers. I have become a friend because of what she does. I have supported her from the second week that she walked in here, because I could see that she knew what she was doing. If anyone was going to lay their life on the line for a while, to drag this company back up by its bootstraps, this woman was going to do it.

'The basis of our affinity is that we are very similar in many ways. We are pretty merciless. We don't mess around. We have very definite opinions. They're not always the same opinions, either, and we argue about things. But I have an abiding respect for what she has achieved, and how she has achieved it.'

Davidson was Media Director at The Australian Ballet when Gielgud was appointed. She was considering leaving the company before Gielgud arrived, but Pelly told her Gielgud was streets ahead of the other applicants, and suggested Davidson give her a month to prove herself. In that time, Davidson stayed very near to Gielgud, and after a couple of weeks said she was in. 'This girl really knows what she's doing. This is what we need.'

What Davidson perceived in Gielgud was that 'she had a very clear view, a mind like a computer. She has a real overview. She's project-oriented. She cared about people, and cared about the company. [At that stage], it wasn't even her company, but that's what she was interested in. She was so turned on by talent. What she cared about was what happened on stage. If there was magic on stage, then she was prepared to put 90 per cent of the effort into it.

'She made a lot of mistakes in the beginning, because one does. She was in love with this thing and so she put herself on the line. She didn't have the experience yet of knowing that you can't do that, because they don't know what to do with it. Anyway, she has certainly learned it now.

'But in those early days, she listened to everybody. And everybody knew better than she did. And they all told her, including me. I cared so much about the company itself. I was horrified at the standard I found when I came back here in 1980. It was just so far removed from what I remembered the company as being, and what Peggy's vision for it was. And this woman, I felt, had the intellect, background, contacts, knowledge and caring to pull it up by its bootstraps, all over again.

'I always go round the bend when I hear, "This is such a wonderful company because the talent is so great." That's a lot of hogwash. It's what you *do* with the talent that makes the difference. It's in her blood, to know what to do with whom and when. I don't mean she's some sort of saint, some sort of perfect person who never makes a mistake. But she makes a lot fewer mistakes than most people I've ever seen.

'And that works against her a bit, I'm sure, that no matter what they do to her, it doesn't make a blind bit of difference to her. If the work's good, it's what comes out of them. If the dancing's good, she puts up with everything. I had the same patience with my company, exactly. I understand exactly what she feels.

'I said to her, "You're going to be the sort of artistic director that hundreds of people are going to cry over at your funeral. But meanwhile, they're all going to shaft you to death, unless you stand up and look them in the face and tell them to sit down. She's done it a couple of times. But each time it took weeks of revving her up.'

One of the other shocks Gielgud remembers from those early times was when one of the most promising male dancers, still in the Corps de ballet, somewhat defiantly, according to her, told her one day that he wanted to be a real estate agent instead. She felt it was bravado on his part, and his way of telling her to back off. But, indeed, working in real estate was exactly what he ended up doing. She was again shocked when he asked for time off during the week so he could move house. Gielgud thought he should do it at the weekend. Her dismay with him was compounded while he was still with the company, when one night she told him he was going to dance a Principal role. Instead of jumping for joy, he asked her if he would be paid more for it. Some of this sounds like rather petty matters, but it demonstrates the difference in attitude that Gielgud experienced when she felt some of the company did not care enough about their work.

Sir Robert Southey was Chairman of the board of The Australian Ballet from 1980 to 1990. A former federal President of the Liberal Party and prominent Australian business figure, he is a straightforward man, with a deep belief in ethics and fair practice.

As Southey moved closer to the company, he came to

realise how uneven it was in dance quality, despite having an excellent Corps de ballet, which he now believes to be the best in the world. He is careful not to diminish the contribution of Peggy van Praagh. She was right for that age, but, 'I don't think that the ballet under her had anything like the approach to perfection which it's had under Maina.' In the 1960s and 1970s it was the only permanent dance company in Australia. 'It was a fine company. It had some great successes, mostly with guest artists,' though there were two or three outstanding Principals, 'and the average ballet-goer, who wasn't seeing the great overseas companies every day of the week, said it was marvellous, thought it was marvellous – and it was very, very good. But it was certainly in poor shape in the late 1970s and early 1980s. And then, of course, we had the strike and, as you can imagine, that didn't improve the standard of dancing.'

Walter Bourke was with The Australian Ballet as a 15-year-old boy when the company was formed, and has retained a great passion for it. He left as a Soloist and went overseas, then came back as a Principal. He supported the dancers during the strike, then was appointed the dancers' first representative on the board, which resulted from the strike. He was then running a restaurant in Carlton, with his wife, Maria, who had also been a leading dancer. He now has a couple of restaurants in Melbourne, the most famous being Walter's Wine Bar, in Southgate, beside the Yarra River, just a stroll away from The Australian Ballet, where he is now a Director on the board.

A robust and forthright person, who speaks with

feeling, he reflects on how The Australian Ballet has grown to become one of the world's best companies. 'The Australian Ballet has given me a tremendous direction in life.'

He describes it as having been a different company when he started. 'I think there was more maturity at the top end, particularly in the senior dancers. If we looked back over the repertoire, it was probably an older company in those days, with a lot of experience from different areas. A lot of the people had been in and out of musicals, whereas today they've all come through the Ballet School. I felt very lucky to have people like Garth Welch and Karl Welander around. They were very experienced dancers. As a 16-year-old kid, you learn a lot from that.'

He says of the board, 'It was pretty well unanimous when we interviewed Maina Gielgud that she was the right person. And I think that's been pretty accurate.'

As the Dancers' Representative in the early days, he and Gielgud 'had a very close relationship, and a fairly positive one.'

Speaking of the way the dancers had earlier been treated badly, 'just used', Gielgud says that when she came to the job, 'I didn't want to know too much about the background. I could certainly sense the wariness, which I couldn't understand, because I was there for the dancers. When I heard that they had a dancers' representative elected on the board, I thought that was part of what an artistic director does.'

She was puzzled by what to her was the contradiction between the dancers' sunny side and a darker tinge of suspicion of authority, of resisting what were considered by them to be unreasonable demands by the Director, and perhaps worst of all, a reluctance to star, in case they were considered 'ambitious' by their colleagues.

'Part of my recognition of that was that you can't deal with it in the way that your instant reaction would tell you to. To some degree, you've got to go along with it, and look at it from their point of view. If you're in the Corps de ballet, and dancing some Solo roles, plus a Principal role, well, yes, it is extra work. And if recognising and rewarding that [extra work] is an incentive and relieves the burden – consequently producing harder work, with goodwill – then it's worth providing the incentive. So I suggested, and the Administrator agreed, to Corps and Coryphees getting additional money if they danced a Principal role.'

Bourke says there were several very good dancers who had been previously with the company but at the time of the interview (1995) were not there.

'I think for the good of The Australian Ballet it should not have happened. I think a lot of that has to reflect on the handling of Maina, how Maina handled those particular people. Most of the time I spent defending her, because for a lot of the time the dancers' gripes were very trivial, and could be very easily looked after without too much trouble at all. That's pretty much par for the course in ballet companies. But then, there's a certain degree of stubbornness there, that I wish had had more flexibility in understanding.'

He refers, for example, to the dancer Liz Toohey and

her partner David McAllister, whom he considered 'probably one of the most exciting couples this country has ever produced. And Maina would never accept it.' Gielgud, in response, says she sent them to the 1985 Moscow International Ballet Competition, where they had great success and were invited back to dance with the Kirov, the Bolshoi and other companies. But on their return, Bourke says, Gielgud 'refused' to promote them to Principal rank. Gielgud's version makes the fine distinction that she 'did not' promote them.

Gielgud says, 'There was pressure exerted on me to promote them (but *later*), and I refused to do so, because I did not feel it was correct. Toohey, however professional, was not a Principal in my opinion, and David not *yet*. I certainly would not have promoted anyone just because I was asked to by influential people.'

Bourke continues, 'And personally I had a real problem with that, and a lot of other people did too. I could never understand that. I guess that was a part of where I started to lose a bit of my real respect for her.'

Toohey later left, and today there is still some residual ill-feeling towards Gielgud about it, with her name still surfacing in discussions about disputes with Gielgud's judgment. Gielgud says Toohey was an extremely good dancer, but simply not Principal material. McAllister is now a Principal, and one of the company's leading male dancers.

Bourke describes Gielgud as having been very spoiled by the amount of talent being turned out by The Australian Ballet School, like no other in the world. If someone was out of line, she simply moved on to the next one, but not out of spite or anything nasty. 'Maina couldn't resist young talent.' It would be one of the main issues when people criticised her methods and policies as Artistic Director. Generally, though, Bourke says many supportive things about how hard Gielgud has worked, and the many achievements she has accomplished for the company.

Paul De Masson, one of the senior members of the company, remembers that in the second half of the 1970s, the work ethic was sloppy. 'There was very much a Norwegian sort of attitude: "We're here, and we're here to stay." There was no threat that if you weren't pulling your finger out, you could go.' He is referring to a Scandinavian system by which dancers are permanently appointed, and then put on a pension.

'The company was so unsettled in lots of ways. No one was really putting their foot down. At first, Maina brought an edge with her, not because she's a disciplinarian as such, but because she was devoted to dance. She wanted it done properly. That's what discipline is, not as in bashing something with a stick. It's because she sees what she wants, and she wants to achieve it. So she'll push and push and push until she gets it.

'As a dancer, I was always a supporter of her in one sense, but I've always disagreed with lots of things about the way she personally managed me. She was right in one sense, but I felt that it was interfering with my life – she had to push me more than I wanted to be pushed myself. In retrospect I think she was probably right, and if I'd been pushed a little sooner in my life, in that manner, I probably would have been a better dancer, technically and physically. I was rebelling against her, because I'd grown into this safe situation with The Australian Ballet, that I think a lot of people were.'

De Masson says that before Gielgud came to the company, dancers expected to stick to their job descriptions, 'and slowly, people with ambition got themselves into doing higher position work'. Then Gielgud arrived, and 'starts pushing people'.

'I always thought that her motives were good. A lot of it was due to respect, because I knew what she was capable of on stage. I knew how disciplined she was as an artist herself. I always knew she was doing what she felt was the right thing.'

He communicated this to other dancers, 'when I got a bit older, and got more understanding of what had happened'. During Gielgud's troubles with the company, he became one of her staunchest defenders.

Colin Peasley is the only one who has been dancing with The Australian Ballet since it started. Having previously been Ballet Master, he is presently the manager of the company's education programs. 'I'm still listed as a Principal Artist, because I do character roles on stage. Any old man or old woman that you see walking across the stage is me.'

A volatile, earnest person, still keeping the figure and nervous energy of a dancer, he can be very funny when he starts rattling off stories and relating crazy theatrical conversations, though he realises that after twenty years on the ballet staff, he 'may have been becoming a little bit tetchy.'

In his words, the first time he saw Gielgud, he thought she was 'wonderful'. This was because she offered to take classes for me, during a period when the workload was very heavy. 'And she was very good. She also came in and said a very interesting thing to me. I thought it was right at the time, and even in hindsight, I must say, I still think she was on the right track. It just went wrong. She said she wanted to develop a family atmosphere in the company. She thought that was the way out of the problems we had been having.' A previous Artistic Director, Anne Woolliams, had tried to instigate it, too, having been so impressed by the family atmosphere created by John Cranko in the Stuttgart company. 'But it's something you can't develop. You can't put it on from the outside. It must just grow from the inside.' Peasley says there was unity, like a family, in the beginning, with Peggy van Praagh.

Nonetheless, 'Maina came at the right time. The company had had a nervous breakdown. We had the famous five-week strike, and the big clean-out through the whole of the company. All the ballet staff except me were basically caught in the mess when it hit the fan. So she came in where she could really have a new beginning. And that was her biggest strength in the beginning, and the fact that she wanted this really nice relationship with the dancers, which I found very appealing, and I thought would work.

'But now I realise it takes a bloody lot of clever thinking to make that sort of thing work. It's ordinary human nature: you go into a room, and you've got five dancers there, and you say, "hello". Some of them will come up and be very friendly back, because it's their nature; others will go, "how do you do", and somebody's got their own problem and they don't even talk to you at all, and they turn around. You go in the next day, and the same people do the same thing. You go in the next day . . . Eventually, you start to gravitate to the people who talk to you. If you come in and just take a class or rehearsal in a businesslike way, those sort of situations don't come up.'

In Gielgud's case, it applies, 'particularly if you're a solo woman, who really every night goes into the theatre. The poor darling has to go because she's not a very "house" type of woman. You know what I mean. You can't see her sitting over a stove whacking up a bloody pasta or something. She doesn't do things like that. A cup of black coffee, and that's probably it at home, and a dead chicken that's been there for three weeks. No, no, no! So Maina goes out and eats. It's hard for a single man to go to a restaurant; you feel a bit stupid going in there, with everybody's surrounding tables, and saying, "A table for one, thank you", and sitting down there and eating, and everybody's having a good time. Bad for a man; worse for a woman. A woman always feels very strange going into these restaurants.

'So she'd say, "Oh, I've been meaning to talk to you about your career; wouldn't you like to come and have a meal with me?" It was company for her – no skin off her nose – a couple of dollars for a meal, somebody to talk to. And she would talk about work. And again, you get those people who are really nice to be with, and those people who say, "Oh, yes, I'd love to come", and those people who say, "Oh, I'm terribly busy tonight, and I can't go out and . . . next Wednesday? I don't know. I've got a busy week . . . " So, again, you gravitate to people.

'You can see what's going to happen, can't you? You've "got favourites". It's just the way things work. And before you know where you are, "Oh, darling, you know what happened with him. We know why *he* got the role, don't we . . . " He would have, anyway, because of the fact that he could do it. But we're all in there, bitching ourselves.

'Every artistic director who has been here has had what I would say were favourite dancers – preferred dancers is a better way of putting it. They had dancers they preferred to other people, as dancers. So, this is what people are calling "favouritism", you see.'

Actually, Gielgud herself makes no bones about having 'favourites', saying it is perfectly natural, because they are better dancers. It is the same in all ballet companies. Just the same, she now rarely goes to dinner with any of the dancers.

Some dancers alleged that Gielgud sees the company in terms of very specific categories: those she likes very much, those she admires, those she is fairly indifferent towards, and those she dislikes. Another description was 'gods, demi-gods, others and devils'. Another popular term for those who have done best under Gielgud is 'The Chosen'.

One person said that while they believed Gielgud could be badgered, at the same time dancers did not have the confidence to go in and talk with her. 'They do their talking with their bodies.' Another said that Gielgud was always aware when she had hurt someone's feelings, and was better with this person afterwards because she had come to realise that she could be blunt with them. 'We have a mutual understanding.'

Another dancer said that when they told Gielgud that they were having doubts about their dancing, they found her to be sympathetic. 'She kept asking me how it was going.'

Yet another, when talking about Gielgud giving them special attention, said, 'Most of the time it was fine because I have genuine affection for her in that sense, so I can't blame her.' But it did have an effect on the company morale.

And so it goes on, with there being probably as many different feelings about Gielgud as their are people in the company. Quite often people were ambivalent about her. Stanton Welch said, for instance, that outside of ballet she was a great friend whom he loved and respected. But inside ballet, he did not always agree with her tactics. 'It's too involved. No matter how much you like someone as a person, it gives you rose-coloured glasses. It kills as much as it grows.' He spoke of her stubbornness. 'She runs the *whole* show.' At the same time, he has learned much from seeing her work with other people. He does not regard talking about her as being bitchy. 'She teaches you not to flinch. Maina is an artist, completely . . . she's got her bag of demons. Her thing is obsession with work.'

A member of the company who is not a dancer said Gielgud does not seem to be able to trust people readily, and has to control everything. Also, she seems to them more concerned about 'backs and ankles', rather than what goes into the whole production of a performance.

In her defence, Peasley says, 'Maina is coach, teacher and director – all of this – unlike most. The Artistic Director has to have so much judgment, and that's why there aren't many good ones in the world.'

Wendy Walker, who works closely with Gielgud, says, 'Maina is very good at letting people have their voice.'

Lucinda Dunn, a Senior Artist who admires her greatly, says, 'I listen to her, and she'll listen to me. She has so much to offer and to give. She knows what to do, but how to do it better. She knows, and I really trust her, and I think that she trusts me.'

A more recent arrival to the company says of any attempt at a personal relationship with Gielgud, 'It's a bridge to her that's not to be crossed over.' Another, more senior dancer, says Gielgud had not understood the personal side of her particular life, so she has not bothered to bring that side of her into her relationship with her. On the other hand, Gielgud had not tried to stop her when she left, asking her to keep in touch.

A third dancer, who has been there for some time, is critical of Gielgud, while at the same time saying that professionally she is a remarkable woman. 'Personally I dislike her greatly. When I joined the company I thought I was going to make her my friend. There's such a lovely side to her that people really don't get to see. There are so many contradictions in her. She can be cruel and yet she can be compassionate. She seems to get turned on by people who have to fight back after they have injuries. On the last day I will tell her that all our years together were wasted.'

There is also a much-publicised story about Gielgud, in which it was alleged that she engaged in 'kissing and cuddling' certain dancers. A witness who says they saw Gielgud walking along a corridor with a first-year boy in the Corps de ballet did not like what they saw, though there was no suggestion of any impropriety, simply her behaving inappropriately in the circumstances. 'A hug is one thing; smothering is another.' A dancer commented that Gielgud being seen hugging people made others think, 'Why not me? What have I done?'

Privately it became pretty nasty when a member of the board once said that he 'knew it for a fact' that she was having an affair with a younger dancer. When told about it, Gielgud was flabbergasted, and flared up in a storm of distress. She was so upset that she spoke in French, her first language: 'Ce n'est pas mon genre!' (It's not my style!) Noël Pelly, when discussing the principle of such matters says, 'You don't mix with the merchandise.'

Peasley explains how natural it is in the ballet world for someone's hand to be held for a moment, or a head to be put on somebody's shoulder, or a joke to be shared. 'But it instantly looks as if there's some sort of lecherous thing happening behind there. It's "lust", and, "There may not be a casting couch in The Australian Ballet, but, my God, it's not far behind."

'Do you realise what we're getting into here? This is how these things get out of hand, and how they can be used by anybody who's a little bit worried about their career. Dancers touch a lot. They don't have the same problem with it, unless they're going to read something into it. Dancers work with their bodies all day long. If it was a company full of nuns, well, yeah, but these are people who run around with no clothes on, and they've got no hangups about their body at all. So you'd be very unlucky for them to think you were sexually harassing anybody here. It's just if you want to make something out of it. And it can be either sex.'

It is true that at the Ballet Centre you are constantly surrounded by young people with superb bodies. Even the ex-dancers on staff are hardly decrepit, either, including Gielgud, who is often seen dashing to take a class or rehearsal in her working togs, looking as comparatively energetic and excited as the next dancer.

There is a marked, almost bizarre, contrast between the very new Ballet Centre building with its modern fittings and furnishings, and the classical dance tradition going back centuries, with young people everywhere, often in flimsy dress, chattering away and flitting about as unselfconsciously as you like. They are aware of themselves, certainly, as anybody in their place would be, and competitive in their comparisons with each other. But their mind is mostly on the work itself – the dance. Nobody seems to take any notice as they skitter and scamper along the carpeted corridors like urban nymphs. Ballet people are much more broad-minded than most.

It is all part of life in the hive of the centre, perched as it is on the edge of the busy vehicle throughway dividing it and the Arts Centre, where huge interstate semi-trailers thunder through day and night, rumbling the office section, which is on that side. The eight studios are immune from this, being on the opposite side of the building. From there you hear only the sweet sounds of music, either on a tape or from rehearsal pianists, who seem to play everything from classical to bebop with equal aplomb. Located at the end overlooking the Arts Centre, Gielgud's office seems to shake even more than the rest.

Jonathan Kelly, Gielgud's longtime dancing partner and friend, has some views on the manipulative powers of dancers, and how her showing feelings for them could be misconstrued.

'You have to put it in a realistic context. Here you had a woman who was dedicated to her job, and her personal life is her own business, but there was obviously not much time for that, given the fact that she was dedicating 100 per cent to the company. So, obviously, she looked for friendship and warmth from her work colleagues, I think, in retrospect, in rather – she would admit – a naive fashion. There was not a sexual connotation to this. It was a question of warmth, friendship, a bit of contact, which we all need. I think, to a degree, some of the individuals in the company cottoned on to that. Dancers are extremely clever at finding out – as all people are in those circumstances – the different ways of exploiting different situations, and I think, in that sense, to a degree, they did that.

'I think that ultimately one would have to say, for all of that, she was the boss, and a more distant approach would have been better suited, given the fact that she was working with dancers, who can be very exploitative. I think probably the old adage, "A little distance goes a long way", is very true, probably in any situation, but particularly with dance, where it's very hard, because you're with the dancers all day. A familiarity is always there.

'I don't mean that as a criticism of dancers, *per se*. I think it's a natural tendency that human beings have, particularly people who are trying to make a career in a profession that's extremely demanding, physically and emotionally. It is perfectly normal for dancers, a lot of the time, even if it's subconscious, to use any means to get a leg up, so to speak.

'I loved working with Maina, because we were on the same wavelength, artistically, interpretively. We could talk about what we wanted to do with a character, and we could evolve our way of doing that without any sense of animosity or one-upmanship, or anything else. We were working on something and we were both determined to do our best. And in those terms, she was a very exciting person to work with, because she has a great brain.

'I was absolutely mad keen on Maina getting the job. She was my ex-partner, and I knew her, and, of course, I genuinely saw and knew that Maina would be an excellent Director, because I could think of no one who would work as hard at it as her. I also knew that she would know every impresario, choreographer, and, just as importantly, every critic. I knew she would come with an enormous portfolio of experience, willpower and discipline. I knew she would be a very competent director, and there are so few of them in the world – and I mean just competent.'

Kelly was a Principal with The Australian Ballet for four years from 1982. But he slipped a disc in 1983. He says, 'I found it more and more difficult to work between then and 1986. We didn't have the treatment that we have now. I really couldn't work around it. My technique was going down. My interest was going down, because I was in my thirties, and I knew that my time was limited as a male dancer. I retired and left the company, and came back on the staff. I used to coach all different ranks, but mainly Principals, and teach class.'

Kelly said any sadness he felt at that time came from a strain that developed between Gielgud and him between 1983 and 1986, when he was acclimatising to the fact that he would not be able to go on. 'Maina was trying to urge me on. It must have been very difficult for her, because she had the dilemma that I later saw, with hindsight as a staff member, that often, when a dancer has lost interest, no matter what excuses they make, ultimately there's very little anyone else can do.

'But, at the time, I felt I could have had a lot more support from Maina. I don't think in those situations I behaved my best. I know that I didn't. But on the other hand, in a certain way, I don't think Maina did, either. She might not feel like that, but I do.' Their friendship suffered from it, for a while, though in the end Kelly went back to the company and joined Gielgud's staff.

'I might add that I was one of the only ones who was vocal in her support in the press, and within the organisation, which was pretty surprising.' Kelly feels a fundamental flaw occurred in the early years of Gielgud's appointment. 'What she did with the company was pretty extraordinary, and, God knows, no one could have given more. If ever you can say that someone gave 110 per cent, I can truthfully say this woman did that, as far as this organisation is concerned. But I do feel some of the problems that developed towards the end could have been avoided to a certain degree if the board that was then in power guided her by not giving her such leeway in the first five, six, seven years of her directorship.

'Because one was so blinded by Maina's achievements – I suppose it's easy to say this in retrospect, probably we'd all do the same – it would have been better at that stage for a little bit more rein to have been put on her to that degree. I think the board could have helped more. It wouldn't have been easy, and Maina by no means would have welcomed it, but I think in the long run it might have helped her more.'

Admitting certain bias, because he had at the time raised some objections to her casting, 'I felt that she didn't value the Principals who were there enough. Of course, I was pushing my own barrow, because I was one of those Principals, getting a few years on, aware of younger talent rising through the ranks, that was being avidly pushed in every way.'

As to Gielgud's much-publicised and criticised attention to promoting the younger dancers, he comments, 'In retrospect, I don't think she was misguided at all. But it did raise the ongoing problems of personal skills. You have to be able to deal with people on different levels in different ways, and I don't feel that Maina has always been able to deal successfully with mature artists. I think she can now, but it's actually a skill that has been forged in the latter part of her directorship. I don't think there was the need initially. She had so much support that she could just do what she wanted to do.'

At the same time, 'The fact is that Maina was the Director, and it's up to the dancers to get the most out of that situation. If the dancers can't cope with it, then it is far better that they leave.'

Steven Heathcote, an outstanding Principal Artist with the company, came into it from the school at the same time as Gielgud started with the company. A strapping boy from the small sheep town of Wagin in the south of Western Australia, he has grown enormously in his work, showing not only brilliant technical expertise, but also a strong dramatic flair. He would have to be called one of the company's 'stars.' At thirty-one, he is in his dancer's prime.

Of his first impressions of Gielgud, he says, 'I thought she was exceptionally eloquent. She seemed someone who was very focused, which she is. She seemed very pleasant. I hadn't thought about it then, when I was young, whether she was approachable or not. Her enthusiasm, her vision for the company was certainly coming across to the dancers, and everyone felt that. For me, it was a good feeling. For some others who had been in the company for quite some time, it could have been quite unsettling, because they would have experienced life under quite a few directors, and during a very turbulent time with the company.'

He denies any possibility that he would put himself down, as in preferring to be seen as just one of the boys. 'No. If I'm asked to do something, I'll step up and do it. Cockiness is very dangerous; confidence is not. I've had to be confident over the years, because, for starters, leaving home early, I had to be assertive about where I was going, and how I was going to get there, from a day-to-day as well as a career sense.'

It is clear that he could be, like Gielgud, strongly self-directed. Indeed, their time together has been at times something of a battle of wills. He once reportedly described Gielgud as overbearing. He sounds regretful now when discussing the incident, which must have hurt Gielgud a lot; not that she would ever admit it.

'I think by using the word "overbearing", it probably represented that sense of smother that I used to get from Maina. Her wish for you to be just the best you could possibly be used to get almost suffocating.' But, hearing the word repeated back to him later on, he says it sounds very out of context.

He says the differences between Gielgud and him arose over his wish to have a balanced life. 'I must admit, that's where I have come up against some personality differences with Maina. I mean, all through the years, we've had a very good working relationship. She saw me from a very early time, and saw that I had talent, in her eyes, and decided to start to mould that to her specifications.

'And I think it's been a learning experience for her, too, because she's realised along the way that you can't mould two different people in the same way, because they don't fit the mould, necessarily, and everybody has their own way of going about things, and their own path to get to the same point.

'One of the conflicting things that we came up against was when Maina would say things like, "Why can't you be more like so and so?" – who perhaps was a guy who was in there an hour before class, warming up, and was in there every lunch hour, bang, bang, bang, and just used to pour every ounce of time and energy into his dancing. And I said, "Well, the first thing is that I'm not him. I'm me. And the other thing is that if I were to pour myself into dancing to that extent, I'd run the risk of cutting off my enjoyment of it."

'I think it took her a while – maybe it still is, I don't know – to understand that, for me, as a different person from the person we were talking about, I needed my outside stimulus. I needed my friends, my time, my fresh air, my breathing space, in order to come back and be able to focus on the increasingly big and responsible workload that I was running into.'

Yet he also volunteers that Gielgud was worried because she must have seen that his technique 'was not natural at all, and that it really needed work, and still does. That's why I'm still doing work [on it] now.

'I think between Maina and myself, what had to happen was a real compromise. I had to come up to her required level of concentration and commitment towards improving technique, and I think that she had to come up to my level of at least understanding that I was not an obsessive person with what I do. It's her complete life, whereas for me, it's not; it's my complete love.' Of course, he wants to be a great dancer.

'Sure, sure; but again, there's not just one way to get to the top, you know. One day, when we were rehearsing, I was so frustrated with everything, I just felt I wasn't getting anywhere, and I said to her, "I've got to start working things out for myself. I can't keep being spoon-fed, because I'm not learning anything. It's just being force-fed, and I'm not digesting it properly." I think I've probably come out with a few things like that, and Maina's not quite known what to do.'

He says matters between Gielgud and him have never been 'bad'. 'They've just been difficult because maybe she's felt that my attitude towards her has been ungrateful, in that I haven't taken on board everything she's suggested.' He appreciates, though, that if Gielgud had not cared so much for the company, she may not have done as much for it.

'Oh, sure. I think that Maina and I have been very good for each other, and I think that we've both done some good things for this company, and we've both learned a lot about people, and how to manage them. Her people management has become a hell of a lot better since she first arrived, that's for sure, because [then] she was the sort of person who, if she didn't know how to deal with someone, would rather just pretend they weren't there. Now I think she's probably more apt to face them and talk about things.'

He says the question of Gielgud's talent is difficult. 'She's definitely talented, but I believe that her huge strength lies in the ability to partition her mind. And this is what gets confusing for the rest of us, because we can't do it. But she can split her mind into ten pieces, and be functioning on all those ten places at the same time. It's scary. It's like, which one do I follow? You get it just talking to her. You can see the central strain of her conversation – what's she's saying – and then she goes off onto this plane, and then one under here, and one up there, all connected to that middle stream.' Gielgud certainly has a powerful concentration, which matches her determination. Speaking of that intense Gielgud focus, Heathcote says that just as she is telling the dancers that they take their skills for granted, he has often wondered the same thing about her. 'In a way, she expects everyone else to keep up, and we're like . . . "Ooooh, hang on, Maina! You lost me three paragraphs ago!"'

On whether he believed Gielgud's superhuman efforts were for the benefit of the company entirely, or whether there was also ego involved, he says, 'I've asked her the very same question, quite a few years ago. I made a statement. I said, "There could quite easily be other people's perception that what you're doing with us young dancers is for your own kind of accolades, glory, or whatever." And she said, "That's completely untrue."' Indeed, without exception, the people interviewed agreed that Gielgud has acted in the best interests of the company. Many went further, and said she has had no thought for herself.

Heathcote continues, 'But I think that she's also human, and being human, people like to be patted on the back for doing good things, and I'm sure that she takes great delight in taking credit for producing dancers like myself and . . .' He mentions several other male dancers.

Gielgud is equally candid about Heathcote. 'Steven's had everything from the minute "go", and can only see what he can see from that perspective. I realised early on that he needed to work really hard on his technique, while he had already tremendous gifts as an actor and in his sense of movement, and could probably go up to the top rank. He also had this need for a very separate life, an equal personal life to his professional one. Without it he probably wouldn't have continued to dance.

'I did get to realise that he and other dancers all have different ways of functioning. Some need 100 per cent involvement in their career, but many feel the need of an outside life – which can either fuel or be negative to their ongoing professional development.'

She refers to him as 'more than anyone, the extraordinary contradiction. Steven is your normal boy-next-door, but he's also an extraordinary artist.' She says he knows he has this talent, and has an artist's soul. 'He thinks he can balance the two [lives], and to some degree he has. But he was one of the dancers to whom I wrote a long letter, trying to make them conscious of the additional demands that a talent such as theirs requires.'

Those letters to various dancers from her would be the basis for part of the list of complaints against her, along with the good luck cards she sent to all solo performers on first nights, which, again, led to talk of favouritism. The letters were seen by some dancers as an interference by Gielgud in their lives.

'I told Steven he had been born with all this talent that other people would kill for, and "you have to do your bit, and be *seen* to do it. There are other people in the company who work ten times as hard. Think of it in terms of developing what you have to the maximum." I gave him a long list, but tried to make it as simple as possible, because he was very young at the time – eighteen or nineteen. The list told him what a *real* dancer would do, how they would go to class *every* day, how they would take time to warm up before, how they would be really focused on what they were doing; think and prepare for both rehearsals and performances.

'He was not doing every class. He was often ill, because he was not looking after himself. In class, he was as vague as anything. He had difficulty remembering steps and stringing them together. However, he's always been totally professional when he's rehearsing or performing, a capacity, again, which I admire very much.

'He didn't actually perform particularly well in his first year, until one day in Canberra when he did a performance, and I went, "Wow!" And then I started looking more, watching, seeing what he was and wasn't doing in terms of work and focus, noting the incredible instincts. He did Mercutio that first year [in *Romeo and Juliet*], and the acting ability was just astounding.'

Gielgud says Heathcote at the time appeared to be confused by her letter. 'I don't think I probably come across as I would like to, especially to those who are . . . I was going to say . . . less passionate than I am. Perhaps I pride myself on being able to compromise and do this balancing act and walk the tightrope. But while I'm doing that, I'm still treading it just a little bit too far in certain directions, so some people resent it.'

She believes she operates gently between pointing and pushing. 'I'm not pushing to the extent that I think it's going to go over the brink. But I'm pushing as far as I dare, for, so to speak, a higher purpose. I'm trying to take into account the personality of the person and how far is too far. And I'm trying to give a realistic appraisal of the potential, which I think will make the difficult work palatable. But then, what is palatable to me may not necessarily be palatable to others.

'The biggest lesson I've learned is that it is a complete fallacy to say, "Treat others as you would be treated." That's something to put right out of one's mind, because other people's reactions are different. What's interesting for me is not necessarily interesting for other people.

'I have confidence in myself as far as knowing what the potential on paper of a person is, what they are capable of physically and artistically. I look for that instinctively, and I look at people, even people I don't know, who have nothing to do with my job, and try to imagine them in twenty years; how they will look, how they will talk. I also do it in reverse, as to how they must have been when they were children. To see this is a gift that I believe I have. And sometimes it's a dangerous one, of seeing how people could develop if they go in one direction, or another. It's pretty scary when you see both possibilities, and how the direction they choose can make such a difference to the outcome of their careers and lives – and it hinges on so little.'

Gielgud touches on another of the grievances which were made against her: that she had denied her dancers their need for mentors.

In the case of The Australian Ballet, 'All the dancers, and until recently, our present Principals, who are in the middle of their careers, people of thirty-one and thirty-two, will still say, "We didn't have any role models; Maina deprived us of them." This is because I didn't bring in these "wonderful dancers" that they imagined should have been the Principals. Instead, I gave them opportunities to do Principal roles themselves. I *would* have brought in role models if there had been any around anywhere in the world who I thought would be suitable. In fact, I've now brought in Li Cunxin, who's a first-rate role model. He's three years older than they are, and he behaves as enthusiastically as a 19-year-old. In the early days, there were people in the company who were very good dancers, but who were dissatisfied and left soon after. They were not necessarily good role models in terms of their attitude.

'I knew that the new generation of dancers in the company were already dancing better than anybody I could bring in. I'm there to be the caretaker of their careers while they're in the company, and while I'm in this position I need to point, pressure, push, draw – whatever it is, because that's my duty – not me, Maina, but the Artistic Director of this company.'

Lisa Bolte joined the Corps de ballet, from The Australian Ballet School, ten years ago so she, too, has been with

Gielgud through much of her term of office. Bolte is now a Principal, and popular with the public. At twenty-eight, she is approaching the prime years of her career. She is slightly, but strongly, built, with that deceptive sense of fragility that modern young female dancers have.

'I've enjoyed from the very beginning being coached by Maina.' This includes her first full-length ballets, and first Principal roles. 'So I think a lot of the way I've grown into being the dancer I am comes from how Maina has coached, and her time and her patience, and her openness of mind, her suggestions of different ideas. I think I've had a wonderful time in the company as far as that goes. I think I've probably reaped her best years, from when she's been most comfortable in the company.

'The most special thing I first did was *The Sleeping Beauty* – Aurora – and Maina coached me on that for quite a bit of the time before I actually made my debut in it. It was really extraordinary for me, because we really had to delve into the character – into the technical aspects, and really polish them, and get it very stylised so that I felt as comfortable as I could be with my first performance. So I went out feeling quite confident that I could just believe in myself, and enjoy my first performance in the role. I knew I had a lot to learn after that, but I'd just turned twenty-one, and it was the best twenty-first birthday present I could ever have had.'

In Bolte's coming of age with Gielgud, she seems to have come quite close to her professionally. 'I think so. I probably have enjoyed that more than some. I've always enjoyed her classes, and mostly . . . enjoyed the challenges she gives you there, and in rehearsals. I think that she's a fairly natural actor and, even though I may not feel the same things that she feels, I'll always value her opinion.'

She agrees that it is unusual, as she has done, to stay with the same company for ten years.

'I think it probably is, a little bit, in our company. You wouldn't leave a company when you're enjoying doing [ballets such as] *The Sleeping Beauty* and *Giselle*, and I've done all the classics here, including *Romeo and Juliet*, *Don Quixote* and *Swan Lake*. It is why I dance. I've only just started to feel comfortable in modern [dance] after ten years. I've always felt a natural in classical. And I enjoy [the fact] that Maina does a lot of the classics, and has a passion for them. And I think it's given me a passion for them, and an eye for detail, and a want to keep growing in the classics with my life. And I really can see that that can happen.

'When I was younger, we worked on individual steps a lot, rehearsing different ones. She could always feel that you could go a bit further. It was a very strengthening process, because I tended to be a bit weak, and the more I did them, the more they would come into my body.'

'I never find with Maina that she really makes you do it in a certain way. She just always suggests a way, and if that doesn't work, we'll try something else, until we find something I feel comfortable with. You have no fear of the work, because you're on top of it – you've found what suits you.' Nothing like some of those ancient Russian teachers who used to shout at Gielgud when she was a girl? 'No, she's not really like that. She's fairly strong when she

42 With Miranda Coney (now Principal Artist) in rehearsal (1984)

43 The Australian Ballet during class on the stage at the Teatro del Parco, Nervi, Italy (1992)

44 Rehearsing her production of *Giselle* (1986)

45 *Don Quixote* in Marseille with Rudolf Nureyev (1972).
'An unforgettable experience.'

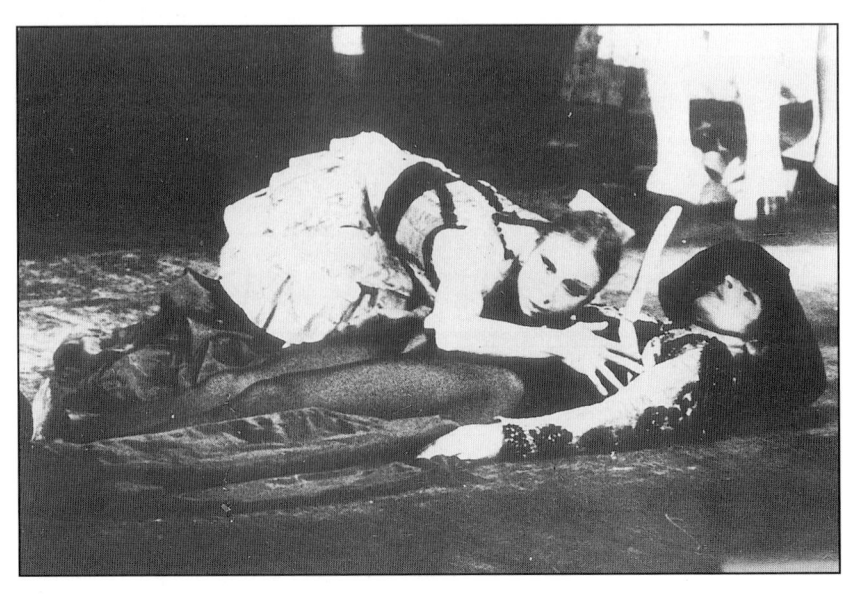

46 *Don Quixote* in Marseille with Nureyev (1972)

47 Nureyev on his last visit to Australia, in 1991, took a class with The Australian Ballet. The feet belong to Andrew Murphy.

48 Erik Bruhn, acknowledged as the greatest *danseur noble* of the century. Just before his death in 1985 he staged *La Sylphide* for The Australian Ballet.

49 Picasso surrounded by (clockwise from bottom) Gielgud, Mercedes Serrano, (unidentified), Natalie Krassovska, Nicolas Polajenko, Vasil Tupin, (unidentified), Daphne Dale (1958)

50 Last night of *Noir et Blanc* in Peking with Chou En-lai, after a performance of 'La Cigarette' (1965)

51 First night of Bicentennial Gala of *The Sleeping Beauty* by The Australian Ballet at Covent Garden, 1988. From left: Miranda Coney, Lisa Bolte, Kathleen Reid, Gielgud and H. M. Queen Elizabeth. Taking *The Sleeping Beauty* to Covent Garden was considered to be 'taking coals to Newcastle', but it was very successful.

52 With Ian McRae, General Manager of The Australian Ballet, and Gielgud's friend Betsey Sawers

53 With Sir Robert Southey, Chairman of The Australian Ballet board (1988)

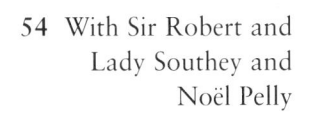

54 With Sir Robert and Lady Southey and Noël Pelly

55 'Young Generation' Cruise (1988)

56 With Steven Heathcote, Anna de Cardi and Brett Morgan, in Bangkok

57 With a great Danish teacher, Johnny Eliasen, and Noël Pelly

58 Christmas party in Australia. She is given a role (1983)

59 With Alessandra Ferri, one of the greatest dancers of our time, on Sydney Harbour

60 Fiftieth birthday party at Ian McRae's house in Melbourne

61 Curtain call at the 1988 Royal Gala Performance of *The Sleeping Beauty* at Covent Garden with The Australian Ballet. With Christine Walsh, John Lanchbery and David Ashmole

62 Taking a bow at the Maryinsky Theatre during The Australian Ballet's first tour to Leningrad in 1988. The orchestra pit has emptied because there were so many curtain calls!

63 From left: Edna Edgley, Gielgud, Mary Duchesne, Gary Norman in *Romeo and Juliet* in 1988 at the Maryinsky Theatre

64 While with Festival Ballet (1973)

wants to make her point, and I think in some ways I've learned to become a little bit stubborn, because sometimes I think that I'm right.'

On whether Gielgud has given her room to move, she says, 'Yes, I think so, actually.' As for some people saying she has been possessive and not let them be themselves: 'I guess at times I've found that. But, at the same time, you always want what you can't have, don't you, and I'm sure that if I was in a company where I didn't have that interest, I would want that; I would really crave that sort of nurturing. I'm glad I've had the time, and someone there to make sure that I have got the detail, and persisting like that, because I think it will help you have a longer career, and to keep searching yourself.

'I went to Canada last year [1994] and, even though I'd done the roles before, they told me, "You're here; this is how we do it here; this is what you do.' It was really very strange, and that's how their Principal dancers work. They all do the same version of *Swan Lake* as the next girl. With Maina, you do *Swan Lake* in the traditional way, but different steps are changed, depending on your type of body and emotion, and so you go out there feeling you're doing your *Swan Lake*. It becomes you, and it become more real, than someone's else's imprint. I think a lot of other companies don't have the freedom that we have here.'

14

THE TROUBLES

No one knows the full story of the extraordinary situation which led up to Gielgud losing her position with The Australian Ballet. While the narrative can be readily documented, the themes of it, the reasons behind the behaviours of the many individuals involved, are as diverse as those people, and much harder to identify than the actual account of the events. Gielgud herself, who has taken an understandable interest in her fall from grace, is unable, even with all her meticulous attention to detail, to put all the pieces in place.

She was bewildered by her abrupt, spectacular and for her, most unwarranted, unwanted and premature removal as Artistic Director. She believes she had more to do before she finished her time with the company.

But the second set of key players, the members of the board of The Australian Ballet Foundation, suddenly withdrew their support of her. There is strong evidence to suggest that a concerted campaign was staged to destabilise her position, fuelled by leaks to the media. Implicit in some press coverage was the feeling that an aloof English woman, who had too much power in the Australian performing arts world, had got her comeuppance.

Then there are those people, some of them well-meaning towards her, who believe that her fourteen years was enough, but abhor the way that it was done.

Maybe if Gielgud had been more political, she might have saved her skin, although she says if she had been cynical back then, she would not have lasted as long as she did. She is more cynical now, she says. Perhaps it would be more true to say that she was more open to attack because earlier she had so much power, and so, when the move against her came, it was absolute.

As has been described earlier in some detail, she has her flaws, mainly revealed in her determination, admittedly a very powerful one, to do what she believed to be right, on behalf of the dancers and the company. There has been some lack of communication here, some misreading, though no one has questioned her motivation, more how she went about it. She was someone from the formal old world, who had grown up in the tradition of ballet as a whole life, coming to the informal new world of some Australians who, for a variety of reasons, ranging from a real need to be free to sheer bloody-mindedness, were telling her to back off.

Gielgud's single-mindedness and obvious high intelligence have rubbed a few people up the wrong way. She has made it easier at times for people to criticise her for being a bossy-boots.

The other key players, the dancers themselves, have shown an ambivalence towards what has occurred. The picture has become blurred by the publicity given to the departure of a small number of important dancers, after relations between them and the Artistic Director became virtually unworkable. On the one hand, as many have said, some dancers did not like what they perceived as her enforced intimacy – albeit professional – some felt it crossed over into the personal. On the other hand, they end up agreeing that they would not be where they are today without her constant vigilance and determination.

There is pettiness in this sorry tale, too, which, while tedious in its detail, has some importance as examples of the way things can break down between people who work together. They became lightning rods for deeper, darker issues, such as whose will would prevail, how much would people respect themselves, and jealousy and envy among the company.

And, just to complicate the choreography and accompanying clamour even further, there has been some other critical opinion, not of the Gielgud style, but of her choice of repertoire. There have been complaints about the need for the company to be 'less classical' and 'less old-fashioned' and 'less Anglophile', and 'more Australian' and 'more modern', all of which Gielgud resoundingly rejects.

Ultimately, though, the most telling issue has to be about ends and means. Was Gielgud artistically in charge, or was she not? If so, should her authority have been absolute? And, despite the criticisms from the board and the dissident dancers, has her position not been more than vindicated by the great work that she has done with the company?

There is so much speculation about the demise of this Artistic Director that it would fill a book in itself, though a lot of the day-to-detail would not mean much to anybody outside the immediate situation.

All performing arts companies have their people problems. This is to be expected: they are made up of such passionate, committed, exposed, and often vulnerable people. And there is no doubt The Australian Ballet has had its share of woe. It was there before Gielgud came – the worst being the 1981 strike – and earlier artistic directors suffered for it, some of them also leaving in reportedly not the happiest circumstances, either. And no doubt it will be there again in the future. The ballet world, for all its beauty, can be very bitchy. But, as Principal Artist Lisa Bolte says, 'Maina gets blamed for everything.' She adds, 'I think that's what probably happens to an artistic director.'

Bolte, with great insight, explains what it is like being in such a company. 'It's a lot of people with a lot of ambition. All the people who are here have got a lot of dreams about what they want to do with their lives. You put them all in a room, and if Maina doesn't quite push them how they dream they could be, then that's when there are going to be problems.

'I've been able to stand up for Maina because she has pushed me, and she has thought my work is worthy of being pushed.' This was even despite Bolte having a lot of injuries. 'So I've reaped a lot of benefits from her, that maybe other people have felt they've deserved. Other people are probably quite angry.'

From all the evidence in this fascinating tale of intrigue, of which this is the first full account, it would seem that Gielgud's real problems began around the middle of 1993. She had been having trouble with about half a dozen dancers, one of whom allegedly threatened her to her face that they, 'will go to the media and tell them everything'. It mystified Gielgud, who says, 'I didn't know what they were saying.' Another dancer was reportedly heard declaring loudly that they were going to 'see her out.'

As well, relationships were not good between Gielgud and two talented Principals, husband and wife Greg Horsman and Lisa Pavane, and they left for London amid a blaze of bad feeling and even worse publicity. Indeed, their departure would become a constant spearhead for future complaints about Gielgud not looking after her Principals enough to keep them. They have been quoted as saying that, in retrospect, they felt the place under Gielgud was being run like a schoolroom.

Also, Gielgud decided finally in July 1993 that she would not keep on the dancer Christopher Goldsworthy. The situation had been worsening for some time, with Goldsworthy, according to Gielgud, not fitting into the company repertoire any more, and asking her for more senior roles, and her telling him he was just not suited. Some time previously, Gielgud says, she was approached on his son's behalf by Goldsworthy's father, Professor Ashley Goldsworthy, who is the Dean of the Business School at Bond University on the Gold Coast. Like Sir Robert Southey, he, too, has been federal President of the Liberal Party. Southey was more than ready to talk about Gielgud and her achievements, and her 'being squeezed out', while Goldsworthy would not be interviewed.

When contacted by the author in July 1995, Goldsworthy sounded cheery enough, if with a possible edge in his voice when told the intended project was a biography of Gielgud. At the end of a brief, brisk conversation, he wished the author well with the book, but he remained adamant that he would not talk. He said he had been 'poorly treated' in the press. The author suggested that being interviewed for this book would give him time and space to put his case fully. To this he responded that he considered the whole matter too unimportant.

A month before this conversation, he had spoken publicly when interviewed by Peta Koch, the dance writer of the *Courier-Mail* in Brisbane. In an article headed 'Goldsworthy plotted to oust Gielgud', the writer, after describing him as the man 'credited' with orchestrating Gielgud's downfall, then reported him as admitting he had been agitating for some time to have Gielgud removed.

The article continued:

Professor Goldsworthy, who has had little to say in the media about his role in the sacking in the lead-up to Wednesday's crucial election of board members, said he hoped the newly elected board would now be able to 'get on with the job'.

Goldsworthy was the Dancers' Representative on the board for seven years from 1988, when he took the position from Walter Bourke, and since then was annually elected unopposed. He resigned in 1995, amid a report in March that year in the *Australian* that some dancers had lost faith in him, and it was unlikely he would be re-elected. The newspaper said, 'The dancers were unhappy with his handling of a dossier of complaints about The Australian Ballet's artistic director, Ms Maina Gielgud.'

A letter sent by Goldsworthy to the dancers themselves in March said he believed it was now appropriate for him to step back and let someone else look after their interests. At the beginning of a long paragraph outlining a list of better conditions achieved for the dancers, he said, 'The Board has now put in place an orderly process of succession for the Artistic Director . . . '

Goldsworthy ran unsuccessfully for a new position of director on the board, writing to members of The Australian Ballet Foundation seeking support for his candidacy. After presenting his history as Dancers' Representative, and his diversity of experience as a senior executive in business, the public sector, professional organisations, education, politics, science policy and the arts, he said (in part):

> Ballet for me has been a fabric of my life, with a wife and daughter as ballet teachers and a son who danced

with The Australian Ballet for thirteen years. I was also a Director of the Queensland Ballet from 1985 to 1994.

It is important that the Board [of The Australian Ballet] comprise a diversity of experience, *but* within the framework of an understanding of and sensitivity to ballet, particularly in respect of the dancers.

The role of the Board is to ensure the long-term growth and development of the Company. This requires Directors with the capacity and experience to formulate a vision for the future, and the integrity and commitment to see that through.

The Australian Ballet is too important to become subject to factional or divisive interests, either internal to or external to the Company.

In the June 1995 *Courier-Mail* article, Goldsworthy said:

'I hope the media circus is finished and that the board will be able to get on with the job.

'I have been agitating for quite some time to have a new Artistic Director appointed and to set the company on an appropriate artistic course and I'm confident the board will now do that.

'I think it's important the board make sure an appointment is announced no later than the end of this year.

The article continued:

Professor Goldsworthy said it was a matter for the board whether Gielgud would be directed to leave earlier but he was confident the decision for her to leave would not be overturned.

He was further quoted:

'I'm fully confident the board will implement the decision taken in December [1994] to appoint a new Artistic Director and I'm quite certain that is what is needed.'

It was at the December meeting that the board decided Gielgud's contract would not be extended beyond 1996.

The story in the *Courier-Mail* reported that Goldsworthy was not at the Annual General Meeting at which the five directors standing for re-election were returned. 'He said he did not regret in hindsight his decision not to publicly explain his crusade against Gielgud.' The article concluded:

> Board chairman Timothy Cox in his address to The Australian Ballet Foundation's annual general meeting on Wednesday said 'Controversy has surrounded the company for over two years with many charges being levelled at Maina for her management style.'

Sir Robert Southey, a close friend and supporter of Gielgud, says of Goldsworthy, 'He was the main source of the working against Maina.'

Southey describes Goldsworthy's campaign to take the job of dancers' representative from Walter Bourke in 1988, when Southey was still Chairman. 'The first thing we knew about that was when we were shown a CV which he'd put around among the dancers, and it was designed to impress – as everything he does is designed – full of the sorts of things that would dazzle a young dancer.'

Southey says Goldsworthy resigned as Dancers' Representative when it was realised that he was not going to be re-elected because of the 'dossier'. Southey points out that he [Southey] was no longer on the board at the time, but he understands the dossier was 'collected at the request of Fred Millar, who was the Chairman until late last year [1994]. And Ashley was the main collector of the dossier. It was really his dossier.

'What game Fred was playing, I don't know. I must say... he's vastly better known as a businessman than I ever was. He's a successful man, and I'm fond of him, and he was completely loyal to me for eleven years as my deputy, so it's a bit rough for me to be picking holes in him, but, whatever the motive, it seems to me that he worked this up with Goldsworthy.'

The author attempted to interview Fred Millar, but without success.

Piers Akerman, a senior *Daily Telegraph Mirror* columnist in Sydney, who wrote many stories about the troubles of The Australian Ballet, reported in February 1995 that when he interviewed Professor Goldsworthy,

> He said he did not bear any animosity towards Ms Gielgud, nor did he think the fact that his son

Christopher had been dropped from the ballet last June may in any way have influenced his feelings towards her or presented a possible conflict of interest when the board considered her contract.

He also said he had not been involved in preparing any dossier or file of complaints about Ms Gielgud from members of the company on his own initiative or at the direction of the former chairman, Mr Frederick Millar, who holds directorships in a number of companies including TNT and Ansett, and who resigned [from the board of The Australian Ballet] in December [1994].

'That's irrelevant,' he said. 'There was no file. There was certainly no conflict of interest. I'm merely one of the board.'

Akerman also quoted Goldsworthy as denying that he had been involved in any bid to oust Gielgud.

For her part, Gielgud says Goldsworthy Snr spoke earlier with her about his son in her dressing room in Melbourne, at a meeting which he requested with her. 'He said, "I'm here as a father, not in the capacity of dancers' representative." He asked me what I thought about Chris; what his future was.

'And I told him absolutely honestly, as I had with Chris *many* times. You see, Chris asked to meet with me regularly a couple of times each year. He was extremely ambitious, and believed his talent entitled him to roles to which he was generally considered unsuited, not just by me, but by those casting ballets from outside the company.

At first, I tried to be kind, because he was so hard-working. But then I felt it important for him to understand his career limitations.

'When his father came, I said, "I know your son is enormously hard-working, but he's not going to go up in this company. I don't believe he would elsewhere, either. But if he feels that strongly – and I can say this to you, I have difficulty saying it to him because he would just think that I'm hoping he will leave – he should try elsewhere because, who knows, perhaps people may see what I don't."

Gielgud says Goldsworthy listened to her. 'He was very civilised. He said that his son's dream was to be a Soloist. He was a Coryphee already, because I had promoted him earlier because of his seniority, and because he did a certain amount of that type of role to a reasonable standard. And he worked so hard. That's why I kept him.' When Gielgud told Goldsworthy that his son could not be promoted, she says, 'He said something to the effect that being a Soloist was his son's ambition, and if I promoted him, he would just go away, happy.'

Then, in July 1993, Gielgud realised that she could give Christopher Goldsworthy only another twelve months' work, because after that there was not the repertoire for which he would be suitable. 'I let him know that this was the case, to give him as much time as possible to make plans for the future.'

There was some unrest in the company, but Gielgud says that at the time she knew she was supported by almost

THE TROUBLES

everybody on the board, despite Goldsworthy Snr having compiled a list of dancers' complaints against her. She heard that he told the dancers he wanted to hear all their problems, that nothing was too small. He also got the dancers to sign a statement, not a petition, that the morale was low in the company. 'It was true,' she says, 'morale was low. There was this small group of malcontents, and nobody dared to be themselves, and nobody could be happy. How could one be?'

Then, during the company's tour of Japan in November 1993, Millar told her that, with her agreement, he would have a meeting with the dancers, by himself, when they all got back to Australia, and try to get to the bottom of it.

Gielgud remembers a previous occasion back in the mid 1980s when Millar came from Sydney to Melbourne to address the dancers – Southey was away – at a time when 'there was a really strange atmosphere, and problems, and senior dancers complaining. He told them basically to shut up and get on with their work, and it worked, to a degree, anyway.' So Gielgud thought Millar would use his proposed private meeting with the dancers the same way and, while it was unorthodox, she agreed to it.

It was also in Japan, on the last night, that Millar, according to Gielgud, raised with her the question of changing the renewal system of her contract. She says he told her that from 1994 it would be renewed annually, unless the board decided to end it. (Previously it had run for three and a half year periods, renewable every year, with either side having an option of giving the other a year's notice.) He said this would still enable her to make plans for the company, and it seemed to him more logical. Gielgud says Millar added that she might get an offer from elsewhere that she could not refuse, being a young lady who had done so well, and would obviously want to go further. She might get an offer from The Royal Ballet, or American Ballet Theatre. Millar, says Gielgud, also said the board would not get in the way and would release her as soon as was practical.

'And, you know, like a fool, I didn't feel until quite recently that this was most odd,' says Gielgud.

Back in Australia, the morning before Millar's meeting with the dancers, Gielgud was contacted by the '7.30 Report' on ABC TV, asking if she would do an interview, supposedly, she says, about the Japan tour. Gielgud found the questions in the prerecorded interview 'very odd'. 'I was asked about the morale of the company, and weren't people here happy. The program people were also asking the dancers leading questions.' Gielgud became wary and warned the company's publicity officer, Jill Rivers. 'There's something very odd going on; please be careful.' Steven Heathcote was one of the dancers interviewed. Gielgud says that some of the people involved were later very embarrassed. 'It was bad for me.'

The dancers' meeting with Millar lasted about three hours. He then came to see Gielgud. She says, 'The Chairman sat down in my office with a very, very serious face, and said, "Well, Maina, this is a very serious situation. I hadn't realised that almost unanimously, the dancers

THE TROUBLES

feel extremely strongly about certain things."' Basically, there were criticisms of her management style, and concern about low morale in the company. It was said that Gielgud 'was around too much', including watching every performance.

Gielgud found what Millar was saying beyond belief, so much so that she started to 'relax' with the conversation, upon which Millar said, 'I'm absolutely serious, and you have a problem.'

Millar honoured a promise he had made to the dancers not to mention any names, but Gielgud says she knew from what he said, 'who had said what'. Millar indicated that Gielgud might be surprised if she knew what had been said by dancers who might normally be expected to support her totally.

He also mentioned one dancer suggesting, with the best intentions, that it might be a good thing if Gielgud did a management course. Gielgud says that in fact she had already discussed interesting management strategies with the dancer in question, who had been telling her about her husband's firm's involvement in this area.

It is worth diverting from the main stream of the story for a few moments to consider the implications of a psychological and management program being implemented by the company and including Gielgud.

There had been some discussion at the board level about management training. Noted Melbourne personnel and corporate consultant Larry Holmes was suggested by one of the directors. Gielgud was very interested. She had previously brought in Rob Kirkby, a sports psychologist, to speak to the dancers and to be available from time to time to individuals.

Holmes met with Gielgud, and they established a good rapport. Then, just before the company left for its United States tour in September 1994, Gielgud and Holmes met the then Administrator (now called General Manager), Ian McRae, to consider the possibility of Holmes working with the dancers. They discussed the fact that at the time of performance, elite athletes, including dancers, relied 80 per cent on the mental process and 20 per cent on the physical side, including technique. Both Gielgud and McRae saw this as an opportunity to do something new, interesting and challenging within the company.

Whilst in Washington DC, Gielgud and McRae met with Fred Millar, then Chairman, and Timothy Cox, the Deputy Chairman, to seek their approval on engaging Holmes to work with the dancers in the agreed context.

A program was then brought into operation, run by Holmes. He first met with the dancers, to achieve their optimum performances, with an emphasis, according to Gielgud, on them taking responsibility for their own careers. The dancers completed a psychological type of questionnaire.

Holmes at one stage had a day and a half with all of the dancers and ballet staff together.

The Australian Ballet, which has shown considerable insight and foresight in implementing the scheme, must be one of the only performing arts companies in the world to bring in such a strategy.

THE TROUBLES

While the proceedings were confidential, it is clear that Holmes' impact on the company was very positive, with the result that the dancers suggested that his work be extended into other areas of the organisation to improve communication between departments, and to facilitate a better understanding by everyone of what other people in the organisation did. Holmes also worked extensively with the heads of departments. The program in fact extended to the whole company, in the name of improving communications. There were two retreats with him which were reportedly most beneficial.

The process concluded in September 1995 with a meeting of the entire Australian Ballet organisation, again conducted by Holmes. In effect, this was a half-day training seminar, which also included nearly all members of the board.

Gielgud herself became very keen on the scheme, developing a high regard for Holmes and his methods. The program produced an analysis of her own psychological profile, which is even more interesting when applied with hindsight after what has happened to her. It classified her as an 'INFJ' personality type, meaning she has predominantly the four elements of introversion, intuition, feeling and judgment. According to the assessment, 'INFJs trust their own vision, quietly exert influence, have deeply felt compassion, are insightful, and seek harmony.'

The assessment said that the contributions of INFJs to their organisations were to provide future-oriented insights directed at how to serve human needs; to follow through on commitments; to work with integrity and consistency.

They prefer jobs which require solitude and concentration and they organise complex interactions between people and tasks.

Their leadership style was to lead through their vision of what is best for others and the organisation; to win cooperation rather than demanding it; to utilise a quiet yet persistent course of action; to work to make their inspirations real; and to inspire others with their ideals.

Their preferred work environment contains people strongly focused on ideals that make a difference to human well-being; provides opportunities for creativity; is harmonious and quiet; has a personal feel to it; allows time and space for reflection; and is organised.

The potential pitfalls with such people are that they may find their ideas overlooked and underestimated; they may not be forthright with criticism; they may be reluctant to intrude upon others and thus keep too much to themselves; and they may operate with single-minded concentration, thereby ignoring other tasks that need to be done.

The suggestions for development for people of such a profile are that they 'may need to develop political savvy and assertiveness skills to champion their ideals; may need to learn to give constructive feedback to others on a timely basis; may need to check their visions with others; and may need to relax and be more open to what can be accomplished in the present situation.'

The analysis also lists their order of preferences in daily life, in order of priority, as intuition, feeling, thinking, and sensing.

Gielgud says that in their discussions after the

dancers' meeting, Millar told her of their allegations of her as being interfering, and asking them to dinner. 'There reportedly were one or two who said they liked going to dinner with me, but they were supposedly shouted down by the others. Then someone else talked about my telephoning dancers at home, and interfering in their medical matters at home.'

Gielgud says there was normally two-way communication between her and doctors about dancers. She did not normally telephone dancers at home unless there were very important and urgent matters to discuss.

The allegations of her 'kissing and cuddling dancers' came up not at that meeting, but later, in the media.

The matter of her contacting the parents of dancers was raised at the meeting. 'I told the Chairman, "Yes, I have talked to parents. If somebody looked as though they were going to be anorexic, or some serious thing, of course I felt it was my duty to ring up the parents."'

Millar also told her that some dancers felt there was not sufficient discipline in the company. Gielgud was surprised by this. However, she said she would be happy to implement further rules and guidelines which she felt could be generally helpful, and in fact later did so. Gielgud says it is curious, in retrospect, to find that 'too much discipline' was one of the main problems Pavane and Horsman complained of a few months later. 'I was very aware, and mentioned this to the Chairman at the time, that there could be a danger of my taking some of these recommendations too far, and being "damned if I did and damned if I didn't". Indeed, this prediction came true!'

Of her feelings at this time, including about Millar himself, Gielgud says, 'I tend to react slowly to things. I tend to take them at face value, and then think about them. I had expected him to come back and say, "Look, it seems there are a few problems, and I think we need to sort this out," or, even more likely, "Well, we all know who those troublemakers were, and what the reasons were, and I told them to shut up and do their work."

'I told him, "Yes, I do watch all the performances, and I watch many rehearsals and classes. It's what I believe an Artistic Director must do. If one doesn't, and makes career decisions without close knowledge of the dancers' *work*, as well as their performances, one runs the risk of being even more unfair than is inherent in the selection process, which of course, by its nature, is subjective. And, you know, all the companies in the world complain that their Directors are *not* there."

'He also told me about the vote. He said he had asked the dancers something like, whether, if they had the choice, they would want me to stay. Reportedly, half the dancers there voted that if I changed my management style, they would want me to stay. Only two dancers wanted me to go, regardless.'

Gielgud says Millar told her he thought the entire company of dancers had been present at the meeting, though some press reports later said they were not all there.

'Then, when he said, "Clearly, you're going to have to change your management style," I said, "Well, I will, if it's a problem. I've been trying to do what I thought was best for the company," . . . all the time thinking, "Is this going to change the work, the performances?" I told him I was just trying to get the sort of atmosphere that is easier for the dancers to talk to me and be – I suppose – a family. "But, if they don't like that, well, I haven't done it for myself, so I'll change it."

'At the end of probably three quarters of an hour, I said, bemused, "Well, if you really believe that, if this is what the dancers are saying and feeling, well then, okay, I'll be more formal. I'll wear red instead of green if they prefer. It's not going to affect me." More discipline, more formality – not a problem – and I implemented it.

'In retrospect, I am now inclined to wonder if it was expected that I would say, "Well, I'm not going to change my ways." But I had no conception of that at the time. And then, almost immediately – the next day, I think – things started appearing in the media – the anonymous phone calls, the meeting that had happened . . . '

Then in mid 1994 there were the much-publicised resignations of Horsman and Pavane, about whom Gielgud had told the board there were difficulties. There were complaints in the press about her handling of the company. Gielgud says she continued to be told she had the full support of the board, but Ashley Goldsworthy was still reporting that there were problems needing to be addressed. She says he was asked what these were. He replied that he did not have the material with him, and was asked to get it together. This was where the 'dossier' came into the story.

The board decided to meet in Sydney, at Millar's TNT building, on 25 August, without the Administrator or the

Artistic Director present. Gielgud says she was assured privately that Goldsworthy was going to be put in his place, which would be difficult if she was there. She later heard reports of the meeting indicating that Goldsworthy was kept outside, 'although there are theories that this was done for show.'

Knowing none of what had happened in Sydney, Gielgud was next given a message that Millar would like to see her in a building in St Kilda Road, to tell her about the meeting. 'As I went there, I felt very nervous and very sick, for no particular reason. I didn't really think that it was peculiar to see him outside of this office [at The Australian Ballet], as, in retrospect, it was.

'Eventually, I was ushered in, and in a very few words, he said, "Well, we had our meeting, and I want to assure you that this has nothing to do with Ashley Goldsworthy. He was not allowed in the meeting. I asked him to stay outside, and in fact he was absolutely furious when he eventually came in. He was very angry because we kept him out for two and a half hours, at the door. But, in the course of this meeting, well, I'm afraid the board has asked me to ask you to resign."'

Gielgud says this information has not been previously revealed, until now, in this book. She continues in a voice remarkably steady for the content of information she is conveying. 'This was 27 August, and I was deeply shocked, but very calm. I said, "Oh, really? Well, for what reason?" He said, "There's no discipline in the company." I repeated this, and said, "Surely you can't be serious. What do you mean, 'no discipline'? The company's acclaimed everywhere, as one of the world's leading classical ballet companies." Then he said, "And there's no respect for you amongst the dancers." I asked him, "How is it possible, in that case, that we produce the quality of performances that we do?" He said, "It's well known that the dancers talk to you and behave towards you without respect." I said, "Well, I'd like some time to think about this, if there's any suggestion of resigning. And certainly I request the possibility of meeting with the board and answering the criticisms, the allegations."

'And that's pretty much it for that meeting. I was very shocked, for obvious reasons, but also absolutely amazed at the timing of it, because this was just prior to the overseas tour to Washington, where it was Festival Australia Week. And I could not see what they would get out of it, except that it would be bad for the company to announce such a thing at that time – just ridiculous.'

When Gielgud later told Ian McRae what had transpired, he said, 'Oh dear. Yes, I thought something like this could happen.'

Gielgud continues, 'A day or two later, Millar and I talked again, on the telephone. I said that whatever decision I came to, certainly the timing suggested was quite impossible for the company.'

Then followed the September board meeting, at the Ballet Centre in Melbourne, which Gielgud attended, having reiterated that she wanted to have a chance of answering 'the so-called allegations'.

Meanwhile, Gielgud had been shown a copy of the 'dossier'. 'It contained a litany of concerns, so to speak, from the dancers; they were a regurgitation of the so-called problems that had come up over the years. It also contained an unsigned petition for the reinstatement of Christopher Goldsworthy. The whole situation seemed to be like reading a novel, or being in a film.'

Gielgud went to the next board meeting, and answered the allegations. 'I was told repeatedly that Ashley Goldsworthy had nothing to do with this, and that the "dossier" – which was there in front of each of them – had nothing to do with it, that nothing in the dossier was being taken into account, because it was all old stuff that'd been dealt with, and was not relevant. I was also told that "people" felt it was incorrect that my dancers call me by my first name, as opposed to "Miss Gielgud".'

She had sought legal advice immediately after Millar asked her to resign. Her lawyers, she says, 'were pretty horrified at the whole saga'.

After her earlier meeting with Millar, Gielgud telephoned each one of the board members, whom she knew quite well, and asked what was happening, and how they felt about the situation. Only the previous December the board had reportedly expressed 100 per cent confidence in her. 'I got a very closed response. The voices all went like I'd never heard them ever before. They said things like, "Well, we have discussed this at some length, and this is the conclusion we have come to." Very cold. They said Ashley Goldsworthy had nothing to do with it. I also understood that only one of them out of twelve had voted for me.'

Although Gielgud was feeling in great danger, she did

not sense that all was lost because the board was no longer backing her. 'I always knew that I had been extremely lucky to have the support of the board, as I did for so long.'

She did not feel obliterated by what was happening. 'I couldn't be destroyed. I was working. I had my dancers, and they were dancing stunningly. And we had an atmosphere which was better than it had ever been, due, it seemed clear, to the departure of the dancers with whom there had been difficulties.'

So her life, she says, went on. No one was going to see a grieving Gielgud, no matter what she felt, though some of her associates have said she has been deeply hurt by the troubles at the company, and they were amazed at how she kept going. Each Sunday, as usual, she continued to work on her papers.

'The first thing I always do is to turn to my work, when something bad has happened. If I had a drama in my career, I'd rush to a studio, and do a barre, not that I necessarily needed to, but it's just the best washing out. It's just my personality. I find it so hard to understand people who have to go away and do nothing when something dreadful happens. It's just the worst thing for me to do.

'So I did the usual, the paperwork, and so on. I was not going to let them get me down so that I was incapable of doing my job properly. On the contrary, I was going to do it better than ever. Besides, we had an overseas tour to do, and I was not going to let The Australian Ballet down. You just can't drop the rein.'

She says that, having answered the allegations at the

board meeting, she was asked to leave the room while the Directors deliberated once more. She returned to her part of the building, 'being busy, watching class, waiting to be called back, and I was not called back. Then it was lunchtime, and I was told that the board meeting was over. I went downstairs and saw the Chairman at the other end of the room. I think I had a dress rehearsal – it's always on a dress rehearsal day! – and I decided I was not going to go over to the dress rehearsal without knowing what was happening. The Chairman said we should talk, so we went up to a little meeting room. He said, "Well, I have to inform you that the board came to the same conclusion. We ask for your resignation, and we would like it as soon as possible."

'By now we were two or three weeks away from a company tour of the United States, and I didn't know, of course, whether by not resigning I was going to be fired. But I thought, "Well, if I'm sacked . . . I mean, bloody fools, idiots . . . for wanting to do this to the company just before an important tour. I have a clear conscience. I see no reason to resign."'

The tour to Seattle and Washington was a huge success, she says, though of the board members who went to Washington, none of them except Josie Woodgate came near class or rehearsal.

'I found that most puzzling, because one of the things that I said to the Chairman, and then later at the board meeting, referring to the allegations, was, "How can you say there's no discipline and a lack of respect? You haven't been in the workplace, not one of you. I always extend an open invitation, and you're never there, so who are you listening to?" They said they had their ways and means, and it would be meddling if they came in.'

At the dinner on the last night of the tour, there were speeches praising Gielgud, 'and I understood, one way or another, that there was a feeling that perhaps it [demanding her resignation] hadn't been quite the right thing, after all, and perhaps somehow it should be looked at again.'

Yet again, Gielgud was approached by the Chairman, she says, after the overseas tour. He now said it was really the time for her resignation. Again, she asked a reason for it, but this time was given none. She still had no intention of resigning.

She says she was also approached by a group of people who told her they were good friends of hers, and how fond they were of her, and what wonderful things she had done, and how extremely worried they were about her future, and really, it would be much better for her if she resigned.

It was intimated to her that at the forthcoming board meeting some directors would very much like to have her contract renewed for another year beyond 1995, but the majority of the board was totally against it.

'They said, "We would like to have your assurance" – by this time they have realised that I'm not going to resign there and then – "that if we renew your contract through 1996, you will give notice of your resignation during 1995. We would like to take to the Chairman this assurance from you today. We'd like to take it away with us."' Gielgud comments, 'And implicit in that was that if I did not give them that assurance, then I'd be out at the end of 1995. So I said, "Well, I'd like to think about this."'

A few days later Gielgud talked with Cox, the Deputy Chairman, at his request. 'I told him I'd thought about it, "and I don't think in all honesty that I can tell you that I'm going to be ready to resign next year. How can I know? At this moment, I certainly don't see any reason for it."'

That next board meeting was the last one to be chaired by Fred Millar, who Gielgud says had been 'terribly busy' since their earlier conversations about the demand for her resignation. Ashley Goldsworthy was also there. 'Eventually I was asked to leave the room, which is normal procedure when there is discussion about the two chief executives' contracts. I had the lawyer in my office, sitting there in case I felt I needed to bring him in. Three minutes before lunch, which is always at 12.30, I was asked to come and meet in a separate room, with the Chairman and the Deputy.' Gielgud asked for her lawyer to be present, upon which 'Fred said, "I'm not having any dealings with lawyers!"'

Inside the room Millar, according to her, 'now looking tired, said the board had debated at great length, and decided to offer me a year's extension – "But that's it!" – and a new Artistic Director will be appointed to take up duties at the beginning of 1997 – "And there's no going back on that."'

Gielgud, after being offered the new contract, said she 'would like to think about it.' Millar insisted that the board wanted an answer very quickly. Gielgud went back to her office and discussed it with her lawyer. There were unanswered questions and possibly serious implications in the offer. Gielgud spent much time musing on the possible conditions. Millar, she says, had told her that she would retain full artistic control, but she wondered if they were going to be telling her what to do.

Then, toughing it out, she went and had lunch with the board. 'My reaction, whenever there's anything which is so-called stressful, is to make sure I eat and, consequently, sleep. None of that "no appetite" stuff, because that's the surest way of getting yourself into true deep depression. That's my theory, anyway, and it seems to work.'

She found Millar beside her at lunch, and then heard a loud, booming voice: 'Well, young lady, we need to have an answer within the next two or three days.'

Gielgud, apparently composed as she sat eating, told Millar she wanted the offer and any conditions put in writing. She says he replied that he was too busy to have this done. Later that afternoon, though, the offer did arrive in writing. She quickly called a meeting of the dancers, told them she had been made an offer by the board, and was considering it, in terms of what it meant, first to them and to the company.

Gielgud says, 'Having looked at it carefully, and thought about it, I wrote back accepting, because I knew that the next two years could be amongst the best yet, with many of my initiatives coming to fruition.'

Gielgud says she got very good and supportive press at that point. 'I suppose, in a way, I'd become a "victim". Much was made of my having arrived at my "use-by date".'

When Gielgud first joined the company in 1983, its media people wanted there to be a public focus on her, but she would not have it, wanting the emphasis to be on the dancers. Ironically, as it worked out towards the end when it got rough, the name 'Maina Gielgud' became very public property indeed.

The shark ethic of eating the wounded prevailed in sections of the media over the story; but Gielgud refused to play the victim, accounting for herself with a composure that was exceptional, given the circumstances. This made her seem, in jaundiced eyes, even more aloof. Dignity and steadfastness were seen as disregard and highhandedness. Her fortunes were discussed as publicly in news and current affairs programs as blithely as the daily share commodity fluctuations, and with the same lack of feeling. How this public exposure and humiliation must have hurt someone so attached to personal privacy.

Edward Pask, who is one of Gielgud's greatest supporters, had tears in his eyes when he spoke of her bewildering fate. Of some so-called media experts who fastened onto the story with such relish, talking about Gielgud and the company with such familiarity and so little understanding, he said, 'They wouldn't know *Swan Lake* if they fell in it.'

As is to be expected, Gielgud refuses in any way to accept that it was time for a change. 'No, not at all. In ballet, if you've got good choreographers, good dancers and good directors, you hang onto them.'

There has, of course, been much speculation about the nature of her going. Timothy Cox, the Chairman of The Australian Ballet Foundation, in a letter to the *Weekend Australian* in March 1995, said:

Reports in *The Australian* have debated the existence or non-existence of a 'dossier' on Maina Gielgud, artistic director of The Australian Ballet. The facts are as follows.

Professor Ashley Goldsworthy is the dancers' representative on the board of The Australian Ballet Foundation, elected by the dancers. One of his duties is to bring to the board's attention the concerns of the dancers. This he does routinely.

From time to time over the past years, he has reported to the board about complaints made by dancers.

In December 1993 the then chairman of the board met the dancers to hear their concerns. This resulted in discussions with the artistic director which led to some changes in artistic management.

During 1994 there were suggestions that the dancers were raising new complaints. At the board's request, Professor Goldsworthy collected the dancers' comments, but the result did not show anything significant which had not been considered and discussed with the artistic director earlier. The collection was in no way a 'dossier' on Maina Gielgud, and was not the catalyst in the board's decision concerning the artistic director's re-appointment.'

Contacted by the author in March 1996, Cox said Gielgud had 'done a superb job'. He refused to reveal what that critical 'catalyst' was which led to her departure, saying the board did not want a 'public slanging match in any way that would undermine either Maina or the job'. He did add, however, 'We felt that after fourteen years that we did need a period of renewal. We need to invigorate the company, and prepare it for 2000 and beyond.

'I think what happened with The [Australian] Ballet is that the whole issue is headed "Maina", but there were many sub-issues, and they all got a run in the press, which made the whole episode of the change much more emotional than it could have been.'

He concluded by saying, 'We don't have anything to hide.' He said there were 'a multitude of reasons' for Gielgud's going.

Valerie Lawson, the arts journalist who has followed the story closely, wrote in the *Sydney Morning Herald* in April 1995:

> The real reason for the axing of Ms Maina Gielgud as artistic director of The Australian Ballet is because the company's former chairman, Mr Fred Millar, lost confidence in her management style.
>
> The gradual breakdown of confidence between Mr Millar, chairman of TNT, and Ms Gielgud, artistic director since 1983, reached a culmination last year at the time of her unsuccessful application for the job of artistic director of the Birmingham Royal Ballet, and the departure for the English National Ballet of The Australian Ballet's former principals, Lisa Pavane and Greg Horsman.
>
> It also followed tensions between Mr Millar and Ms Gielgud when she failed to promote a former

senior artist of the company, Ms Elizabeth Toohey, who left the company in 1991 eventually to join the English National Ballet.

Ms Gielgud made a veiled reference to this last March when she spoke on television of 'suggestions from people in high places who should have known better to promote certain dancers, and that may also have created problems'.

Mr Millar has been a director of The Australian Ballet since 1979 but retired from the board last December.

A special meeting held at TNT of The Australian Ballet board on August 25 last year sealed Ms Gielgud's fate.

One by one, directors were asked how they felt about her. When it came to Mr Millar's turn, he indicated he thought it was time for her to go. Most directors concurred and the decision to extend Ms Gielgud's contract only until the end of 1996 was announced formally before Christmas.

Gielgud claims she 'was not really keen' about applying for the position of Artistic Director with the Birmingham Royal Ballet, previously the Sadler's Wells Ballet. It happened in May 1994, during the troubles, but before she was asked to resign. Many people, including her mother, advised her to try for it, because the situation for her in Australia appeared so precarious.

Gielgud wondered whether her mother and the others might be right. 'Who knows what might happen? Look at

Peggy, Bobby and Anne Woolliams.' She says these previous Artistic Directors' exit from The Australian Ballet happened very fast. 'So I supposed it would be silly not to put feelers out.'

Further afield in the history of Artistic Directors having troubles with their companies have been Nureyev at the Paris Opera Ballet, Baryshnikov at the American Ballet Theatre, and, most recently, Grigorovich at the Bolshoi and Vinogradov at the Maryinsky. Baryshnikov himself said in February 1995 that he was sorry to learn Gielgud would be leaving the company. 'Only time will show who is right, who is wrong.'

Gielgud applied, and went across to London for an interview, over a weekend, so she would lose no time at work. She considered speaking to the Chairman about it, but then decided, 'rightly or wrongly', that it was her own business. As it happened, while in London, in a cafe near Covent Garden, she ran into Matthew Trent, a dancer who was about to join The Australian Ballet. Gielgud told him she was there on her own business but the word got out, and she says she subsequently told the media of her application and the reason for it.

The resident choreographer of the Birmingham company, David Bintley, got the job, as Gielgud believed had been intended, but the incident was held against Gielgud on the grounds that she was fickle.

It might come as a surprise to Gielgud, but Noël Pelly, a close and loyal friend, nonetheless believes her time with the company had been enough. 'One has got to be realistic.

Fourteen years is a pretty strong term. I think dancers need a change. I think audiences probably need a change of repertoire.' But he was greatly distressed by the way Gielgud's departure from the company was handled by the board.

'My own personal view is that the thing should have been settled by a private conference, saying, "Look, you've had a fair term, you've done a fantastic job, but we think it's time," and then to be able to go out and announce that she's going to stand down at the end of next year [1996], with all the appropriate dignity and celebration, instead of coming out with things like "Gielgud Sacked", which I think has been pretty horrendous.'

Pelly said one of the big issues had been Gielgud's refusal to promote Toohey to Principal Artist, despite being asked first by Toohey herself, and then by Fred Millar. Toohey is one of Pelly's best friends, and it was a difficult situation for him. But he agreed with Gielgud, telling her, 'If that's your decision, that's your decision.'

Pelly says there is nothing that makes The Australian Ballet really any different from other companies, where it is common for dancers to query decisions. The departure of Pavane and Horsman 'was considered a catastrophe by some members of the company. Here were your two leading dancers who were going because they objected to the discipline imposed by the Artistic Director.' There is a tradition in ballet that people move around. 'But some people blew that up. One of the problems is that you've got only one major classical ballet company here, and when there's a move, all eyes are on that. If you're in Europe, you've got a ballet company in every city.' He says that in Europe the comings and goings of dancers would not rate a mention, but in Australia it was always made out to be Gielgud's fault, without anybody bothering to check on the real reasons why individuals came and went.

Pelly says he believes that what Gielgud has done during her term 'was perfectly natural, although I don't think an Artistic Director should see every performance. I think the tall poppy syndrome only applied after the series of complaints. Things gradually mounted. Then, the thing came of "We've got to get rid of her. So, what do we do? We start up a campaign."'

Colin Peasley says the continuous supply of dancers from The Australian Ballet School is the envy of the world. There are Australian dancers everywhere now, and in principal roles. Peasley believes half the reason Australian Ballet dancers have left the company has been because of a little dissatisfaction, and half because the grass is greener, 'and, golly gosh, if you're not going to tour the world and see it and be a gypsy when you're twenty, twenty-one, twenty-two, twenty-three, twenty-four, when are you? When you're thirty? No, darling, no. That's when you want to go home and start settling down and thinking, "Bugger the car, dear; I want a house."'

During Gielgud's troubles, Peasley says that when people contacted him, 'I was very neutral about the whole thing, and they didn't want that. They wanted people who would either jump up and down one way or the other. I'm not interested in all that . . . because I've been through it too many times.

'And really, I think the problem in the company was a company problem. I didn't like it being out in public. They're doing it with the cricketers at the moment [November 1995], manufacturing all this carry-on, because it sells papers. And they do this about everybody. They take some small thing, and they keep building it up and building it up, and, by making it "them and us", they can make it into a big thing, and this is horrible.'

Walter Bourke says the company is no different from any other in the movement of people, their feelings, the criticism of decisions, and the carping. 'I've seen it in some of the greatest opera houses in the world. Even some of the great people seem to all have a time when the down sides to them are tolerated and seem unimportant. And I guess then, there comes a time when the change seems to be necessary. There's no fast rule on whether it's ten or twelve years. But a person does seem to have a time when they are at their most effective. I think the last one ever to realise it is yourself, which I suppose is perfectly natural, particularly when in some ways you're still seen to be succeeding in the overall scheme of things.'

He speaks of Gielgud being very dogmatic. 'She's had some good people around her over the years, and few of them, I think, she's ever listened to.' He includes himself in this. 'And I think people who are good leaders are often not good listeners. It's an admirable part of it . . . [that] . . . they're always full of so many ideas, it doesn't seem to be necessary. But there are different times when there needs to be some balance there, or to have someone in between, who can say to you, "Hang on now, someone else has actually said something that might be worth throwing into this whole jigsaw."

'It's interesting how you learn. I've found even with myself now, I apply a similar sort of thinking to my business. I'm full of ideas, and I'm a pretty dogmatic person also. But I've tried very much, recently, to actually listen to other people. I think the modern-day business is one where you involve staff more, and do listen to them, because a lot of them out there [in his restaurant] have got some pretty smart ideas.'

He personally understands Gielgud making telephone calls to dancers' parents, because they came from her real concern. But he resented the notes to dancers, because they were personal, but became company property.

He says the company has been through 'extremely exciting' years with Gielgud. 'We've learned a hell of a lot. And I hope, more than anything . . . that next year [1996] is going to be an exciting year. And I hope that we're going to have the chance to probably say "Thank you" properly.'

There should be no anger. 'We achieved an enormous amount in these last twelve years, and there's a lot of things that have been brought into place by Maina Gielgud and I hope they're going to stay.'

Suzanne Davidson has caught some of that anger, deflected onto her because she supported Gielgud. 'She can't win, once they've decided – this mythical "they" – that she's got to go. She's bad news.'

Many supporters of Gielgud have said they were amazed she did not walk out on the spot when the board made its decision. Davidson says, 'Yes, but you can't. You see, I couldn't have walked out, either. Only a mother does this. Mothers put up with a great deal from their children, and still love them, and still are there. And those children, whilst screaming and carrying on at the mother, know that she will still be there. It's exactly the same relationship.'

She does not agree with those who think there will be much weeping when Gielgud has gone, when people realise what they had. 'They will only realise it when they begin to suffer from it, from what they haven't got. And they will; they will. You see, you can't learn a lesson for someone else. They have to learn their own lesson.'

Of the complaints that Gielgud sometimes did not give some people room to move, Davidson says it is the same criticism that people have of their parents while they are growing up, including the accusation that a mother is too possessive. 'Of course. Don't forget that you see these kids at an age when, if they were at home instead of in a ballet company, they would have this same problem.'

Gary Norman believes there was more maturity when his generation joined the company. At times he has felt it was a shame when students in their third and final year at The Australian Ballet School – where he teaches – are taken into the company to replace injured people, and then do not return. It would be better if they are given opportunities to go with the company for certain periods, to help their transition into professional life.

'Today's dancers are different. They need to have an existence apart from their career. They learn to become individuals a lot earlier. But they also need to have their social life, whereas probably when I first joined the company or the school, I didn't need that as much. Maybe our way of thinking was a bit more in line with Maina when she first started. But now . . . they don't want to be closeted. Maybe that's one of the temperaments of the Australian dancer – they don't want to be closed in.'

On the question of whether Gielgud actually understands, he says, 'I don't know. It's a difficult thing. It's a credit to her that she has such a strong direction. Maybe . . . she didn't realise that people needed to have something else other than the dance. Perhaps that was where it started to become undone a little bit too much. Maybe she didn't . . . let them go as much, because that's the way Maina was, and that's the way I was, as well! But when I'm working with young people . . . I can see that they want it, to have that little bit more freedom.'

Jonathan Kelly, who was one of the few people who spoke up publicly for Gielgud during the troubles, ventures that in terms of human relationships we all sometimes learn a bit late. 'But I don't think it helped that, in a sense, there was a feeling that she was able to run amok for a long time before there were certain sorts of grievances, which by then were huge. It should have been raised and dealt with far, far earlier. But when they were raised initially, because Maina was in such a strong position, with the phenomenal support she had by the then board, they were just swept under the carpet.

'All dancers, everywhere, whinge and moan. But I do feel that actually some of the failings that have been heaped on Maina should actually have been shared by the organisation as a whole. I think they rather ran away and obfuscated their duty.'

'People have the right to other lives, and will have them. I think Maina has to adjust to that, in any company that she directs, be it here or anywhere else. But I think the reality is that it's actually more the external forces that make that a problem, such as competition. The dancers here work extremely hard, and are very dedicated, but we have one major classical company, which means very little competition, compared to overseas companies where it's enormous.

He believes what has happened will probably hurt the next stage in Gielgud's career. 'The easiest way of putting someone down is to disparage them. With Maina, it's that she shows "favouritism", and is "intrusive" in their lives. So there's some sort of sexual connotation there. It's also painting her as someone slightly loopy.'

In his defence of Gielgud at the time, Kelly says it was an in-house matter, and better sorted out by the parties involved, and for all the people on the outside to stop trying to derail the organisation and undermine Gielgud's management. He believes the strongest opposition to Gielgud came from those with the highest levels of influence, both within and outside the company.

'In many ways, it's still a man's world. For a woman like Maina who hasn't got kids, who can't talk about things that other people can relate to very easily, who leads a very dedicated existence, that puts some men off. But it puts women off even more. I'm talking about the people who would like to feel that they have a sense of power within an organisation, without feeling that they actually have to do the work. You often find women who flit around the various cocktail parties and God-knows-what, and feel that this is a cudgel they can take up, and it's good to have a stance on an issue. Very often they're behind the scenes. And they're within the organisation at other levels, too, because they like to feel that, yes, they could be the power behind the throne, but, no, they don't want to spend eighteen hours a day actually doing the job. I think it's a very Australian thing to knock tall poppies.'

Paul De Masson says every company is the same, in so many ways. 'Even in Festival Ballet, people used to bitch. But I think the different thing with Maina is that she gets so personally involved with what she's doing. I was quite outspoken about things that I felt about her. I probably did my fair share of bitching as well. After I left the company, I wasn't involved necessarily with all the bitching, because I just had a soft spot for her always, because she's always tried to help me, and she's always been a part of my career. She was very much in that era before me, but I feel like I just made it in my career, to be on the last leg of a very wonderful era that's not there any more.'

Sir Robert Southey, who retired as Chairman of the board in 1990, describes some naive enthusiasts 'who join the boards of arts companies, partly to help, and probably also partly for kudos, and who haven't the faintest idea of what being a director is, and haven't made the distinction between directing and managing'. He says there 'was a constant attempt at interference' by the board towards Gielgud, 'which didn't get very far while I was Chairman.'

Southey speaks of the need to back the Artistic Director, because she is producing the results. 'And I backed Maina even in cases where probably I secretly didn't think she was right [on matters of detail, not principle]. There were people sniping at her all the time, and I was quite used to that. I tried to improve the method — that sounds rather conceited — but I tried to improve the attitudes of the board, and their professionalism as directors, and I think to some extent I did.'

In February 1995, in a shock move, Southey resigned as Chairman of the national council of The Australian Ballet. Southey wrote a private letter to the Chairman of The Australian Ballet Foundation, Tim Cox, which was subsequently leaked. In this letter, Southey expressed his extreme disgust with the board which 'over the past year ... has hardly covered itself with glory'. He wrote of the events of December 1994 being the 'culmination of a long, determined campaign of destabilisation'. He spoke of slander against Gielgud, who was 'kept in ignorance' and 'given no opportunity to answer her accuser or accusers. In other words, there was a clear denial of natural justice.'

Cox has since rebutted these remarks.

Southey took the board to task for damaging consequences that were likely to follow the December 1994 decision,

... to the board's reputation, to the company's artistic standing internationally, to the maintenance of a healthy relationship between dancers and management, and not least arising out of the perception that the board will be similarly unwilling or unable in the future to protect the next artistic director ... from slander and guerrilla tactics ...

'We all know that anyone, however good, can stay in an organisation too long; and a time comes when, in everyone's interest, a change will be intelligently and sensitively arranged in full consultation.

'But to force Maina out in a hurry when she is at the height of her powers and the company has never performed better, was just plain foolishness. Some spoke of the indignity to which Maina was exposed: but it seemed to me that her dignity remained intact, while those humiliated were the members of the board who were responsible,' he says.

'... key members of the board deceived themselves as to the determination and ruthlessness of those seeking to undermine the artistic director, and allowed themselves to get bogged down in untruths and half-truths about a "lack of discipline" (!) and dancers "leaving the company in droves"(!).'

Southey said that the board had clearly neglected its duty to counter the slander.

Today, he says that there has been previous sniping at Artistic Directors as part of the tradition at The Australian Ballet, and mentions van Praagh and Helpmann having

THE TROUBLES

been discouraged – to put it politely – to stay on. Gielgud agrees with this, and includes Anne Woolliams in this group. Helpmann once told Pelly, 'The higher you jump, the further they pull you down.'

Southey, who declares that he and his wife, Marigold, have great affection for Gielgud, and describes her as 'a person of enormous probity', says he believes 'that she's one of the most intelligent people I've ever met.' He agrees with the description of her showing obsessive behaviour. 'That adjective would certainly, at some times and in some respects, be applied to her. And sometimes it's one of her really important qualities.'

On whether he thinks it is time for Gielgud to go, he says, 'No, I don't.' Later he adds, 'All good things must come to an end. I think . . . it's too hard for any organisation to have the same head for too long. You want change, and that's human, and that's a situation we live with. If the retirement had been properly phased and foreseen, and so on, fine . . . What angered me about the board's decision was that it gave a win to all the . . . little people creeping around doing nasty things. They can go away feeling that they finished her career here. Well, they did.' As to whether what happened has hurt Gielgud's career overall: 'I don't know what her career now is. But I wouldn't have thought so. I think the ballet world knows her, knows her quality, and I think a lot of them know how she's been treated.'

He describes what happened to Gielgud as her having being 'ditched' and given 'the shove'. He says, 'I would say that she'd have to have been very badly hurt. But . . . she's never said that to me. In that sense, she's very private. She keeps her own counsel to a remarkable extent. That's another thing – after all, most women don't. That's another thing that might set her aside, perhaps make her less approachable than some of the other girls around the place.'

Suzanne Davidson has this to say: 'Every successful artistic director I've known has been an autocrat. She's no killer. However, she's more of one now than she was before, and I can tell you, if ever she can be convinced to take on another company, they will really benefit from it, because she's not going to put up with all the undermining next time.'

Ian McRae was shocked by the board's handling of Gielgud's going, and told the Chairman and Deputy Chairman, 'I said the whole thing could have been handled very, very differently and I was appalled at the way it happened. I think it's probably fair to say that some of them feel the same way.'

He was interviewed on 3 November 1995, when the press responses appeared to the company's launch of its 1996 season.

'Some of them are saying The Australian Ballet was at last taking their advice and doing all these interesting, exciting things. And Maina is really irritated by this, and I don't blame her for one minute. Noël and Maina, and then she and I, have shared a vision as to where the company is going, and that takes time. You've got to have all the circumstances right. We are on this path now, and it's been obvious where we're going. We've felt very committed to it. To start to get there, and then have people say that sort of thing, I think, is terrible. A lot of the vision that Maina has had for this company is now starting to come to fruition.'

McRae says he feels really sad that she is going, but also understands why people might feel it is time for a change. 'I trust her judgment. She is the Artistic Director, and I feel that if you don't agree with the policies of the Artistic Director, you get a new one, and I suppose that's what the board has done.'

Former dancer Beth Baird, of Toowoomba, Queensland, who in May 1995 issued her own extensive 'dossier on the board' in favour of Gielgud, in which she addressed many of the issues, documented much of the history of the dispute, and answered the criticisms against Gielgud, including the allegations of many dancers leaving. Baird lists comparative figures for turnovers of dancers in other comparable companies in the same six years: Royal Ballet – of 88 dancers, 54 have left (61 per cent); National Ballet of Canada – of 67 dancers, 47 have left (70 per cent); English National Ballet – of 74 dancers, 60 have left (81 per cent); and The Australian Ballet – of 59 dancers, 37 have left (63 per cent).

'Also,' reports Baird, 'of the forty-seven dancers who have benefited from The Australian Ballet's scholarship program, thirty-one are still with the company (81 per cent).'

Edward Pask believed Gielgud was still in a state of shock, because she did not know why she was being made to go. 'She's done her job brilliantly, maybe too brilliantly. But Maina will survive.' Pask believes the entire Australian

Ballet Foundation will miss Gielgud when she has gone, 'more than any of them will ever know. I think an awful lot of them won't admit it, though.'

Despite realising that her time at The Australian Ballet was over, Gielgud, in an extraordinary twist, decided to reapply for the job. She says she did this partly because she found the job description for the new Artistic Director, in her eyes, exactly matched what she had been doing with the company. She was, of course, also genuinely interested in retaining her position. But also she wanted to ensure that 'They were never going to be able to say, "Oh well, she wasn't interested. She didn't even apply."'

Right up to the end, there was a strange sense that perhaps, deep down, she believed that somehow she would be given back her job. When she reapplied, she hoped to be considered to stay in the position until the year 2000, the year of the Olympic Games in Sydney, for which she had already started working on 'some exciting plans'. She was asked to attend an interview with the job's headhunter, who met her in Melbourne, and asked, incredulously, why she would want to come back. 'It's because I haven't finished my job.' The search committee did not interview her.

In November 1995, Cox announced that the job was going to Ross Stretton, the Canberra-born Assistant Director of American Ballet Theatre. A former student of The Australian Ballet School, who danced with the company up to the level of Principal Artist until leaving in 1979, Stretton reportedly got the job by just one vote, ahead of Graeme Murphy of the Sydney Dance Company.

THE TROUBLES

In his statement, Cox said the company and its audiences 'owe Miss Gielgud a tremendous debt for her extraordinary work, and I hope she will always be close to the company.'

There was general agreement in the media that a good choice had been made, though the response did not have any real edge of excitement, more a sense of relief that the Gielgud dispute was resolved. This is not to prejudge Stretton, about whom one of the major qualities acclaimed seemed to be that he is Australian.

In Gielgud's early years at The Australian Ballet, she had an assistant, Petal Miller-Ashmole. Later, she spent some time searching for another, and in 1993 felt she had finally found the person who seemed ideal. It was Stretton. According to Gielgud, he had been on the verge of coming, but then was offered the position of Assistant Artistic Director at the American Ballet Theatre.

Bryce Hallet, writing in the *Australian Magazine* in early January 1996, in a preview of the year of dance ahead in Australia, said:

> Maina Gielgud may have received her marching orders from The Australian Ballet board but she remains an influential figure in dance. With poise and steely determination, she has headed the company for 14 years, extending its international reach and weathering highly publicised battles at home with customary cool. The subject of inspiration and respect – and a target of envy and scorn – she will step aside at the end of the year. Given the rich, diverse promise of the

repertoire, 1996 will probably be remembered as her most triumphant year.

As the year progressed, and the reviews of the company's new repertoire became more and more glowing, it became clear that Gielgud was having a very good year indeed with The Australian Ballet, even if it was her last one.

15

GOOD TIMES

Gielgud at first finds it hard to discuss what she perceives to be the great moments of her years with the company, because she says they were continual. As well, though, 'That's difficult to talk about, because what would be the obvious highlights – the exterior ones – are not necessarily the same ones for me.' After further prompting, she finally launches into a litany of her good times. As usual, her entire focus is on work.

'On the first nights, I usually feel I'm glad it's over. It's great if they're successful. But it's also the time when you realise what you haven't seen in the rehearsals prior to the first night. It's also one of the very frustrating things, directing a company that performs as much as this one does, because just at that point when you really know how you could develop the performances further, you're already rehearsing the next productions. You have so few hours in the day. You're desperately trying to find time – steal time – to give notes to the dancers and stage and technical staff – time that isn't actually structured to be used for that.

'But it's also the time when the dancers and the ballets are developing through being performed and being in contact with an audience. So some of the most exciting stuff happens actually after first nights are over.

'Some of the highlights would have been the times when I've realised we can acquire a certain ballet, or when new exciting works are being choreographed, such as when I got Glen Tetley to create a new ballet for us, *Orpheus*, as well as all the countless other ballets that we got, like Béjart's *Four Last Songs* and his *Songs of a Wayfarer*, as well as Balanchine's *Apollo*, Cranko's *Taming of the Shrew*, and lately, MacMillan's *Manon*.' She is also 'very excited' about having been able to bring one of the most famous contemporary choreographers of his time, the Czech dancer Jiří Kylián, to come to Australia and work with the dancers. Gielgud laughs about Kylián's having been so fantastic that one of the company's top dancers, Miranda Coney, went away and worked with him further. Coney, a Principal Artist, has since returned.

'One is always taking those risks when one is bringing the best people to work with the dancers, whether they be teachers or choreographers. The same thing with dancers going away on scholarships and exchanges.' One of Gielgud's greatest innovations has been to introduce a scheme by which up to eight dancers a year go overseas on scholarships, something few other companies around the world do. She is so involved in it that when she takes her annual leave at Christmas, she has often spent much of it with the dancers, to help them around when they are in Europe on their scholarships.

'For me, it's all I love to do, to introduce people to other people, and other interests, other artists. It's a perpetual holiday. It's like all my job – well, most of it, except the social part. If you play tennis, it's very hard work, and you expend a lot of energy, and you're having great fun. That's what my work's like. I don't believe in the word "stress". It's all in the mind.'

Developing her theme on what it could mean to the company to have dancers exposed to outside influences, like teachers, choreographers and guests, Gielgud says, 'I think you gain far, far more than you lose. Occasionally, a dancer will find that they want to go elsewhere. But I think far more would have left if it hadn't been for those possibilities.'

Gielgud started an exchange program which has taken off with several top international companies, by which dancers go to perform all over the world, in exchange for dancers of the other companies dancing with The Australian Ballet. She sees this as a wonderful way for dancers to work with other companies, and for other audiences, without the dancers having to leave their home company. The salaries for the dancers continue to be paid by the home company, while the host company pays their travel and living expenses. Since all ballet companies have times when some dancers are not being cast to the maximum of their capacity, this can be a wonderful inspiration, coming at a time which could otherwise be fallow.

'I love my dancers.' This made it all the harder for her when in 1993 she was accused of being too friendly with them, resulting in her agreeing to take a more 'formal' approach. 'I had a slight concern that I was not going to know them as thoroughly, and perhaps not be able to look after them as well. But I've realised by this time that there is very little you can do to persuade teenagers or dancers in their early twenties that it's good to read, or that it's interesting to go to the theatre, unless they are attracted to this in the first place.'

One night at the Ballet Centre, there was a film and lecture on Anna Pavlova organised by Edward Pask, the company's archivist and historian. A man of both precision and passion, he has a great love for ballet. A large crowd of 200 people turned up, many of them members of the Australian Ballet Society, which organised the event. Strangely, none of the dancers was there. When asked about it later, one of them, a Principal Artist, looked dismayed, and said they had not known about it. But this hardly explains why none of the sixty-four dancers came.

Pask's talk was full of sentiment as well as information. He has a special interest in Pavlova, the great Russian dancer, who was born in St Petersburg in 1881, and died in The Hague in 1931. She came to Australia on several tours, where Robert Helpmann studied under her company and became inspired. Pask, whose father met Pavlova in Australia, repeated many of the first-hand descriptions of her – the clear skin, and eyes that missed nothing – and the stories – the way she talked with everybody, and how she was drawn to the swans in Melbourne's Botanic Gardens.

Pask was accompanied by one of the company's rehearsal pianists, Russian-born Emma Lippa, who played Chopin with much feeling, to match the mood of the night. Pask has some rare footage of Pavlova performing. Who could ever forget seeing the old, jerky, and very moving images of her 'Dying Swan', the most famous dance solo in the world?

Pask spoke of the discipline of dance, and the prevailing influence of Pavlova, and how her charisma has endured for sixty years.

Sitting there, in the half-dark, watching that translucence coming from her dancing on the screen, with a portrait of Dame Peggy van Praagh looking down, and Gielgud at the front, completely absorbed, we became once again very much aware of how much ballet is in Gielgud's blood.

There was heartfelt applause when Pask mentioned Gielgud as a special guest, leaving no doubt where the sympathies of those people lay. Afterwards, people gathered for supper, the main part of which was, predictably, that peculiarly Australian dessert known as the pavlova.

Gielgud herself was very much influenced early in her life by Pavlova, about whom she read an enormous amount, including a biography, *Dancing Star*, sections of which she knew word perfect.

The next day, she says, 'I'm sentimental about anything past, whether it's mine or somebody else's, or ballets, or whatever. So I get very nostalgic and very tearful, very easily, and emotional, and all that. I really wanted to dance last night, actually, because of Emma Lippa's beautiful piano playing, and that doesn't happen to me often now.'

A special highlight for Gielgud at The Australian Ballet was the visit of Galina Ulanova to coach Pavane and Horsman in *Giselle*. Most famous for her own portrayal of Giselle, she was one of the finest ballerinas to come out to the West in the 1950s. Dozens of other great teachers, 'all good friends of hers', have also come during Gielgud's time, including Christine Anthony, Sonia Arova, Irina Baronova, Wilhelm Burman, Rachel Cameron, Johnny Eliasen, Rosella Hightower, Gelsey Kirkland, Irina Kolpakova, Gilbert Mayer, Pyotr Nardelli, Magdalena Popa, Jürgen Schneider, Evgeny Valukin, Violette Verdy, Eileen Ward and many others.

Gielgud says so many of her good times 'have been in the rehearsal room, passing on roles to dancers doing them for the first time, or reviving those ballets, and then doing them for the second or third time around, when they've grown into them, when they feel comfortable. Then one can go further with them.

'There have been so many great moments of discovering aspects of the characters in roles. One of the wonderful things about a large percentage of Australian dancers is that they are as at home in the studio as [they are] on stage, interpreting and using their artistic skills.

They don't save themselves for the stage. They're not self-conscious. You can have just extraordinary atmospheres, and just special, special moments when a couple of Principals are rehearsing *Onegin*, for instance. I can remember Fiona Tonkin and Steven Heathcote rehearsing that ballet, and just moving me to tears, time after time, in the rehearsal room, as well as in performance.'

Speaking of the spirit of the Australian dancers, whether it reveals a generous nature, Gielgud says, 'I think it's just an unselfconsciousness, perhaps. I don't know where it comes from. It's not something that I've been able to explain. I don't think it was just good fortune with the first generation that I worked with, although I do find the present generation are equally talented, but perhaps not quite as artistically mature. Interestingly, in another sense, it makes the present generation more inquisitive, more probing, more focused, looking for it, whereas many of these others seem to have such a natural gift that it was almost as if they felt that they didn't need to search further. Sometimes that could be frustrating, because it was wonderful and one wanted it to go further.'

By contrast, people in other countries tend to hold back in rehearsal, particularly young dancers. 'Sometimes they just don't have it in them, even in performance. When you go overseas and see performances, you wonder why they don't use all that technique that they've worked for years and years and years to acquire, or then they only use it for its own sake. They often seem to have lost the plot.

'It's what attracted me to this company in the first place – that I felt the kindred spirit. It's the *theatre* they're interested in, not just steps. So we belong together, because it is clearly what both they and I believe it is all about. They not only believe it, they put it into practice.'

It was impossible to generalise about whether what she encountered in her beginning with the company was raw material. 'There were some people, like Fiona Tonkin or Steven Heathcote, who were such natural actors and artists, that I felt, while admiring and appreciating that side of things, that the polish and technical style was what needed focus, and they might have glossed over. With others, and particularly later on, there were some young dancers who needed most attention on their stage craft, the stylistic side and acting. In general with the classical ballets, between Jonathan Kelly and myself, we gave them all their coaching before their first performances of the classics. That's when you educate them to know what that particular ballet and classical role is about, what its stylistic demands are, what the boundaries are in terms of what is "done". I try to get that across before their first performances of these roles, [such as] *Swan Lake*, *Giselle*, *The Sleeping Beauty*, *Don Quixote* and *La Bayadère*. It's important to stay as near as we can know it to the first intentions of the choreographer, technically, stylistically, because these steps are mucked about with a lot. It's a little easier to get and retain the choreography for the female. But I'm also talking about the Corps de ballet. For male dancers it's much more difficult because all that's got merged into a pond, the kind of steps that are showy. It's now very rare to see a sense of style and interpretation of the classics, or any differentiation between the roles. So it's very, very important to me that those things don't get lost – and they *are* getting lost everywhere.'

As to what she has achieved with The Australian Ballet: 'One of the things that is highlighted is that the dancers *do* differentiate between the styles; the obvious ones are between contemporary and classical works. But also between classics. *Swan Lake*, *The Sleeping Beauty* and *Giselle*, for instance, use similar steps which *must* be performed entirely differently. There is also the fact that discipline must be used for the purpose of being free. Once the discipline has become a part of you, then you can be yourself within it.

'And that's so enormously difficult to get across to a young person nowadays, because what they want to do is throw away the discipline, and *just* be free. I think that appears in all walks of life. The initial reaction to any discipline can often be to feel restricted. Sometimes dancers who start out in classical technique will decide that they just want to do contemporary dance, because they don't want to be "restricted".'

Meryl Tankard told a story to writer Rosalind Reines in the December 1993/January 1994 issue of *Mode* magazine, which shows that Gielgud might not be so hardline in her tastes as her critics would have her.

Tankard, the Artistic Director of the Adelaide-based Meryl Tankard Australian Dance Theatre, a contemporary company of considerable national and international reputation, began her career as a classical dancer. After finishing a six-year ballet diploma in six months, she was finally taken into The Australian Ballet in 1972, where she spent three years in the Corps de ballet. She did not like it, feeling she was part of a machine, which meant using all her creative ability just to turn into a swan or a fairy. To her, classical ballet came to mean masochism, as represented in the image of a pink pointe shoe bathed in blood. One of her teachers even went so far as to strap her foot to her knee so she could learn to pirouette.

Tankard won a scholarship to Europe, where she joined the famous Pina Bausch Wuppertalen Tanztheater. She performed with Bausch for six years, touring the world. She also worked with the equally modern, though even more wild, English dancer and teacher Lindsay Kemp. Tankard later returned to Australia, established her own company in Canberra in 1989, and was appointed Artistic Director in Adelaide in 1993. Her work has become a big talking point in the modern dance world, not the least for the way she uses past experiences to produce themes and stories, and sets her dancers free to express themselves.

Probably her most popular work is a piece called *Two Feet*, which takes a hard and humorous look at the world of classical ballet. It contains two characters. One is Olga Spessivtseva, a Russian ballerina whose obsession for perfection sends her into an insane asylum. The other, a contemporary character based on Tankard's experiences and those of other dancers, is called Mepsie. Here in the show there is much parody as Mepsie goes on a torture bar, with one leg tied up on it, and talks about what her ballet teacher did to her.

After seeing the show, Gielgud wrote to Tankard and

said she loved its subject matter. Tankard commented, 'Isn't that interesting; out of all the people, I thought she would have rejected me because I'm not doing classical ballet, but she's really embracing me.'

Tankard admires Gielgud a great deal, and in 1996 was back with The Australian Ballet, as a guest choreographer, with a new work of hers included in the company's season for the year. It is the first time she has choreographed for them. In the advance publicity she is billed as 'one of Australia's leading contemporary choreographers', while her style itself is described as 'idiosyncratic dance-theatre'.

Speaking further of dancers wanting to break away from what they see as the strictures of classical work, Gielgud says, 'They do not understand that in really good contemporary dance you also have – if you look at it this way – restrictions, or boundaries, or a discipline, a style, a framework, and it's up to you what you do from there. This is the task that is set, I think, in life as well: you're within that framework, and how much can you actually include *and* go beyond it?

'Some dancers here now understand that. Of those who do, some will have great importance for the future of dance, in that they will eventually become teachers, coaches and directors. They will pass on their understanding of something that has been terribly lost.' She says she is delighted by the way the company's dancers perform. 'Time will tell how much stays. The Australian Ballet is the most thriving classically based ballet company in the world, because it not only has the dancers, but also its own choreographers, and that simply can't be overestimated.

'There is a crisis worldwide of classically based dance, and just as there was a ballet boom in the 1970s in America, it now seems to be showing the way to the rest of the world in the decline of ballet.

'Ballet companies are providing dancers with less and less employment. We employ our sixty-four dancers for the full fifty-two weeks a year, but a big company like the American Ballet Theatre is now down to twenty-six weeks, the last time I heard. It's a very serious crisis when dancers are working for only half a year. Audiences are getting less responsive. Some people will tell you that's because there are hardly any big stars around. Less people are going to the theatre.

'Joffrey Ballet in New York has closed. In England, also, there is a box office crisis, and who knows what will happen. People are asking whether it will recover. It's a bit of a chicken-and-egg situation. One doesn't know where it started. The Russian companies – the Kirov and the Bolshoi – are not doing as well as they used to, and the houses are not filled any more in Europe or America. When you see those companies, their work can seem dusty. Consequently, the performance can be unexciting. Perhaps as a result, the audience doesn't come as much.

'There's also a merging of styles throughout the world, so there's not much difference any more between seeing a Russian, French, Danish or American company. That also means that there's less excitement about seeing a company that's touring internationally. The expense involved in running a ballet company is not getting any less. Conditions for dancers are better, but then if you're looking at twenty-six weeks' employment to get better wages and better accommodation and *per diems* during the twenty-six weeks, and you're on unemployment for the rest, has it really changed?'

Ian McRae says, 'We do feel strong in ourselves. The company's great strength is in its financial security. We have some good reserves, and they need to be safeguarded.

'We are a stand-alone company. We tour a lot throughout Australia, and, that, of course, creates a very different environment.' He is comparing it to many companies in Europe, which have much less independence because they are under the control of the opera houses. 'If you're a dancer and you work at The Royal Ballet in London, then primarily your performances are at Covent Garden. You go home from work, you have an outside life, outside friends. If you're in The Australian Ballet, you spend twenty-six weeks away from your home. That means the forming and maintaining of relationships and partnerships is very difficult, and it creates tensions for those who do. It's something we need to have in the back of our minds all the time.'

The Australian Ballet has a budget of about $16 million a year, of which $9.5 million comes from box office, making them very dependent on that. The Federal Government, through the Australia Council, gives them $3.5 million. Over the last decade, the state governments, who used to fund them, have one by one decided that The Australian Ballet is a national company, and not their problem, even though it tours more than any other arts company in the country.

McRae says all arts companies struggle, but The Australian Ballet has not had a tradition of losing money. 'I think this company is in a much more secure position than most other ballet companies in the world.'

On whether that has improved or not in the time of Gielgud, he says, 'I would think we are in a healthier financial position than we would have been when she became Artistic Director. The big difference is that we have this building. Maina has had an effect in the sense that she chooses the repertoire, and the dancers, and, in the final analysis, The Australian Ballet is what you see on stage. This is what gives it the right to exist: its credibility.'

McRae, a sensitive, cultured and gently spoken man, has had to walk a difficult line during the troubles, with his obvious affection and high regard for Gielgud, his loyalty to her as the other authority who runs The Australian Ballet, his own relationship with the company, including the board, and what he believes to be best for the organisation.

'The relationship with Maina has been wonderful for me, I must say. She's a strong, very focused individual. However, such a concentrated focus can be a two-edged sword: great strengths can sometimes create their own weaknesses, which on occasions can actually come back and bite you around the other side.'

He agrees that The Australian Ballet is world-class. 'I think it is as good a company as you'd get anywhere. I would temper that by saying that we don't have the great superstars which other companies have. Some people say it's not important, and Maina has concentrated on building an ensemble. It's quite interesting. She says she wants to develop stars, but I actually don't think she behaves in that way all the time, because she's constantly wanting to discover new talent, pulling people up and challenging them very early in their careers.'

McRae believes the relationship between General Manager and Artistic Director 'needs to be absolutely a partnership – in a sense, a marriage – between the two positions, because the company pivots around those two people, and there needs to be a really good understanding between them as to what the vision is that they're trying to achieve.' He says that he and Gielgud have always been able to work things out, with no power play about who is in charge.

'I think Maina feels that I procrastinate on some particular things. That's the way she sees it. My view is that we're actually not quite at the point where we're agreeing, and unless we need to make a decision tomorrow, there's no real need to force a confrontation on the issue.'

On the issue of people leaving the company, most Australian Ballet people interviewed felt that, despite the bad publicity about the departures, the situation has been not really different to that in other ballet companies. Indeed, Gielgud has produced tables proving that.

'A few years ago, I predicted people leaving, because of an overload of talent, a buildup of people from senior down,' she comments. That build-up of talent occurred after Gielgud joined the company. She says she had predicted the safety valve of people wanting to go elsewhere, and reiterates that it has been perfectly normal.

Typical of such reports was one she made in August 1992:

> Looking at the talent in the junior ranks and counting on long careers (at least another 10 years, hopefully, for our current principals and senior artists), it is inevitable that I will not be able to provide *all* these talented individuals with opportunities at the right time. I'm fully aware that at different stages during the next few years, dancers will wish and, indeed, need, to leave, and go to companies where they may find these opportunities. Naturally, I hope I'll be able to keep the most talented. I hope to, and perhaps I can, find a way of exchanging or eventually loaning dancers to other companies for a period of time, rather than losing them altogether.
>
> But, without doubt, some of the young dancers will have to make their careers elsewhere in the hope that they realise their full potential. I'm saying that there will be an inevitable turnover within the company, and this is in the nature of the beast. It is my job to maintain a fine balance in the standard of the company between the most experienced and talented dancers, and the most talented up and coming ones.
>
> To do so will ensure the highest all-round standard of performances for the audience to see on a continually developing basis. It is vitally important, of course, that we nurture and keep those with that rarest and intangible gift, star quality, a great

responsibility, particularly as we are blessed with more dancers with that halo than any other company in the world.

In 1994, she produced a table showing the number of performances by principals and various other ranks.

> This was in response to the claim that it's mainly the younger dancers who perform, and that the principals don't have enough performances. As you can see, out of 206 possible roles to be danced by principals, 161 were danced by principals or guests, 28 by senior artists, [only] 11 by soloists and 6 by coryphees. Out of 206.

Further to the criticism that she forced senior dancers out by giving junior ones the roles – for which they were supposedly unready – and did not give dancers role models, Gielgud produced another report, in 1990:

> In the light of the critical and public acclaim received, I need to ask myself about it and about us. Here are some random thoughts: 'The Australian Ballet should be of major importance in keeping the traditional classical repertoire alive, over the next decades.'
> Our youngest dancers presently do have role models to look up to, and aim even to surpass one day. That's important, but equally so is the fact that our top dancers show a growing interest in the talent among the young generation and help them. If I had

anything to do with that, it is probably one of the things I'm proudest of. It didn't exist before.

The 1990 memo continued:

Perhaps our present leading senior dancers do realise that I appreciate them, and know that we need them, and that I am giving opportunities to young talent *as well as*, and not *instead of*, continuing to develop them. That is the case, and it's also why I'm continuously on the lookout for opportunities for both juniors and seniors in the guise of displays, workshops, exchanges, etc. One must also be aware that young talent should not be blocked, and that this generation is far more ambitious, generally, than the last.

Consequently, we are far more likely to lose dancers to other companies overseas if we are not careful. Personally, I believe it is inevitable that some *will go*. There's already more talent than we can properly develop. Obviously we must keep the cream ... without spoiling them.'

Another report, in 1994, said:

Some facts and figures which may be of interest regarding the company we have: Twenty-five dancers have been with the company five years or more, 14 have been here seven years or more. All our principals have been in the company seven years or more. All our senior artists have been here more than six years.

In our company of 63 dancers, we have only six whose range of repertoire is restricted for various reasons. These dancers are not usually cast in ballets requiring a classical physique and technique – nor in some ballets by contemporary choreographers. They tend to be used for more demi-charactere roles.

Possibilities for the future, rank by rank: Amongst our three senior artists, all these could go to principal. Amongst our 12 soloists, one should go to principal, if all goes well, two dancers perhaps could, and four or five dancers should go to senior artist... Of nine coryphees, two [perhaps] should go to principal, two could go to principal, three could go to soloist. And in the 30 Corps de ballet, six or seven boys could go to principal, five or six girls could go to principal.

In 1996, Gielgud feels that the absolute majority of present Senior Artists and Soloists have the potential to become Principals. She comments on this with feeling: 'I mean, it's incredible, and that's why I put it on paper. In most companies in the Corps de ballet, you're very lucky if you find *one* potential Principal.'

McRae is asked for his views on the complaints about people leaving the company during Gielgud's time. 'No company likes to lose good dancers, although there is a natural turnover – everywhere. I believe we are thin at the top, and I think Maina will probably feel that as well, at the moment. It bothers me, yes.' Gielgud does not agree.

He says he has basically agreed with Gielgud's decisions,

'because the result at the end of the day is excellent performances, and a company of which we all feel proud. However, I do think that Maina finds it difficult to deal with people who disagree with her. I don't know why it is. There is this image of Maina as a very tough lady, and in some respects she is. But I also feel that Maina is a very vulnerable person, and has difficulty in communicating some of the tough decisions to a dancer.'

For her part, Gielgud, the stubborn romantic and eternal stoic, says, 'I still wake up every day incredulous at my good fortune.'

EPILOGUE

THE LAST DANCE

The coming down of the curtain on Gielgud's long season with The Australian Ballet might give her one dreadful moment of desolation as she stands by herself on the empty stage after what she calls a very golden age of her life. Ahead for her is the hour when she must face and deal with her own personal appraisal of her time in Australia – her successes and her failures.

 Meanwhile we will not find her lingering or languishing in the wings. She has too much pride for that, as well as too much to do. She will seek to make her departure from the company as dignified as possible, holding tightly inside her whatever hurt she feels after having had her time so unceremoniously curtailed.

She is invited one last time to reveal more of herself, to speak frankly about what she feels on departing the company. Her response, however, is typically restrained, leaving many unanswered questions about what she really feels and thinks. While she seems to want to go in a state of grace, the head nun leaves the order without making a final confession.

Is she being coy? Does she want only 'positive' feelings – which she is always saying are the only ones that count – to prevail? Certainly, she has consistently deflected any suggestion that she has been hurt by her removal from the company. At the same time, in the latter part of the interviews, she has talked a lot more about friendships. When it is suggested that she is trying perhaps to counter earlier impressions that might have made her seem too anti-social or strange, she says she had always intended to include 'many people of importance' in her account. She adds that in the early interviews, 'I had at first talked mostly about my career, thinking this was the most interesting thing about my life.' Late in the piece, she supplies a huge list of names of people to whom she makes glowing tributes. Many of these are from The Australian Ballet.

The departure was not expected to be easy because of her pain and because it would be so public. The company decided to send her off in style by giving her not one but two lavish farewells. These took the form of gala performances as tributes to her: in Melbourne in September, and in Sydney in December.

In early August, the company launched another, more

lasting tribute: the Maina Gielgud Fund, to celebrate her achievements and honour her in perpetuity. It reportedly came about in response to a large number of people wanting to do something by which she would be remembered. The Fund brochure says her contribution to The Australian Ballet has been 'immense'.

> She has re-established the company on the international stage and consolidated its reputation as one of the world's finest classical dance companies. This capital Fund will be for the preservation of classical ballet – a subject close to Maina Gielgud's heart. Income earned from the Fund each year will be used to support a specific, classically-based project [which will] keep the spirit of classical ballet flourishing.

Many people have said they believed she had been deeply hurt by the circumstances of her departure from the company. When asked what it felt like to be given two gala performance tributes, despite the fact that her contract has not been renewed, she says, 'It did seem a little strange to be told of these ... a bit like obituaries! I did ask, "Please, no dinners in honour of, no speeches of thanks from the board!" Performances are different, and I think these will give me a lot of pleasure, because they have been my prime concern, the performances and the dancers.'

As to whether she has any feelings of bitterness or sadness about the board, she says, 'Not really. I suppose I am a bit odd that way. It is a matter of how one uses one's energy. I actually believe that most of the board of the time believed they were acting in the way they should, and I believe they were misled and misguided, that's all.'

She is equally even-handed about how she sees the nature of her virtual dismissal, saying, 'My contract was in fact renewed for an extra year, at the same time as the decision was made not to renew it after that. "Sacked" or "contract not renewed"? They are only words. The facts are the same: beyond 1997, I will not be continuing my work of developing this company and its dancers and choreographers, and there was much I still wanted to do, and many unfulfilled plans for the years up to and including the Olympic Games. That is all I have ever cared about in this saga.'

Earlier in our encounters, while she was going ahead planning the company repertoire for 1997, she had much to say about what she hoped her successor would do, whoever that would be. Once Ross Stretton was named in November 1995 as the next Artistic Director, though, she would not discuss it.

The impending abyss of Gielgud leaving The Australian Ballet in December 1996 was suddenly offset in July that year with the news that she had been appointed as the new Artistic Director of The Royal Danish Ballet, taking effect in March 1997. The highly prestigious position is with one of the oldest ballet companies in the world, founded in 1775. Gielgud is the first-ever woman Artistic Director, only the third person from outside the country to be appointed, and the first one this century.

While the news of the appointment was very well

received, there have been inevitable questions. Bryce Hallett wrote in the *Australian* on 2 August 1996:

> When asked why The Danish Ballet hired her, Gielgud shrewdly replied, 'I would say they wanted me because they see someone with 24-hours-a-day dedication as a plus.'
> ... Gielgud said the opportunity to take charge of The Royal Danish Ballet did not diminish the sadness she feels in having to part from an exuberant, confident and maturing company she loves and now ranks as 'world standard'.
> Whatever the much publicised resignations of dancers, boardroom battles and artistic management flare-ups of two and three years ago, Gielgud leaves the AB in good shape, in promising hands and with her once-tarnished reputation intact.
> Her '24-hours-a-day dedication', discipline and obsessiveness – qualities which led to her being held to stricter account, and ultimately, her replacement by the AB board amid intense lobbying – are now wanted in Copenhagen's Royal Theatre, home to the company.
> She has been hired also to introduce new repertoire to complement Royal Danish's staple August Bournonville fare. (The AB has two works by the choreographer in its repertoire – *La Sylphide* and *Konservatoriet*.)
> While some dance commentators expressed surprise initially about Gielgud's appointment because of

the stark contrasts between the two companies, particularly in terms of repertoire styles and traditions, it has quickly become apparent that – in temperament, personality and work ethic – the AB artistic director is well suited to lead a company of this ilk.

Gielgud is not certain what hurdles might emerge in her path in the first several months, but she is alert to the instability and management problems left during the brief stint of her predecessor, Peter Schaufuss, who 'at his own wish', according to Royal Theatre's general manager Michael Christiansen, left the company a year ago. For the AB director, the journey ahead promises to take her from one hot seat to another, if not from the proverbial frying pan into the fire.

The former director of The Royal Danish Ballet, Peter Schaufuss, featured in The Weekend Review of the *Weekend Australian* of 10–11 August 1996. He was in Brisbane to dance a few performances of *Swan Lake*, Act II, with the Queensland Ballet.

The article, by Lee Christofis, reported that his departure from The Royal Danish Ballet, where he was for two years, generated controversy, as did his earlier leaving the English National Ballet, where he had six successful years as Artistic Director. Schaufuss, while saying there were many good boards and chairmen, then said, '. . . most . . . are well-meaning amateurs'.

Bearing in mind his apparent ability to be outspoken, his remarks about The Royal Danish Ballet have some interest when we wonder about Gielgud's possible future there. The article said, 'At RDB he was in a strait-jacket.' It then quoted him:

> 'The [European opera house] general-director system is just as difficult to work with as a board ... The Danish company is one of the oldest and they're very much set in the way they have been for 200 years ... The Administrative side of that job is much greater than I anticipated when I was offered [it] and I never had any time free to spend in the studio.'

The article continued:

> Australian Ballet supremo Maina Gielgud replaces Schaufuss at RDB next year. How might she, coming from a position of tremendous freedom, expect to cope there? 'I've no idea, to be honest ... I think she'll find the job very difficult.'

She is asked how The Australian Ballet compares now to when she joined it in 1983. 'I think it has become the company it was in embryo when I started; one of the most beautiful, perhaps the most, in the world. A company is only as good as its dancers, its choreographers, and the ballets it stages. Our dancers understand *performance*, and they now also understand to some considerable degree the commitment and work ethic a dancer needs to have. Every one of our dancers is developing; there is no dead wood whatsoever, and none stagnant. This is almost unheard of in the ballet companies of the world today. I envy my successor!'

One of the senior dancers who is a friend of Gielgud says they feel fine about the change of Artistic Director. 'We get to move without having to move. It's a natural process.'

Several people in the company have commented that Gielgud appears more relaxed now that she is leaving, trusting people more, letting go her previous iron grip. One person near to her says she has changed a lot. But has anything shifted in her?

Her answer is, 'Not really much different from before. I have always felt that there is not enough time to do all the things I want, and I have *always* been aware of my good fortune in working with marvellously talented people. One cannot rush the development of dancers; each has their own pace, so it is not as if I can "rush" through anything extra before I leave.

'I am perhaps a *little* more cynical about people and their motives, but not really that much – there is always too much to do, and not enough time and energy to do it in, so practically, I cannot waste energy concerning myself about whys and wherefores. It takes all I have to do the things I feel need doing, having questioned myself about my own motives.

'I learnt very early on, in my first few months as Artistic Director, and to my intense surprise at the time, that not all talented people feel the need or the duty to utilise their talent to its utmost. I am as sad, but a little more patient now, with those that don't.

'I always recognised and loved the fact that everyone is different, and consequently should be handled differently. I still believe that is the greatest challenge. (And, of course, one makes mistakes and misreads an individual's signals at times, however good one's intentions.)

If everyone is treated just the same, and their individual talents, pace and sensitivity are ignored, it is easier to read a "policy", so it would have perhaps gone down better if each dancer had been treated like a pawn on a chess board. But I don't believe we would have the company we have now, if I had given in to that "easier" way.'

'Once I get on the aircraft – it doesn't bear thinking about, yet I will have to get on with my new challenge – of course a large section of my heart will always stay here with my beloved company, whatever the future holds, but I am realistic enough to know that only very few people will keep in touch; it is the nature of our profession. I also know that some will always be there, whether we communicate regularly or not. I will look back at this time as what I have always known it to be, a very Golden Age, for me in my life certainly, and also I believe, through the team work of all those who have been involved, for The Australian Ballet.'

There is also the issue of what artistic style she has brought to The Australian Ballet, with one of the harsher criticisms being that while it is now one of the leading classical companies in the world, it has at times become something of a replica of The Royal Ballet.

She is asked if the inclusion of more modern works in

the 1996 repertoire has been in response to those critics. Gielgud responds: 'I have neither tried to, nor brought a type of artistic style to The Australian Ballet. It was said in the time of Dame Peggy van Praagh that the company was similar to The Royal Ballet, through the type of repertoire she brought, and her own background. Partly because of the extraordinary capability of the dancers to adapt to different styles, and perhaps because of my own very diverse background in different companies, I made a prominent feature of this *stylistic diversity*, and that has been much remarked on. Very few people have found anything remotely like The Royal Ballet in The Australian Ballet, except perhaps in some of the repertoire we share.

'The planning of this year's repertoire, as is necessary in the planning of such in a ballet company, started about five years ago in a practical sense, and in broader terms from the very beginning of my term. For instance, I started negotiation for the bringing of a Forsythe work about twelve years ago, [and] I have planned for works new to our repertoire by Jiří Kylián as a regular addition since 1983. The search for (one, and we ended up with two) resident choreographers also started in 1983. The use of Australian choreographers who usually work with companies other than The Australian Ballet has also been a regular part of our repertoire throughout my time with the company. I have no doubt that each of our new works is going to be exciting, interesting, and probably controversial in the best sense of the word.

'It does annoy me that people could imagine that you bring a repertoire... "in response" to something. It takes time to build, and it has to be done with the bricks available at any given time.'

Stephen Baynes says the company has arrived at a big fork in the road. The overriding criteria with regard to repertoire has been very much to do with what dancers were there at the time. 'Maina has realised that there has to be more than the constant repetition of the old warhorses such as *Swan Lake* and *Giselle*.' The problem is that while people want to develop new repertoire and work with interesting choreographers, there is not the time available, of which there has to be a great deal, and quality time at that.

In reply to a question about what she would like to be remembered for, she says, 'I hope that the present dancers and choreographers, and then later those that continue working in dance as teachers, ballet staff, archivists, critics perhaps, will remember and pass on a bit of the heritage so that classically based ballet will remain living and breathing. Perhaps occasionally, someone will think, "Now I know what Maina meant." That would be nice.' She says the meaning of this remark is 'in the context of things I have said or promoted in class, rehearsal, performance, attitude to classical ballet as a career and a vocation – things that often a person only understands years later.'

This is more than a hint that she feels she has been misunderstood. But it refers only to her as the Artistic Director who tried to instil a sense of family in the company underlined by her intense puritan ethic. Things went out of balance as she sought to introduce her old-world ballet tradition into the Australian way of challenging authority. She has been prepared to sacrifice her life to her art, while for some of the company it was a large part of their life, but not their whole life.

For her part, Gielgud says, 'I don't really care whether anyone "understands" why I tried to promote a family feeling or not; it was to be a means to an end, of helping communication. The reason for my being here was to achieve the best possible standard for this ballet company, and to help dancers to understand, share and care more about the tradition of classical ballet and to love and respect it and their stage – also for some of them to understand that ballet can be a way of life, a yoga, a very fascinating never-ending journey.'

Being someone who is solitary, eccentric, strong-willed, extremely talented and with a high intellect, are characteristics which suited her as a performer, but did not necessarily lead to great social skills. How much Gielgud might also feel misunderstood as a person is hard to determine because she insists on deflecting too much attention from what she prefers to keep hidden. She says she does not really mind what personal impression of her she leaves behind. She also once said it was very hard, if not impossible, to hurt her. But it sounded too defiant to be totally convincing.

She now adds to this, 'The way I feel is that I can only get badly hurt by a very few people – those for whom I have tremendous respect and admiration. It is difficult for others to hurt me.'

As the outsider, one who did not fit the mould, she

was the pale-faced woman who went every night to watch The Australian Ballet. To the public perception, she came and went in the theatre without most people ever having a real sense of her, except for only what mattered to her, what could be seen in performance. She was in the crowd but not of it. This became a metaphor for her time in Australia.

Another memory of her will be when she worked in her beloved studio, her one true sanctuary, with all those mirrors at each end, and the images of her and her dancers reflecting back and forth into infinity, each seeming to hold and possess the other.

How much the reaction to Gielgud is a mirror of other people's concern, criticism, envy, admiration and appreciation is a matter for history and her dancers and their audiences to decide.

What she sees of herself in the mirror is between her outer self and the inner one, which she will not let us see. Whether she will continue, as Maurice Béjart once told her, to 'fly away far, very far', is between her and her gods.

She once lightheartedly remarked that she would still be going at ninety, probably in some studio in New York. To this could be added that she could well be still alone, while still immersed in her passion, which is only for dance.

PICTURE CREDITS

Every effort has been made to trace copyright holders of photographs. The publishers would appreciate hearing from any copyright holder not acknowledged.

FRONT COVER: Photo courtesy of *Herald Sun* (Melbourne)
BACK COVER AND SPINE: Photo courtesy of The Touring Office, London
PICTURE INSERTS (numbers refer to numbered captions of photos):
The following photos are from the personal collection of Maina Gielgud: 1, 2, 3, 4, 5, 6, 7, 8, 9, 10, 11, 13, 14, 15, 16, 17, 19, 20, 23, 24, 26, 27, 28, 29, 31, 34, 36, 37, 38, 39, 40, 46, 47, 48, 49, 50, 52, 53, 54, 55, 56, 57, 58, 59, 60, 62, 63, 64.

Other photo credits: 12: Rosemary Winckley. 15: Alain Béjart, © Editions Rene Joly, Brussels. 18: Gilbert Tourte, Cannes. 21: Walter F. Stringer. 22: Nanette Carter and Christopher Köller. 25: Photo Traverso, Cannes. 30: André Bilet, Cannes. 32: The Touring Office, London. 33: James McFarlane. 35: The Old Vic, London. 41: James McFarlane. 42: Jef Busby. 43: Lio Arippa, Genoa. 44: James McFarlane. 45: Claude de Garam, Marseille. 48: James Robinson, photo bequeathed on his death to The Australian Ballet. 51: Desmond O'Neill, Surrey. 61: Express Newspapers, London.

INDEX

Throughout the index, Maina Gielgud is noted as MG. Numbers in italics refer to photograph numbers. Italics are also used for names of ballets, stage shows, films, books, poems, magazines and newspapers.

ABC TV ('7.30 Report'), 282
Academy of Choreographic Art, 104
Akerman, Piers, 278–9
Akers, William, 202
Aldous, Lucette, 34, 157–8, 199, 205
Alexander, Floris, 118, 132
Alexander, Ron, 10, 12, 13–14, 38–40
Alhambra Theatre, 94–5, 97
Ambassadors, The, 218
American Ballet Theatre, 29, 169, 202, 282, 302, 316–17, 330
American (Chicago), 127
Anderson, Reid, 205
anorexia, 36
Anthony, Christine, 324
Apollo, 320
Arts Centre (Victorian), 251–2
Arova, Sonia, 106, 324
Ashmole, David, *61*
Ashton, Sir Frederick, 34, 203, 208
Aszpergercwa, Aniela, *52*
Attard, Vicki, 36
Auric, Georges, 65
Aurora, 168, 184, 207, 267

Australian, The, 275, 299, 341–2
   Magazine, 317
Australian Ballet, The, 1–46, 345
   Artistic Directors, 18, 57, 66, 97, 102, 104, 199–200, 225–6, 245, 275–7, 302, 312–313, 316–317, 342
   artistic style, 347–9
   board of Directors, *53, 77*, 230, 238, 275–7, 289–97, 310–11
   Centre, 19, 26, 112, 252, 322, 332; *see also* premises
   class and rehearsal, 20–4, 25–7, 43–6, 228–9, 324–5
   dancers, 9–16, 17–19, 20–2, 27–34, 35–8, 40–3, 44–6, 91–2, 118, 181–2, 192–3, 231–2, 239–44, 254, 256, 261–2, 264–7, 315, 326–7, 333–7
   dismissal of MG, 269–318
   exchange program, 321–2
   Foundation, 270, 275, 277, 298–9, 311, 315–16,
   funding of, 331–2
   guest choreographers, coaches, conductors and producers, *20, 34, 47, 48*, 178, 320, 324, 329, 348
   guest dancers, 153, 175, 199–203, 204–7, 210–11
   historical tradition behind, 64–7
   Maina Gielgud Fund, 341
   management of, *52, 57, 58*, 230, 234, 300
   national council, 311

INDEX

Australian Ballet (*cont.*)
  performance rate, 29, 39, 330–1
  premises, 19, 26, 203, 227, 251–2; *see also* Centre
  productions, 1–2, 6–11, 12–14, 206, 320
    Beyond Bach, 5, 11, 14
    Checkmate, 202
    Don Quixote, 201
    La Fille mal gardée, 34, 203–4
    Giselle, 21, 266, 324
    Las Hermanas, 5, 15
    In the Middle, Somewhat Elevated, 5, 15
    Onegin, 6
    Romeo and Juliet, 204–6, 232, 266
    The Sleeping Beauty, 22, 40, 51, 61, 199–201, 265–6
    Squeaky Door, 140–1
  psychological and management program, 283–6
  scholarships, 321
  status of company, 3, 240, 329, 332
  on tour, 43, 62, 3, 6, 103, 123, 230–1
  work ethic, 243
Australian Ballet School, The, 202, 235, 240, 304, 307
Australian Ballet Society, The, 332

Bahen, Peter, 206, 230, 234
Baird, Beth, 315
Baird, Paula, 34–5
Baiser de le Fée, Le, 175
Bakst, 65
Balanchine, George, 31, 65, 143, 168–73, 209, 320
Bal de Nuit, 121
Balfour, Maina (Mary), 53
ballet dancers:
  diet, 37–8
  injuries, 4, 38–41
  lifestyle, 17–46
  personalities, 41–44
  physical condition, 4, 10, 36
  training, 4
Ballet de l'Étoile, 105
Ballet des Champs-Elysées, 87
Ballet of Marseille, 153
Ballet of the Twentieth Century (Ballet du XXème Siècle, Maurice Béjart), 129–48
Ballets Russes du Colonel de Basil, 66, 86

Ballets Russes de Monte Carlo, 68, 87, 108, 125, 174
Ballets Russes de Sergei (Palovich) Diaghilev, 64–6, 71, 88, 130, 169; *see also* Diaghilev, Sergei
Ballet Today, 146
Bari, Tania, 144
Barnes, Clive, 142
Baronova (Irina), 68, 89, 324
Baryshnikov, Mikhail, 22, 302
Baudelaire, 136
Bayadère, La, 326
Baynes, Stephen, 5, 32–3, 349
Beau Danube, Le, 176
Beaumont, Piers, 217
Béjart, Maurice, 23, 79, 130, 136, 351
  artistic style, 132, 133–4, 147, 193
  Ballet du XXème Siècle (Ballet of the Twentieth Century), 129
  ballets;
    on Baudelaire, 136
    Bhakti, 133–5, 175
    Le Concours, 79, 148
    Four Last Songs, 16, 138, 320
    Mass for the Present Time, 132
    Ni Fleurs, Ni Couronnes, 135
    Ninth Symphony, 131, 148
    Les Noces, 15
    Rite of Spring, 129–30, 144
    Romeo and Juliet, 131, 132, 148
    Rose Variations, 196
    Songs of a Wayfarer, 320
    Variations pour une Porte et un Soupir (Squeaky Door), 140–1, 175, 203
    Webern Opus 5, 141, 148, 175, 185
  classes by, 30
  MG leaves company, 143–5, 147, 167–8, 188
  permits performances, 147, 148, 154, 168, 174–5, 189
Belgrade, 214
Benois, 65
Beriosoff, Poppa (Nicholas), 101
Berisova, Svetlana, 38, 67, 101, 172
Berlin Opera Ballet, 167–73; *see also* Deutsche Oper Ballet Berlin
Berrett, John, 7
Besobrasova, Marika, 86, 88
Beyond Bach, 5, 11, 14
Bhakti, 12, 133, 175, 214;
  film, 135
Bintley, David, 302

354

INDEX

Birmingham Royal Ballet, 208, 300–2; *see also* Sadler's Wells Royal Ballet
Black Queen, 208–9
Black Swan, 23, 34, 160, 219
Black Tights, 94
Blue Bird, 71, 90, 207
Bolm, Adolf, 65, 69
Bolshoi Ballet, 19, 67, 136, 175, 242, 302, 330
Bolte, Lisa, 40, 51, 31, 264–7, 272–3
Borovansky Ballet Company, The, 66
Borovansky, Edouard, 66, 125
Bortoluzzi, Paolo, 131
Bourke, Walter, 239–43, 275, 305–6
Bowman, Andrew, 44–6
'Boyo', 41
Brandreth, Gyles, 52; *see also John Gielgud: A Celebration*
Breuer, Peter, 181, 190, 207
Britanny, 216
Bruhn, Erik, 48, 29, 109
Brussels, 55, 139
Buckle, Richard, 145, 169, 172, 184–5
Burman, Wilhelm, 111, 324

Callas, Maria, 139, 172
Cardi, Anna, 56
Cardin, Pierre, 215
Cameron, Rachel, 71–2, 324
Canadian National Ballet, 209
CAPAB Ballet (Cape Town), 214
Cape Town, 214–5
Carrison, Guy, 10
Carroll, Lewis, 56, 223
Carter, Andrew, 11
Casado, Germinal, 134
Cata, Alfonso, 111
Cauley, Geoffrey, 9
Central Ballet of China, 123
Centre de Dance Classique, 30, 86, 108, 111–2, 130
Chase, Alida, 206
Chauvre, Yvette, 219
Checkmate, 202, 208–9, 219
Chenciner, Robert, 216–8
Cherce Partenaire, 106
Chesiere, 5
China, 122–4
Chou En–lai, 50, 122
Christofis, Lee, 344
Christiansen, Michael, 344
Churchill, Winston, 54
'Cigarette, La', 50

Cocteau, 65
Coliseum Theatre, 201
Coney, Miranda, 42, 51, 320
Concours, Le, 79, 148
Courier-Mail, The (Brisbane), 274–7
Covent Garden, 51, 61, 230, 302, 331
Cox, Timothy, 277, 296, 298–300, 311, 316–7
Craig, Gordon, 7, 52, 53
Cranko, John, 6, 204, 205, 245, 320
Croese, Francis, 7
Cuevas, de, Company, 11, 85, 87, 90–1, 94, 96, 101–3, 105, 122, 150, 169, 174
Cuevas, Marquis de, 91, 96, 100–1, 103, 108
Cuevas, Marquis de, Company, *see* Cuevas, de, Company
Cunxin, Li, 264

Daily Telegraph, The (Sydney), 215, 224
Daily Telegraph Mirror, The (Sydney), 278–9
Dance and Dancers, 138, 173, 225
Dance Magazine, 127
Dance News, 214
Dancing Star, 323
Dancing Times, 134
Dale, Daphne, 49
Danilova, 69, 70
Darrell, Peter, 219
Darsonval, Lycette, 89
Dauberval, Jean, 203
Davidson, Suzanne, 58, 81, 163–4, 235–8, 306–7, 314
Dayde, Lyane, 122
Deane, Derek, 220
de Cardi, Anna, 56
Debussy, 65, 136
De Masson, Paul, 41, 21, 192–7, 243–4, 310
Deutsche Oper Ballet Berlin, 156; *see also* Berlin Opera Ballet
Dévéney, Ella Téven de (MG's maternal grandmother), 50
Diaghilev, Sergei, 65, 103, 143, 174; *see also* Ballets Russes de Sergei (Palovich) Diaghilev
Die Burger, 214
Dolin, Anton, 32, 58, 65, 69, 72, 87, 170, 219
Donn, Jorge, 16, 131, 138, 147, 171
Don Quixote, 45, 46, 156–7, 159, 201, 202, 266, 326

355

INDEX

Dowell, Anthony, *10*, 68, 170
Dózsa, Imre, 214
Dubreuil, Alain, 181
Duchesne, Mary, *63*
Dudinskaya, Madame, 138
Duff, Sir Michael, 169–70
Dunn, Lucinda, 30–1, 123, 249

Edgley, Edna, *63*
Edgley, Michael, 219
Egorova, Lubov, 69, 73, 86, 89, 171
Ek, Nicklas, *15*
Eliasen, Johnny, *57*, 324
Elizabeth, H. M. Queen, *51*
Elvin, Violetta, 67
English National Ballet, 220, 300–1, 315, 344
Éspace Cardin, 218
Eugene Onegin (poem), 6; *see also* Onegin
Evansville Press, 127
Evening News (Bolton), 184
Evian, 47
Evina, Madame, 71

Farmer, Peter, *21*
Farrell, Suzanne, 143–4
'Favi' (MG's nickname for father); *see* Gielgud, Lewis
Ferran, José, 114
Ferri, Allessandra, *59*
Festival Australia Week, 29
Festival Hall, 190, 221
Festival of Cuba, 213
Festival of Perth, *36*
Field, John, 219
Fifield, Elaine, 67
Fille mal gardée, La, 27, *28*, *29*, 34, 203–4
'Fin' (MG's nickname for stepfather); *see* Sutton, Nigel
Fitzsimons, Margaret, 9
Fokine, Michel, 65, 69
Fonteyn, Dame Margot, 67, 69, 72, 88, 153, 157, 170, 180, 209, 219
Forsythe, William, *5*, 348
fouetté, 70
Four Last Songs, *16*, 138, 140, 320
Franca, Celia, 208

Gâité Parisienne, 176, 196
Gemini, 210
Ghosties and Ghoulies, 222–4

Gielgud, Eleanor (MG's aunt), 52,
Gielgud, Frank (MG's grandfather), *1*, 52
Gielgud, Sir John (MG's uncle), *9*, 51, 143
biography of, 52
Gielgud, John (MG's great great grandfather), 52
Gielgud, Kate Terry (née Lewis, MG's grandmother), *1*, 52, 53, 60
Gielgud, Lewis (MG's father), *1*, *5*, *8*, 48, 51, 53, 56
Gielgud, Maina, *50*, *51*, *52*, *54*, *55*, *56*, *57*, *58*, *59*, *60*, *61*, *62*, *63*, *64*
adolescence, 59–60, 67, 84, 87–92
approach to ballet, 67, 88, 100, 110, 112–14, 119, 178–9, 329
as choreographer
  Ghosties and Ghoulies, 222, 224
  Little Prince, The, 185
  Soldier's Tale, The, 221
  Steps, Notes and Squeaks (also as producer/director), 190, 216–9
  see also repertoire danced
and The Australian Ballet
  applies for position, 225–6
  as Artistic Director, 2, 18, *57*, 88, 104, 232
  artistic style, 347–9
  asked to resign, 290–7
  attitude to it as a ballet company, 203, 206, 228
  board, 238, 240, 270, 274–8, 283
  contract with, 97, 281, 296
  'dossier' on, 275, 278–9, 291–2, 299
  highlights with, 319–22, 324–7
  leaving, 339–402, 346, 349–50
  The Maina Gielgud Fund, 341
  management style, 2–3, 10–11, 16, 19–23, 233–250, 252–6, 263–7, 270–1, 283, 287–8, 290, 306
  reapplies for position, 316;
  teacher at, 21–7, 43–46
  termination of position, 276, 296–7, 298–301, 311–12
  troubles, 234. 241–2. 247–9, 252–3, 264, 269–318
  views on its dancers, 42, 118, 201, 219–20, 228–9, 230–3, 238, 241–2, 245–50, 252, 256–64, 306–7, 322, 324–5, 329, 333–7
  views on what she brought to it, 345, 347–9

INDEX

Gielgud, Maina (*cont.*)
   British influence, 58
   childhood, *1*, *2*, *3*, *5*, *6*, *7*, *49*, 47–9,
      53–7, 63, 70, 71, 84–5
   companies danced with:
      Australian Ballet, The, 199–206,
         207–4, 232
      Ballet de l'Étoile, 104–5
      Ballet of Marseille, 153
      Ballet of the Twentieth Century
         (Béjart), 129–48
      Berlin Opera Ballet, 167–73; as
         Deutsche Oper Berlin Ballet, 156
      CAPAB Ballet, 214
      Cuevas de, Company, 96–103, 105
      Festival of Cuba, 214, 218
      Grand Ballet Classique de France,
         122–28
      Hommage au Marquis de Cuevas,
         115–122
      London Festival Ballet, 175–78,
         203, 206–7
      PACT, 214
      Roland Petit Company, 93–8
      Scottish Ballet, The, 207
      Sadler's Wells Royal Ballet,
         208–11
   decision to stop dancing, 221–4
   and diet, 38, 179, 222
   doubts about continuing dancing
      career, 219–221
   French influence, 58
   and fortune-telling, 203–4
   health, 99, 125
   home apartment, 19
   Hungarian influences on, 58, 78, 81
   and *I Ching*, 215–6
   imaginary childhood friend, 'Fayelle',
      57
   injuries, 4–5, 121
   joins The Royal Danish Ballet, 342–4
   and love, 115–6
   and mother, 75–92, 203–4, 207, 224
   need for humour, 178
   on Australian audiences, 125
   on life, 181
   personality of, 3, 19, 25–6, 58–9,
      99, 116–117, 232, 236, 260, 271,
      338
   productions by,
      Giselle, 21, 41, 44
      Le Concours, 148
      Sleeping Beauty, The, 40, 51, 61

   Steps, Notes and Squeaks, 35
   psychological profile, 285–6
   Rehearsal Director, London City
      Ballet, 223–4
   and reincarnation, 110, 114
   and religion, 55–6
   repertoire danced:
      Bal de Nuit, 121
      Baiser de la Fée, Le (The Fairy),
         175
      Baudelaire (Mauve Woman), 136
      Beau Danube, Le (Street Dancer),
         176
      Bhakti (Shakti), *12*, 133–5, 175,
         214; film, 135
      Checkmate (Black Queen), 208–9,
         219
      Cherche Partenaire, 106
      Don Quixote, *45*, *46*; (Kitri),
         156–8; (Queen of the Dryads,
         Mercedes and bridesmaid), 159
      The Fairy's Kiss, 24;
      Four Last Songs, 16, 138, 140
      Gâité Parisienne (Glove Seller),
         176, 196
      Gemini, 210
      Giselle, (Giselle), *26*, 170; (Queen
         of the Wilis), 121, 124, 127–8,
         185, 209
      La Fille mal gardée, 27, 28, 29, 34,
         203–4
      'The Greatest Show On Earth',
         gala (Rose Adagio), 169
      Mass For The Present Time, 132
      Ninth Symphony, 131
      Les Noces, 15
      Noir et Blanc, 127
      Prodigal Son, The, 208
      Phantasmagoria, 14
      Raymonda, 209
      Romeo and Juliet (Juliet), 204–6,
         232; (Queen Mab), 132–3, 148
      Rose Variations, 196
      Shakespeare Sonnets, gala (with
         Uncle John), 9, 52
      The Sleeping Beauty, *39* (Aurora),
         153, 168, 170, 174, 184,
         199–201, 207; (Blue Bird, Lilac
         Fairy), 207; (page, nymph),
         102
      Soirée Musicale (pas de deux),
         118, 214–5
      The Soldier's Tale, 221

INDEX

Gielgud, Maina (*cont.*)
   Steps, Notes and Squeaks, *32*, *35*, 190, 216–9
   Suite en Blanc, 122, 171
   Swan Lake (Black Queen), *13*, *23*; (Odette–Odile), 171–4, 193, 214
   Sylphide, La, *25*, 109, 111
   Sylphides, Les, 128, 170
   Sylvia, pas de deux, 89
   Tchaikovsky pas de deux, *31*
   Variations pour une Porte et un Soupir (Variations for a Door and a Sigh), 139; (as *Forme et Ligne*), 140; (as *Squeaky Door*), 140–2, 203
   Webern Opus 5, 141, 148, 185
   reviews of, 124, 127, 134, 135, 138, 142, 145, 184, 185, 214
   shape of nose, *11*, 70, 133, 170
   weight problems, 220–1
   and yoga of dance, 114
   teachers, *6*, *17*, *18*, *38*, 48, 65, 67, 68–9, 71–3, 85–6, 88–9, 101, 103, 104, 107–31, 149–50, 153–4, 169, 171, 180–1, 201, 208
Gielgud, Val (MG's uncle), 52
Gielgud, Mrs Zita (MG's mother), *1*
   see also Gordon, Zita; Sutton, Mrs Nigel; *Zita, Zita Gordon Gielgud, Her Story* by Noël Pelly
Giselle, *21*, *26*, *41*, *44*, 31, 89, 121, 124, 128, 185
Golovine, Serge, 68, 90
Gordon, Zita, 79; see also Gielgud, Mrs Zita; Sutton, Mrs Nigel
Goubé, Paul, 88, 171
Goncharov, George, 69
Gore, Muriel (MG's adopted godmother), 4, 61–2
Grand Ballet Classique de France, 122–8, 130–1, 229
Grand Theatre, *31*
'Greatest Show On Earth, The', gala, 169
Grey, Beryl, 173, 182, 201, 207
Grigorovich, 175, 302
Grüszner, Zoltán (MG's maternal grandfather), 50
Gsovsky, Victor, 88, 132
Guardian, The, 145–7, 162, 167
Hallet, Bryce, 317, 343–4
Hampshire School, *10*, 68
Hampshire, Susan, *6*, 68

Harman, Geoffrey, 9
Harris, Frank, 124
Hart, Pro, 33
Hattemer, Cours, 88
Hawke, Hazel, *20*,
Heathcote, Steven, *40*, *56*, 256–63, 282, 325–6
Helpmann, Sir Robert, 157, 159, 200, 202, 219, 302, 312–3
Hermanas, Les, 5, 15
Herf, Estelle, 146
Herod Atticus Theatre, 103
Hightower, Rosella, *18*, *23*, 88, 103, 108, 149, 159, 169
   Ballet of Marseille, 153–4
   Centre de Dance Classique (Cannes), *30*, 86, 108, 130
   dancing, 90, 108, 112, 122, 150, 219
   and MG, 24, 107–8, 121, 130–1, 171
   productions:
      Bal de Nuit, 121
      Giselle, *26*, 121, 128
      Noir et Blanc, 127
      Soirée Musicale, 118
      Suite en Blanc, 122
      La Sylphide, *25*
      Les Sylphides, 128
   teaching, 109–13, 116, 202, 324
   yoga of dance, 114–15
Hilarides, Marianna, 127
Hoffman, Wilfred, 214
Holloway, Victor, 214
Holmes, Larry, 283–5
Hommage au Marquis de Cuevas, 115, 118–28
Horsman, Greg, 273, 287, 289, 300, 303, 324
Hugo, Jean, 169
Hugo, Victor, 169
Huxley, Aldous, 54–5
Hynd, Ronald, *24*, 175, 219

Idzikowsky, Stanislav, 71, 170
Ile St Marguerite, *25*, 26
Inglesby, 69
In The Middle, Somewhat Elevated, 5, 15

James, Jeremy, 222
Jeanmaire, Zizi, 94–5, 104, 170
Johannesburg, 214
John Gielgud: A Celebration, by Gyles Brandreth, 52–3

INDEX

Joffrey Ballet, 330
Jones, Marilyn, 33, 102, 190, 205

Karsavina, Tamara, 17, 65, 69, 71–2, 73
Kelley, Grant, 43
Kelly, Desmond, 170
Kelly, Jonathan, 182
   with The Australian Ballet, 181, 226, 254, 326
   comments on MG, 188–9, 191–2, 252–6, 308–310
   dancing with MG, 14, 38, 39, 181, 189–90, 196, 213, 214–15, 217, 219
   friendship with MG, 182, 187, 191
   with London Festival Ballet, 187
Kemp, Lindsay, 328
Kirkby, Rob, 284
Kirkland, Gelsey, 324
Kirstein, Lincoln, 142–3
Kirov Company, 90, 149–50, 164, 242, 330; *see also* Maryinsky Theatre
Koch, Peta, 274
Kolpakova, Irina, 324
Konservatoriet, 343
Krassovska, Natalie, 49
Kschessinska, Mathilde, 65, 69, 73
Kylián, Jiří, 34, 320, 348

Lanchbery, John, 175
Laurencin, 65
Larrain, Raymundo de, 96, 102
Lawson, Nicola, 222
Lawson, Valerie, 300–1
Legat, Nicolai, 69
Legat, Nadine Nicolaeva, 69
Legat School, 69
Leningrad, 62
Lester, Keith, 72
Lewis, Arthur (MG's great grandfather), 53
Lewis, Kate Terry, 52; *see also* Gielgud, Kate Terry
Lidova, Madame Irène, 104, 108
Lifar, Serge, 65, 69
Lilac Fairy, 207
Lippa, Emma, 323–4
Lithuania, 8, 51
Little Prince, The, 185
Loggenburg, Dudley van, 181
Lommel, Daniel, 132, 134
London City Ballet, 222–4
London Festival Ballet, 13, 23, 24, 87, 173–84, 187, 192–4, 206, 207, 216, 219, 230
Lopez, Pilar, 170
Lopokova, Lydia, 61, 65, 69
Los Angeles Free Press, 127
Luders, Adam, 25, 181–3, 185, 197

McAllister, David, 31–2, 242
McGrath, Barry, 219
Macklin, Stuart, 44
MacMillan, Sir Kenneth, 5, 172, 208, 230, 320
McRae, Ian, 52, 60, 284, 291, 314–5. 331–3, 337–8
Manon, 40, 320
Markova, Alicia, 87, 160, 172, 209
Markova–Dolin Ballet, 87
Marseille, 45, 46, 108, 157, 163, 192
Martin, Frank, 5
Martins, Peter, 13, 176
Maryinsky Theatre, 62, 63, 31, 66, 68, 88–9, 302
   see also Kirov
Massine, Leonide, 132
Massine, Lorca, 132
Matisse, 65
Maximova, Yekaterina, 175
Mayer, Gilbert, 324
Mayerling, 230
Meck, Mme von, 169
Melbourne, 26, 125, 187, 200, 201, 203, 227
Mepsie, 328
Mercutio, 262
Merry Widow, The, 175
Meryl Tankard Australian Dance Theatre, 327
Messerer, Asaf, 136
Milakovic, Marina, 6–7
Milhaud, Darius, 65
Millar, Fred, 278–9, 281–4, 287–92, 294–6, 300–1, 303
Miller–Ashmole, Petal, 317
Miskovitch, Milorad, 68, 104–5
Mode, 327
Montreal Star, 135
'Mon Truc En Plume', 95
Morgan, Brett, 56
Moore, Lindsay, 225
Moscow International Ballet Competition, 242
Murphy, Andrew, 47, 123, 164–5
Murphy, Graeme, 316

359

INDEX

Nardelli, Pyotr, 324
National Ballet of Canada, 315
Naughton, Louise, 111
Neilson–Terry, Phyllis, 53
Nemtchinova, Vera, 65, 69
News, The (Adelaide), 124
New York City Ballet, 142–3, 168, 169, 173, 176, 183
New Yorker, The, 142
New York Times, 142
Ni Fleurs, Ni Couronnes (Neither Flowers, Nor Crowns), 135
Nijinska, Bronislava, 103, 112
Nijinsky, Vaslav, 38, 69, 103, 169
Nijinsky–Markevitch, Vaslav, 169
Ninth Symphony, 131, 148
Noces, Les, 15
Noir et Blanc, 50, 127
Norman, Gary, 63, 202, 205–6, 231–2, 307–8
Nouveau Ballet de Monte Carlo, 108
Nureyev, Rudolf, 109, 153–4, 160, 170, 302
  in Australia, 47, 109, 153
  bad language, 57, 159
  biography of, 150
  defection to the West, 90, 149, 150
  and food, 38, 155, 163
  health and death, 164, 202
  at Kirov Ballet, 150, 164
  and MG, 45, 46, 153, 156–8, 163, 209
  partners, 106, 150, 202
  productions, 193, 207
  work intensity, 149, 152, 159, 161
  and Zita Sutton, 155–6
Nutcracker, 174, 194, 197, 219

Odette–Odile, 214
Ohn, Gerard, 89
Old Vic, 39, 190, 219
Olympic Games, (Sydney, 2000), 316, 342
Onegin, 6, 33, 36, 175, 325
Open Space Theatre, 37, 38, 216–7
Opera House (Sydney), 25
Original Ballet Russe (Count de Basil), 66
Original Ballets Russes, 87, 108
Orpheus, 320

PACT (Johannesburg ballet company), 214
Palmer, David, 225

Paris Opera, 89, 153, 165, 172, 208, 302
Pask, Edward, 64, 66, 79, 298, 315–6, 322–3
Pavane, Lisa, 273, 287, 289, 300, 303, 324
Pavlova, Anna, 65, 69, 71, 125, 322–3
Phantasmagoria, 14
Peasley, Colin, 27–9, 229, 240–7, 249, 304
Piège de Lumière, 193
Pelly, Noël, 54, 57, 50–1, 72, 75, 78, 81, 97, 230, 233, 236, 250, 302–4, 313
Peking, 50
Peking Opera, 123
Pepita, Marius, 89
Percival, John, 158–9
Perennial Philosophy, The, 55
Petit, Roland, 93–8, 104–5, 114
  see also Roland Petit Company
Picasso, Pablo, 49, 65, 85–6
Pina Bausch Wuppertalen Tanztheater, 328
Plisetskaya, Maya, 172
Polajenko, Nicholas, 49
Pontois, Noella, 153
Popa, Magdalena, 324
Poulenc, Francis, 65
Preobajenska, Olga, 65, 68–9, 89
Princess Theatre (Melbourne), 200
Prodigal Son, The, 209
Pushkin, Alexander Ivanovich, 164
Pushkin, Alexander Sergevic, 6

Queen of the Wilis, 121, 124, 127–8, 185, 209
Queensland Ballet, 276, 344

Rambert, Dame Marie, 175
Raymonda, 209
Ravel, Maurice, 65
Red Earth, 33
Red King, 202, 219
Reid, Kathleen, 51
Reines, Rosalind, 327
Reiter–Soffer, Domy, 14
Renault, Michel, 122
Reznicov, Mischa, 88, 104
Rhodes, Nicole, 41, 140
Riabouchinska, 68,
Ripon, Marchioness of, 170
Rite of Spring, 129, 144

360